FANTASY AND YOUR FAMILY

FANTASY AND YOUR FAMILY

Exploring The Lord of the Rings, Harry Potter *and Modern Magick*

Richard Abanes

CHRISTIAN PUBLICATIONS, INC.
CAMP HILL, PENNSYLVANIA

CHRISTIAN PUBLICATIONS, INC.
3825 Hartzdale Drive, Camp Hill, PA 17011
www.christianpublications.com

Faithful, biblical publishing since 1883

Fantasy and Your Family
ISBN: 0-87509-975-0
© 2002 by Richard Abanes
All rights reserved
Printed in the United States of America

02 03 04 05 06   5 4 3 2 1

DEDICATION

To my friend, Othmar, a brilliant scientist and progressive thinker; an individual about whom I still know far too little, but whose wisdom and insights I look forward to someday exploring. I am indebted to your important work, which enabled me to think clearly and finish this project.

THANKS TO:

Mr. S.Q., esq.
L. Philip
K. Neill Foster
Mr. Tursle
T. Angus
David Fessenden
R.F. Andreas
Patterson
Mrs. Acoon
Juan Prospero
Fletcher
and my wife, Evangeline

CONTENTS

PART THREE:
WELCOME TO THE AGE OF ABRACADABRA

PART FOUR:
DEBATES, DISPUTES AND DECISIONS

FOREWORD

Reading any story "clicks in" the imagination—that faculty of the mind that conjures up mental pictures—allowing readers to experience events, characters, challenging situations and ideas that would never be possible in real life.

And just as real-life experiences are occasions for learning and growing, the vicarious experiences made possible by literature also can shape values, sensibility, beliefs and even personality. In other words, the great power of literature, to borrow Sir Philip Sydney's phrasing, is "to teach and to delight." Of course, to teach *by* delighting means that different works of literature can teach different things.

Interestingly, respectful attention to what a work means has largely given way to an uncritical acceptance of whatever vicarious experience an author chooses to put us through. This is true especially when it comes to children's books. Many parents today are so glad when their child picks up a book instead of turning on the TV that they pay little attention to what the book is about or what it does to their child. Nevertheless, there remains a fair question parents should be asking: "What is being taught by the books my child is reading?"

Richard Abanes' understanding of these issues is clearly evident in *Fantasy and Your Family*—a book that is pro-reading, pro-literature and pro-fantasy. *Fantasy and Your Family* clearly makes a strong case for the value of imaginative literature. At the same time, Richard Abanes makes some distinctions by contrasting what he considers healthy fantasy with unhealthy fantasy. What is a fantasy's meaning and its effect on the reader? Does it make evil repellant or attractive? Does it make a child want to emulate the good characters or the bad characters, or does it blur all moral distinctions altogether? If there is violence, is it presented in such a way that the child sympathizes with those who are hurt, or does it revel in violence so as to give the impression that hurting others is pleasurable? These are just some of the questions this book answers.

And Abanes is no outside observer. He is a self-professed *Star Trek* fan who has himself been nourished by fairy tales, science fiction and works of fantasy. He understands that determining whether or not a book is appropriate for children is not just a matter of isolated imagery—i.e., whether a story has a "witch" or "magic" in it or even whether a story is violent. Abanes knows that to judge a book requires more—i.e., attention not just to its details, but to the specific nature of the vicarious experience it creates using those details. To understand a story's meaning requires not only interpretation, but information and context.

This is what *Fantasy and Your Family* provides. Abanes, for example, discusses the impact of commercialism on children's literature. In order to achieve mass consumption and thus high profits, publishers have been churning out mass-produced, formulaic titles designed to appeal to a child's most immediate appetites. A case in point would be the kiddy-horror novels of R.L. Stine, which merely serve up pointless, albeit titillating, accounts of murdered schoolmates and cannibal parents. How different these slasher tales are from classic horror stories, such as Mary Shelley's *Frankenstein*, which is not only scary but makes an important point about human limits and the boundaries of science.

The Harry Potter series by J.K. Rowling, of course, is better written than Stine's novels, but it has the same publisher—Scholastic Press—and offer similar points of appeal. The main controversy over the Harry Potter books, however, is essentially with regard to the question of whether these absorbing volumes about a school for witches might cause young readers to pursue an unhealthy, real-world interest in real occultism. Rowling's defenders say: "Of course not. Children will not become witches from reading about Harry, any more than reading Tolkien will make them become hobbits."

But Abanes, it seems, has found evidence to the contrary. Judging from what children are posting on the innumerable Web sites for Harry Potter fans, many of them *are* becoming interested in learning how to cast spells and do *real* witchcraft, just like their hero. Abanes also looks at the Web sites of Wicca devotees and other occult practitioners who are hailing the Harry Potter series as a prime recruitment tool. Even more pertinent is the way the children's book industry, in an attempt to cash in on the craze, is turning out how-to books on the occult targeted directly at young Harry Potter fans. Titles like *So You Want to Be a Wizard, Teen Witch, Spells for Teenage Witches* sell themselves with blurbs on the order of *The Witch and Wizard Guide*, which claims to be "a complete guide to doing the magic in Harry Potter using modern Wiccan techniques." These books are often found right next to Harry Potter in the mega-store displays.

Anyone today presuming to criticize a book—especially one so popular as the Harry Potter series—becomes immediately branded with the charge of censorship. Abanes, however, it must be stressed, is *not* advocating the banning or the burning of Harry Potter. Nor does he even say that reading Harry Potter is necessarily harmful to every child. He is worried, though, about these books' effects on *some* children and demonstrates the validity of his concerns by citing child development research.

Supervising how children entertain themselves (the TV shows they watch, the movies they go to, the video games they play and the Web sites they visit, as well as the books they read) is not the job of the government but, as nearly everyone agrees, the responsibility of the parents. *Fantasy and Your Family*, which is exhaustively researched, gives parents the information they need to know in making those kinds of decisions. Moreover, it gives the supporters of Harry Potter their say, addressing their issues point by point. It is a balanced work that Abanes has produced, not just as a sourcebook for the Harry Potter controversy, but in offering a positive alternative in Tolkien's The Lord of the Rings, which is discussed in similar detail, explicating its themes, its imagery, and its salutary effects.

In comparing The Lord of the Rings to J.K. Rowling's Harry Potter, and in accepting the challenge of saying why one is good for children while the other may not be so positive (even though they both contain wizards, magic and scary moments), Abanes illuminates both fantasy works. In doing so, I believe he has helped us move toward recovering the great tradition of children's literature from the wasteland of modern commercialism, adult manipulation and a spiritually impoverished culture.

—Gene Edward Veith, Ph.D.
English Professor, Concordia University

INTRODUCTION

TO BE A CHILD AGAIN

Books fall open, you fall in,
Delighted where you've never been;
Hear voices not once heard before,
Reach world on world through door on door.

> David McCord[1]
> "Books Fall Open"

By the time I had reached the first grade, my love for fantasy and fiction had already manifested itself. *Winnie-the-Pooh*, *Charlotte's Web*, *Peter Pan*, *The Wizard of Oz*, *Tarzan of the Apes*, *Alice's Adventures in Wonderland*—I loved them all. And I still do. Later, I discovered The Chronicles of Narnia and The Lord of the Rings. These works too found their way deep into my heart.

Then, when my father surprised the family with a color TV, I not only learned of cartoons, but of one in particular that would for many years be my favorite: *The Bullwinkle Show*. This series, of course, featured that lovable moose, Bullwinkle, and his sharp-minded friend, Rocky, the flying squirrel. I could not get enough of their antics and adventures.

Most delightful to me was one specific segment of their show, "Fractured Fairy Tales," narrated by Edward Everett

Horton. To this day, I can't help but chuckle to myself when I recall those hysterical twists on classic fairy tales and the humorous lines they contained.

Looking back as an adult, I also see that I learned a great deal from them about right and wrong, good and evil, cleverness and stupidity, and, to some extent, how life works. I remember, for instance, as a third-grader, choosing to not taunt another student— a poor student—thanks to a fractured fairy tale I had seen that contrasted rich nobility with paupers.

A few years later I found another television series that would hold even more influence over me: *Star Trek*. Its September 8, 1966, television debut changed the world—*my* world, anyway. Although my dad would always be my #1 role model, the 1960s sci-fi series presented me with a second male figure to emulate: James T. Kirk, captain of the starship *Enterprise*.

I desperately wanted to be Kirk. Not just be *like* Kirk; I actually wanted to *be* him—a gallant, handsome, strong, brave, tough guy who always seemed to make the right decisions and ended up the hero. And, of course, he always had a beautiful woman falling in love with him. (At eight years old, however, my odd sensations regarding this seemingly positive aspect of Kirk's life were still a bit baffling to me. I would understand more within a few years.)

I can still remember myself in about the fourth grade, turning my miniature rocking chair upside down and sitting at an angle. I'd nestle myself into its underside between two curved supports (the closest thing I could find to a captain's seat). Nearly every afternoon, from 4 P.M. until my mother called me for dinner, I commanded my own starship.

"Mr. Sulu, warp factor two," I'd shout at my stuffed rabbit. "Deflector shields up! Bring us around, Mr. Sulu. Let's give those Romulans something to think about."

An imaginary Spock, stationed in front of my dresser, would invariably turn from his sensors and give a predictable word of warning: "Captain, I must caution you. We are now in the Neutral Zone."

"I'm well aware of that, Mr. Spock," was my usual response. "Lock phasers on target, Mr. Chekhov!"

"Phasers locked on target, sir." (Chekhov never gave me any back talk.)

"Hold your course, Mr. Sulu. . . . Easy. . . . FIRE!"

Of course, I would score a direct hit every time, and the explosion's concussion waves would invariably knock me out of my captain's chair (a perfect excuse to roll around on the floor). Then, after a few congratulatory remarks to my invisible crew, the next mission would begin.

"Mr. Spock, didn't Starfleet Command report Klingons in the Gamma Quadrant?"

"Yes, Captain. At least two Klingon warbirds have been reported, but they may have cloaking devices."

I was thrilled.

"Mr. Sulu. Set a course for the Gamma Quadrant; warp factor two!"

"Aye-aye, Captain."

Thanks to Kirk, I spent most of my childhood longing to be an astronaut. I could not get his words out of my mind: "Space, the final frontier." I just knew that an exciting life among the stars awaited me. But imagination gradually gave way to reality and I eventually became a writer. I still, however, watch *Star Trek* as often as possible.

Today, countless children continue to experience the joy and wonder of fantasy and science fiction on their way to becoming preadolescents, teens and young adults. They, of course, are looking to a whole new generation of brilliant writers with new stories, new plots and new lessons to teach. And Hollywood, now more adept at special effects than ever before, has added a previously unexperienced dimension to children's entertainment—incredible realism and exhilarating images. There seems to be no limit to what can be put on the silver screen, as evidenced by two of the most money-making blockbusters ever to be released: *Harry Potter and the Sorcerer's Stone* by Scottish author J.K. Rowling, and Tolkien's classic, *The Fellowship of the Ring*.

The *Harry Potter* and *Fellowship of the Ring* movies, both of which were adapted from books, have made quite an impact not only on innumerable youths, but also on our entire culture. Their influence, however, has not been without controversy. Many parents are concerned about the books and films in relation to their depiction of occult themes, violence, evil and immorality.

Consider these recent headlines: "Occult Fears Prompt Store Owner To Ban Harry Potter Toys," "Occult Trends in Children's Literature," "Harry Potter Film: Invitation to Join Occult?," "Potter Fans Turning to Witchcraft."[2] With regard to The Lord of the Rings, other headlines are just as illuminating: "Tolkien, Hitler, and Nordic Heroism," "Tolkien and Rowling: Common Ground?," "Movies of Witchcraft and Wizards: Is This Good Entertainment?"[3]

Interestingly, recent evidence suggests that a significant number of young Harry Potter fans may indeed be developing a fascination with occultism. The results of a March 2002 Barna Research Group nationwide poll of U.S. teens between the ages of thirteen and nineteen, for instance, found that twelve percent of those who had been exposed to Harry Potter were interested in witchcraft. Of these teens, "4% said they were a lot more interested, and 8% were a little more interested as a result of the book or movie."[4]

In other words, about one out of every eight teenagers who have seen or read Harry Potter say that the fantasy made them more interested in witchcraft. These statistics certainly represent a minority of teens, but "it still accounts for about 5% of all U.S. teenagers and projects to more than a million students nationwide who claim that the Potter stories have made them more interested in witchcraft."[5]

In light of such information, I have produced *Fantasy and Your Family* with the hope of separating fact from fiction in the controversies surrounding Harry Potter and The Lord of the Rings. The following chapters discuss both the benefits and dangers of fantasy in general, how literature affects children (with emphasis on specific developmental stages) and the place of occultism in modern society. All of these issues are now inextricably linked and must be carefully examined if parents are going to make wise decisions regarding what kinds of literature they will allow their children to read.

This book does not advocate book burning, book banning or rigid censorship. Let me say that again—I am not in any way advocating book burning, book banning or rigid censorship. What I do hope to demonstrate, however, is that a great deal of misinformation and disinformation has been circulating about both Harry Potter and The Lord of the Rings. The result has been nothing less than confusion in the minds of many people—the religious, the nonreligious, the half-religious and even the irreligious.

I believe that the carefully documented information within the following pages will help everyone understand the facts with regard to the many concerns being expressed about Harry Potter, The Lord of the Rings and fantasy literature in general. Some concerns are justified, while others, in my opinion, are not. All final judgments are left up to you, the reader of this book, as you sift through the material in the chapters ahead.

And so I invite Rowling fans and Rowling foes, as well as Tolkien supporters and Tolkien detractors, to journey with me into the wonderful (but sometimes frightening and controversial) world of fantasy. Hopefully, all of us will learn a few lessons along the way.

"Mr. Sulu—steady as she goes. Warp six! Mr. Chekhov—deflector shields up!"

Part
One

WORLDS OF
IMAGINATION

The character of fantasy . . . is that of a fiction
evoking wonder and containing a substantial and
irreducible element of supernatural or impossible
worlds, beings or objects, with which the readers
or the characters within the story become on at
least partly familiar terms.

—C.N. Manlove
Lecturer in English Literature,
University of Edinburgh
(*Modern Fantasy: Five Studies*, p. 11)

THE WONDER
OF FANTASY

Wonder—n., [E]motion excited by the perception of something novel and unexpected, or inexplicable; astonishment mingled with perplexity or bewildered curiosity.

The Oxford Universal Dictionary[1]

Reading is an essential part of a child's maturation into a psychologically healthy and socially adjusted adult. "Growing up without books is growing up deprived," argues Dr. Perri Klass, assistant professor of pediatrics at Boston University School of Medicine, "and with a deprivation that puts one at risk for failure."[2]

For many children, however, reading for pleasure is unimportant; even adults in this day and age tend not to be avid readers. When asked why they do not read, a significant number of persons, young and old, commonly express a belief that stories in books have little bearing on real life. Others assume that reading is not as entertaining as a "good movie." Some nonreaders even say that most literature is boring and just too difficult to comprehend.

But reading need not be an arduous task. If given a chance, it can be one of the most uplifting, entertaining and life-changing activities available on a daily basis. And for library-goers, reading is free. The innumerable worlds, characters and lives resident within good literature can not only enlighten the mind to new perspectives, but also infuse the soul with hope and comfort.

Books can change one's entire view of the world. Why? Because literature, especially fiction, often deals with the perennial mysteries of the human condition. In *The Educated Imagination*, eminent English scholar and literary critic Northrop Frye (1912-1991) observes:

> Literature gives us an experience that stretches us vertically to the heights and depths of what the human mind can conceive, to what corresponds to the conceptions of heaven and hell. . . . No matter how much experience we may gather in life, we can never in life get the dimension of experience that the imagination gives us.[3]

The stories available to all of us through books commonly deal not only with life itself, but also the various ways people interpret life. This can have a profound effect on how we see life; indeed, how we see ourselves in life.[4] Acclaimed English author Leon Garfield (1921-1996) made the following observations in *Horn Book Magazine*, founded in 1924 as America's premier journal of record for children's literature:

> A human being, by and large, is not the most likable of nature's productions. . . . But he has one saving grace. Unlike any other creature, he knows the depths of his own infamy, and, here and there, makes efforts to undo the harm he has done. It is largely through books that he knows these things. It is through books that he discovers himself, and so discovers others.[5]

Hazel Rochman, who won the 1994 G.K. Hall Award for Library Literature for her book *Against Borders: Promoting Books for a Multicultural World*, sees literature as a way of breaking down social, religious and ethnic barriers. She writes: "A good story lets you know people as individuals in all their particularities and conflict; and once you see someone as a person—flawed, complex, striving—then you've reached beyond stereotype."[6]

Books and the reading of them offer nothing less than a window through which one may look directly into the human soul. The written word—like music, art, drama and dance—expresses some of the most intimate aspects of our humanity: joy, sadness, love, anger, desire, suffering and loss. Unlike other forms of creative expression, however, literature merges the art form that is being enjoyed with the one who is doing the enjoying.

There is a marriage of sorts that takes place wherein the story becomes one with the reader, thereby creating a "virtual" experience in the mind. The experience then adds to who we are as individuals.[7] To many persons, such an experience is nothing less than a gift from God. As the Bible says, "Every good gift and every perfect gift is from above" (James 1:17, KJV).

ONCE UPON A TIME

The world of literature consists of two main categories: fiction and nonfiction. Nonfiction has many genres, including real-life stories, such as memoirs, biographies and historical narratives. Fiction also has numerous subclasses, one of the most popular of our era being fantasy. Its close relative, science fiction, which might be best thought of as hi-tech fantasy, has seen a recent increase in popularity as well.

Fantasy as we know it today developed from an immense body of literature collectively known as folklore, a genre which is difficult to define concisely. It is nearly as broad a category as fiction itself, since it includes poems, nursery rhymes, proverbs, fairy tales, fables and folk songs.[8] Folklore is perhaps most simply defined as "all of the great stream of anonymous creation that is the accumulated wisdom and art of everyday people."[9]

Respected children's author Jane Yolen—known widely as the Hans Christian Andersen of America and the Aesop of the twentieth century—finds that folklore has four basic functions: It provides a landscape reflecting real society; it provides a way of understanding other cultures; it provides a means of coping with and responding to reality; it provides a framework for one's belief system.[10]

In other words, folklore always has emerged from a specific group of people as a way of presenting their beliefs, customs, memories and fears to their contemporaries—and to future generations. It is no surprise that folklore has often been referred to as the "cement of society."[11]

TALES AND TALES

The most obvious examples of folklore are folktales and fairy tales, which "come out of the most distant deeps of human experience and human fancy."[12] These two types of stories differ in that fairy tales tend to include some element of supernaturalism (e.g., magical objects, witches, spells, wizards). Both kinds of tales, however, address universal themes such as fear, anger, jealousy, grief, revenge and love—usually with spiritual overtones, notes children's education specialist James E. Higgins:

> The unity of the physical and the spiritual is the basis for all traditional folktales. They tell of immortality, of the souls of beasts and birds and other living things. They tell of perpetual spiritual combat. However, they never leave out the stubborn facts concerning greed and hate; sometimes even daring to tell how these may ride roughshod over virtue and goodness.[13]

Novelist John Buchan (d. 1940), in his presidential address to the Scottish Branch of the English Association, similarly viewed the admirable nature of such tales:

> They deal with simple and enduring things, birth and marriage and death, hunger and thirst, natural sorrows and natural joys. They sprang from a society where life was hard, when a man was never quite certain of his next meal, when he never knew when he arose in the morning whether he would be alive in the evening, when adventure was not the exception in life, but the rule. . . . It was a dangerous world

and a cruel world, and therefore those who dwelt in it endeavored in their tales to escape from it. They pictured weakness winning against might, gentleness and courtesy against brutality, brains as against mere animal strength, the one chance in a hundred succeeding.[14]

It is easy to see why classic fairy tales are widely appreciated and told generation after generation all over the world. Such beloved tales as "Sleeping Beauty," "Little Red Riding Hood," "Cinderella" and "Puss in Boots," along with several others, were first brought together under one cover in 1697 by Frenchman Charles Perrault (1628-1703). He published them as *Histoires ou contes du temps passé, avec des moralities* (transl., *Stories or Tales of Times Past, with Morals*).

Then came the publication in 1812-15 of *Kinder-und Hausmärchen* (transl., *Children's and Household Tales*). It included "Hansel and Gretel," "Rapunzel" and "Snow White." These were collected by brothers Jacob Grimm (1785-1863) and Wilhelm Grimm (1786-1859), who traveled through the countryside asking people to share with them the stories commonly told in the region.

Thanks to the Grimm brothers, fairy tales began being collected by others. Andrew Lang (1844-1912), for instance, released in England a series of color-identified collections—*The Blue Fairy Book* (1889), *The Red Fairy Book* (1889), *The Green Fairy Book* (1892) and so on.[15] By the early twentieth century, folktales and fairy tales had taken on numerous forms:

- *Cumulative Tales* are best suited for younger children due to their typically simple plot and the repetition they use to tell their stories (e.g., "The Three Little Pigs").
- *Talking Beast Tales* feature talking animals that have personalities, habits, strengths and weaknesses reflecting human attributes. These stories tend to be especially entertaining and endearing (e.g., *The Tale of Peter Rabbit* by Beatrix Potter).

- *Realistic Tales*, as their name implies, build a story out of material taken from the here and now. They may be based on real events and people (e.g., "Blue Beard").
- *Humorous Tales*, slightly different than other tales, seem primarily meant to be taken for pure fun and nonsense, with little or no significant meaning (e.g., "Mr. Vinegar," which is about a man who trades his cow at the beginning of a series of barters that in the end leaves him with nothing).
- *Religious Tales*, although rarely heard, do exist within the realm of children's fairy/folktales. They are primarily confined to Europe and often reflect aspects of Christianity. They descended from the morality plays of the Middle Ages.
- *Romantic Tales*, always about two lovers who for some reason cannot be together, usually revolve around their struggle to "live happily ever after." Some form of magic often comes into play as a means of either separating or reuniting the couple (e.g., "Beauty and the Beast").[16]

No matter which form they take, fairy tales and folktales always have the same overall themes.[17] They usually revolve around some hero or heroine demonstrating outstanding courage, loyalty, bravery, cleverness, perseverance or other admirable virtue.[18] The importance of exposing young readers to fairy tales cannot be overstated. Nicholas Tucker, a children's book author and senior lecturer in cultural studies at the University of Sussex, remarks:

> [M]ore than most other literature, fairy stories provide the child with the "knowledge that he is born into a world of death, violence, wounds, adventure, heroism and cowardice, good and evil." ... It may also start providing them with some sort of mental preparation for those more violent aspects of adult society which they will soon also notice, for example by watching television news bulletins. ... In many senses, therefore, the fairy tale world is one of unique meaning to young readers, and as such something always to be treasured.[19]

The true significance of the fairy tale was perhaps best articulated way back in 1910 by poet Richard Le Gallienne (1866-1947):

> The wonder of the world! Perhaps that is the chief business of the fairy tale—to remind us that the world is no mere dustheap, pullulating with worms, as some of the old-fashioned scientists tried to make us believe; but that, on the contrary, it is a rendezvous of radiant forces forever engaged in turning its dust into dreams, ever busy with the transmutation of matter into mind, and mind into spirit—a world, too, so mysterious that anything can happen, or any dream come true.[20]

The real beauty of folk and fairy tales lie in their ability to communicate truths and virtues to children in an uncomplicated way. Children are able to see the reality of good and bad, the consequences of doing wrong, and the rewards of doing right without having to "dig" for any messages. And although there exists little ambiguity in fairy tales, they still leave room for reflection and discussion. Far from being naive or innocent works, fairy tales "have been to the end of experience and back."[21]

The depth of fairy tales can be traced to the fact that they were not originally written for young readers. Sheldon Cashdan, emeritus professor of psychology at the University of Massachusetts, Amherst, explains:

> [F]airy tales were never meant for children. Originally conceived of as adult entertainment, fairy tales were told at social gatherings, in spinning rooms, in the fields, and in other settings where adults congregated—not in the nursery.[22]

So mature are the themes of some fairy tales, in fact, that they never made it into modern-day children's books. Consider, for instance, the earliest known version of "Sleeping Beauty," originally titled "Talia, Sun and Moon." It was recorded by the Neapolitan storyteller Giambattista Basile (c. 1575-1632). After his death, the tale was published with forty-nine other stories he had collected. They were included in a multivolume series, their release beginning in 1634.

In addition to the commonly recognized aspects of "Sleeping Beauty," Basile's tale includes the rape of Talia (i.e., Beauty) by the prince while she lies defenseless under the sleeping spell, her resulting pregnancy and the prince's abandonment of her. Fortunately, the prince eventually returns for her, but only after he has already married another woman—a murderous one with cannibalistic tendencies! The story ends with the evil wife being burned alive on the bonfire she intended for Talia.

And then there is the fairy tale "Donkeyskin," which features as a main element of the story the incestuous feelings a father has for his daughter after her mother dies.[23] He is a king who has been made wealthy thanks to a magical donkey that produces golden dung. The donkey is eventually slain—and completely skinned— at the request of the daughter, who must flee the kingdom or else marry her father. The princess then finds a prince in another kingdom, who marries her, and they live happily ever after. The father finds another wife and repents of his sinful desires.

Such material obviously is inappropriate for young children. Nevertheless, "Talia, Sun and Moon" was widely circulated and very popular for many years throughout Italy. "Donkeyskin" actually was published by Perrault in 1694 in the book *Contes en vers* (transl. *Tales in Verse*). Fairy tales at that time were not yet associated with children. Only after a significant number of the stories were edited and revised did they begin to be marketed primarily for young readers.

Given the origin of the fairy tale, it is understandable that folklore expert Jack Zipes, who also serves as professor of German at the University of Minnesota, would write that fairy tales "emanate from specific struggles to humanize bestial and barbaric forces, which have terrorized our minds and communities. . . . The fairy tale sets out to conquer this concrete terror through metaphors."[24]

The updated and modernized forms of these fairy tales, of course, are much less adult in nature. In their present form, therefore, they can be used as remarkably powerful tools for helping children understand morality and ethics. As Zipes notes: "[K]nowledge of a story's featured 'sin' can, in the context of children's natural curiosity, help make the answers to their questions more meaningful."[25]

Zipes also believes that as children listen to fairy tales and project themselves into various characters, they receive "a stage upon which they can play out inner conflicts."[26] This can be especially beneficial for children needing to resolve tension relating to how they feel about themselves and others around them.

MYTH AND LEGEND

Myths and legends developed as people gathered together, often around an open fire, and infused their own personal struggles and experiences with supernatural elements.[27] Additionally, the storytellers who began spreading myths and legends made their stories far more epic in scope than the folk/fairy tale, usually by setting the story in either far-off lands or mystical regions.

Myths normally revolve around invented characters whose existence explains the mysteries of the world: natural phenomena (e.g., lightning, thunder, rain, wind); the origins of humanity (e.g., creation myths); and the history of religious beliefs/customs. Moreover, myths commonly explain the difficult aspects of life, such as suffering, danger, disease, misfortune and death.[28] Legends, on the other hand, are often based on the life of an ancient ancestor, a regional hero or some other real-life person or persons. And unlike myths, legends serve to highlight concepts relating more to personal human drama and tragedy than to natural phenomena or worldwide issues.

Both story forms are passed down through generations until they gradually become part of a culture's heritage. They usually develop into nothing less than a grand epic that expresses not only the fears of a culture, but also the dreams, aspirations and noblest thoughts of a particular society. Everything from the

changing of the seasons to how the universe came into existence might be incorporated into either myth or legend.

The myth/legend commonly includes thought-provoking and
poignant themes such as love, valor, forgiveness, self-sacrifice,
heroism, dignity and the worth of the human soul. Coloring these
messages are subtle variations in characters, who often interact
with a wide variety of fascinating and fantastic characters—good
and evil—that range from magical beasts (e.g., unicorns) and beneficent deities to demons, witches and monsters (e.g., dragons).

The existence of such wondrous sagas dates back to the very
beginning of recorded history. Interestingly, a significant number of epic tales include trace elements of profound truths and
faith-based beliefs still held by large segments of modern society. Consider, for example, Assyria's famed *Epic of Gilgamesh*,
which is perhaps the oldest known epic fantasy:

> [T]he Epic of Gilgamesh is the tale of a man-god who seeks
> immortality; the tale of the god in the man being betrayed
> by the weakness and corruption of the man in the god.
> Gilgamesh roams a landscape where gods and monsters
> walk abroad, where there are treacherous maidens and pow-
> erful wizards. In the process he encounters the Mood, the
> Ark, and has other fictive experiences which we recognize
> from early Old Testament writings [e.g., a great flood simi-
> lar to Noah's].[29]

Other epics include Homer's *Odyssey*, which tells of Odys-
seus's arduous, but adventurous, journey back to Greece from
the Trojan Wars. We also have the well-known tale of Sindbad
the sailor, whose perilous trip home is described in the Arabian
tale, *One Thousand Nights and a Night*. "Each ancient culture
had its body of fantastic myths and legends—the Roman
Aeneid, the Finnish *Kalevala*, the Persian *Shah Namah*, the
Welsh *Mabinogion*, the Teutonic *Nibelungenlied*, the Anglo-Saxon *Beowulf*, and so forth."[30] For those in ancient civili-

zations, myth/legend helped transform reality into a form they could understand and control through analogy and metaphor.

Within the tales, for instance, one might find the hostile warriors of neighboring villages in the symbolic form of monsters needing to be conquered. Sickness might be represented as curses brought down upon people by either gods or demons. Anything mysterious, frightening or potentially harmful could be explained using the myth/legend. The flooding of crop fields, for instance, might be explained by a certain myth/legend as the consequences of certain human actions in the past against deities of the harvest. At the same time, the reasons for a person's misfortune might be found in another myth/legend that lists the antics of innumerable creatures, both seen and unseen: fairies, gnomes, elves, leprechauns, trolls or goblins, to name but a few.

Myths and legends, unlike fairy tales or folktales, are so all-encompassing that, with few exceptions, they take place within entire worlds separate from the one in which we live. But similar to fairy tales, myths/legends often include deep moral lessons relating to one's conscience, mortality and sometimes even the afterlife. They are prime examples of the kind of stories that have the potential to communicate deep truths about humanity, the world and the metaphysical realm.

Clearly, just because a story contains supernatural beings or bizarre creatures (some of which may be frightening) does not mean it is bad. The important thing is how those characters are portrayed. What are they doing? What are they saying? What is the overall message of the story? This brings us to that form of fiction which is the current cause of so much controversy—fantasy. For some readers, it is the best of all genres rolled into one.

ANOTHER WORLD, ANOTHER TIME

Myths and legends are the literary forms from which modern fantasy has descended. The style of work most directly derived from such ancient stories of imagination is probably best typified by *The Hobbit* and The Lord of the Rings trilogy by J.R.R. Tolkien (see Part Two). Tolkien's imaginative fantasies highlight, in a most profound way, that which has remained the basis of all good fantasy: the "aventures of men in the Perilous Realm"[31] ("Perilous Realm" usually being some kind of alternate reality, separate from the real world).

There is no end to the places fantasy can take us. In *Realms of Fantasy*, science fiction writers Malcolm Edwards and Robert Holdstock identify at least five fantasy environments: the ancient past, the distant future, present-day lost worlds, other planets, and fantasy Earths similar to, but different from our own.[32] Tolkien fondly referred to these secondary worlds as "sub-creations."[33] In the finest fantasy, such places are so realistic, with their own laws of nature, forms of life and passages of time, that they completely consume the reader.

Occasionally this may lead some people to try creating in the real world certain aspects of the places about which they are reading. Such an effort was made, for instance, in the 1960s when Tolkien's volumes gained a cult-like following. According to Edwards and Holdstock, "aspects of the hippy movement can be seen retrospectively as an attempt to turn the Western world into the cosier and more friendly society of hobbits."[34] This is not surprising, since it is in Tolkien's words about the "aventures of men in the Perilous Realm" that we also find our answer to the often-asked question, Why is fantasy so wildly popular?

It cannot be denied that escapism certainly drives, at least to some extent, the joy and excitement we feel as we retreat into a fantasy book's alternate reality. But even more significant is the deep satisfaction we derive from safely immersing ourselves into a place that in many ways is better than ours. Even if that fantasy world starts off worse than our world (as in C.S. Lewis's witch-ruled Narnia in *The Lion, the Witch, and the Wardrobe*), there exists the thrill and glory of ultimately achieving a better world through adventure.

Whatever sorrows may be experienced along the way, the story and the storyteller lead us on as we read. Together with the fantasy hero/heroes, we ourselves meet each dread and the danger they face. And in the end, all of us are victorious. Children's book author Natalie Babbitt agrees, saying, "Fantasy literature lets us share the hero's hopes and eventual triumph."[35]

Fantasy can be highly therapeutic on both an emotional and psychological level. We obtain comfort by seeing evil unmasked, condemned and destroyed. We are offered hope through being shown that at least somewhere, even if it is in another world, good has triumphed.

In reference to this aspect of the fantasy genre, popular fantasy/science fiction writer Ursula LeGuin compared fantasy to poetry and mysticism, commenting, "Its affinity [i.e., attraction] is not with daydream, but with dream. It is a different approach to reality, an alternative technique for apprehending and coping with existence."[36]

LeGuin is only echoing what education specialist James E. Higgins is saying when he explains in *Beyond Words* that through fantasy a writer uses the power of imagination to take readers beyond the material world in order to "lay bare" those realities that are imperceptible to our physical senses:

> His work is expressed—and best understood—through intuition and emotion, rather than through logic. He concerns himself with a spiritual universe. . . . In our "real-everyday world" the great mysteries can only be thought about, puzzled over, or, in parts, studied. Put them into an imaginary world—re-present them—and they can be experienced; they can be tasted and touched, or laughed and cried over. The emotions and senses can be made useful in dealing with mystery.[37]

Fantasy, of course, need not always be a large-scale epic. It can also be somewhat light and whimsical, as is the case of *Winnie-the-Pooh*, *Chitty Chitty Bang Bang*, *Mary Poppins* or Beatrix Potter's *The Tale of Squirrel Nutkin*. Fantasy might also take a more sensitive and sentimental approach—e.g., *Charlotte's Web*. Adventure too might provide the main drive of the story, as in the classics *Twenty Thousand Leagues under the Sea* and *Journey to the Center of the Earth* by Jules Verne. As award-winning sci-fi writer Everett F. Bleiler has commented, "[F]antasy may be almost all things to all men."[38]

Regardless of its form, every kind of fantasy deals in some way with life as it might be in an alternate reality where our natural laws are suspended. In the realm of fantasy, science does not exist as we know it, and magic is everywhere in one form or another. Children respond instantaneously because it activates their imaginations—a key element to healthy maturation. Kids who are never encouraged to enter the fantasy world are, "quite literally, deprived children."[39]

Furthermore, to some extent fantasy can help children to see with spiritual eyes. It trains them to look beyond what's visible toward other possible worlds. In *The Ordinary and the Fabulous: An Introduction to Myths, Legends and Fairy Tales for Teachers and Storytellers*, British writer Elizabeth Cook says that legends, fairy tales and fantasy possess "a sense of the strange, the numinous, the totally Other, of what lies quite beyond human personality and cannot be found in any human relationships."[40]

In summation, good fantasy is well written, tells a great story, has a lot of action and is fun to read. It also should include fully developed characters and rest on recognizable themes. Popular author Madeleine L'Engle makes a much more thought-provoking observation of fantasy, choosing to define it as simply "those things that never were, but always are."[41]

Obviously, fantasy can be extremely beneficial to children. But there remains a problem with fantasy, as with all forms of fiction for young readers. According to recent studies into child development, literature that is good for some kids might not be good for others. These issues will be the focus of chapter 2.

TRUSTING SOULS

Child development specialists recognize that literature helps children realize their potential during a particular stage of development and fosters progress toward the next stage. . . . [Y]es, the books children read are formative in their lives; it is our responsibility to know their books. . . . [W]e need to develop guidelines for choosing the best . . . [because] the books we select influence children in lasting ways.

—Bernice E. Cullinan[1]
former president, International Reading Association

Research into reading comprehension has established beyond doubt that everyone brings his own background, experiences and biases to any book he reads. Consequently, children often understand, interpret and respond to the same piece of literature in different ways. Literature, therefore, that is appropriate for some children might not be good for others.

Adults are no different. Consider the results of a study discussed by Margaret S. Steffensen, Chitra Joag-Dev and Richard C. Anderson in their article "A Cross-Cultural Perspective on Reading Comprehension." They detailed how two groups of adults reacted in divergent ways to the same text—a letter describing an Indian wedding and an American wedding.

The first group (from America) interpreted the accounts as joyous occasions, observing that "the bride looked beautiful and that romance filled the air." The second group (from India) interpreted the narrative more soberly, noting "the hierarchy of the seating arrangements for guests, the importance of the dowry and financial arrangements, and the sacrifice the bride was making."[2]

This kind of subjectivity is even more pronounced in children not only because they are less developed emotionally, psychologically, intellectually and spiritually, but because they have far fewer life experiences from which to draw as they interact with the text they are reading. In fact, studies have shown that it is not necessarily the content that most influences a child's response to any given piece of literature, but the child's personal background, prior reading exposure, life experiences, maturity and overall developmental level.[3] To borrow the insightful words of Bernice E. Cullinan, "[W]e cannot just say, 'This is a good book,' but must ask ourselves, 'Good for whom?' "[4]

MAKING GOOD CHOICES

The criteria parents should use in choosing books for their children and teens clearly go beyond how many copies a popular volume has sold, how many awards it has won or whether a blockbuster Hollywood movie has been made from it. Factors that are equally or even more important include a child's language level, grasp of moral/ethical concepts and cognitive development (i.e., how a child acquires knowledge by use of reason, intuition and perception).

Parents also might want to consider how the child responds to other children, as well as the child's attitude toward books. Even the manner in which a child adopts "feelings and beliefs about themselves" may be relevant.[5] Of course, there is always the "fun" factor associated with any book, which above anything else will probably determine if a child returns to reading when choosing how to spend his or her time.

The trick is to provide children with enough enjoyable literary experiences that reading becomes a habit—one that will broaden their intellectual and emotional horizons for the rest of their lives. A good book for a child, teen, young adult or even a mature reader must be worth the effort of reading. As C.S. Lewis, author of The Chronicles of Narnia fantasy series, noted, "[N]o book is really worth reading at the age of ten which is not equally (and often far more) worth reading at the age of fifty."[6]

But again, a good literary experience is not solely the result of words on a page. There is more to the reading than simple recognition of text via the intellect. Wolfgang Iser, a renowned literature critic, adamantly maintained that a literary work takes on life as it is "realized" by the reader, and then, through that personal realization, the words of the book are "influenced by the individual disposition of the reader, who is in turn acted upon" by the text.[7] Stated another way, the book comes alive.

As previously pointed out, the coming to life of a book should be "fun." But what is "fun" for many children (as well as adults) is not necessarily healthful. Children's book author Elizabeth Fitzgerald Howard comments,

> We read for delight. But at the same time we must read with a discerning eye and mind, with the intention of defining that delight. So on one hand or with one eye, we are reading with a receptive spirit, eagerly and non-judiciously, unconsciously becoming the child that is still with us. But with the other eye, we must go beyond our own delight to the nuts and bolts, the very basic hardware, of how and why this book delights us and what could make it a source of delight for child readers.[8]

It must be remembered that children are not little adults—they need guidance. But in this day and age many children are making critical choices with regard to their own activities, including which books to read. This has led to a troubling reversal of some facets of family structure, with children making decisions that in years past were left up to the discretion of parents.

Children, of course, should be allowed a great deal of input when it comes to their reading material. But the final decision must remain in the hands of parents. The all-too-frequent lament of moms and dads these days, however, is: "Well, I really don't want them reading that book, but what can I do? They're just going to do what they're going to do."

Such a resigned attitude is only helping to create a society of restless and directionless youth. Why? Because this passive and permissive way of thinking tends to extend into even more problematic areas, such as a child's choice of friends, recreational activities and styles of dress (consider, for example, the ramifications of wearing "gang colors"). Parents ought not be afraid to use that necessary, but certainly most difficult of words (the one all kids dread): "no."

As the Preamble to the United Nations' Declaration of the Rights of the Child (1959) reads, "[T]he child, by reason of his physical and mental immaturity, needs special safeguards and care."[9] Choosing reading material for children undoubtedly falls under this guiding principle, and parents must not shy away from acting upon it. To do otherwise could easily prove detrimental—not only to the literary development of children, but also to their spiritual and emotional well-being.

LANGUAGE: A NECESSARY COMPONENT

The most obvious aspect of development that determines what literature is appropriate for a child is language skill level—verbal and written. Material that is too simple only bores children, and they may reject reading altogether as a viable means of entertainment and learning. On the other hand, material that is too advanced could devastate a child's self-confidence, especially if the child's reading difficulties provoke ridicule from peers. At the very least, the result may be frustration coupled with a failure to follow the storyline due to serious misunderstandings of the text.

An example of this can be seen in a study of the responses of fourth, sixth and eighth graders to Ursula Le Guin's *A Wizard of Earthsea* (1975), a fairly advanced fantasy novel. One fourth-grader complained about the long sentences, saying, "[T]hey just rumbled by like a jumbled bunch of words." Other fourth-graders consistently misread "loosing the shadow," which described the character Ged unleashing the shadow of death. One student remarked, "I didn't understand that part about him losing his shadow."[10]

These issues are discussed in-depth by children's literature experts Zena Sutherland and May Hill Arbuthnot, who state in *Children and Books* that even though a certain volume may be a "juvenile classic," such a categorization may mean very little. They warn that if it is "beyond children's understanding or too subtle or sophisticated for their level of appreciation, they can turn it down with a stony indifference which leaves adults baffled and grieved."[11]

A good way to test a young child's development in this area is to read a book aloud to them, letting them take turns reading as you go along. Then pause periodically and discuss the themes and events of the book, checking their comprehension. (This is a critical step, because some children might be able to "read" the words on the page, but not be proficient enough with language to comprehend what they are reading.)

Books take children outside their own personal frame of reference. Therefore, it is important that the new situations, events and conflicts presented in their books are understandable. In this way, the new material can contribute to the database of information the child uses to interpret the world. Fortunately, good stories often place new words and concepts into contexts that naturally explain their meaning. A parent, however, must always be on hand to explain to the child any concepts still unclear.

Knowing Right from Wrong

Everyone has a sense of right and wrong, of morality and ethics, of good and evil. But from where do we get these concepts? That aspect of our development begins early in life and progresses through several stages. Literature helps children, even teenagers, to work through these stages of development and can be very influential in their moral direction. According to researchers who study such issues, the earliest stage (the "morality of constraint" stage) involves obedience to adult rules (i.e., "good" behavior) primarily through fear of punishment. This is why the morality of typical fairy tales is so easily accepted by young children: The stories reflect where they are in their moral development.[12] In *Response to Literature*, published in 1968 by the National Council of Teachers of English, James Miller, Jr., explained how the best books for children include moral dilemmas that elicit discussions of values:

> Literature properly presented should confront the student (like life itself) with a multiplicity of ethical systems and moral perspectives. This expansion and deepening of the student's moral awareness constitutes the education of his moral imagination. It is one important (but not the sole) aim of literary study.[13]

Eventually, as the child develops, the "morality of constraint" stage is replaced by a "morality of cooperation" phase. It is entered gradually as children begin to notice that their actions affect not only themselves, but others—positively or negatively. This new understanding hopefully engenders some degree of mutual respect for their fellow human beings. In addition to realizing that their actions affect others, the "morality of cooperation" stage usually includes the discovery of something called "motive." Children come to see the motives in their own and others' decisions.

Suddenly, with an understanding of motivation, a child can appreciate not only what a character does, but why a character does it. Herein lies one of the most beneficial aspects of literature in relation to the "morality of cooperation" stage—literature facilitates discussions with children that delve into the actions of fictional characters and the legitimacy of those actions. Such talks can help children develop problem-solving skills, enable them to become more secure in their moral convictions, and force them to examine why they believe what they believe. Each of these benefits of literature can do nothing but help a child in future years.

Of course, there is also a danger here. What if a parent's own ethical/moral conscience is not developed? What if a teacher who is discussing morals/ethics with a child seeks to impose his/her own standards of morality on that child, rather than allowing him/her to reach their own conclusions? What if the morals/ethics put forth and glamorized by a story are not compatible with the parents' convictions? Sutherland and Arbuthnot offer several observations and suggestions:

> Children's literature often reflects the values that adults think are important to encourage, and those who select books for children should be aware of the author's values and assumptions as well as of their own. If an author's attitude toward parent-child relationships, sex mores, civil rights, or any other issue is in agreement with our own, we may tend to approve of the book as a whole, but if the values and assumptions are at variance with our own, we may tend to dismiss it, regardless of its other qualities. For these reasons, it is particularly important for us to analyze books [as] carefully and objectively as we can. . . . [I]t is often illuminating to compare a book with the author's other books and with other authors' books on the same topic or in the same literary genre.[14]

There is just no way to avoid some risks when the time comes for parents to expose their children to literature. But if parents are careful about choosing books for their children, the risks are well worth taking.

I Think, Therefore I Read

Literature also is inextricably linked to how children acquire knowledge and make choices in life (i.e., our cognitive development). Great books help young readers mature intellectually, especially with regard to how they process information in the real world around them. Closely tied to how literature helps in this area is the universal practice of personal storytelling. Long before children can read and well afterward, they invent their own stories as a way of dealing with reality.

Adults do it too, since storytelling is a very human act. Engaging in it enables us to process, reflect upon, and put to use all we perceive. Respected language/literature authority James Britton, in *Language and Learning*, described storytelling as "an assimilative function through which we balance out inner needs with external realities."[15] Literature becomes interwoven with this natural form of expression during childhood when kids take symbols and characters from the stories they read (e.g., witches, fairy godmothers, giants, trolls, wizards, etc.) and adapt them for use in their own personal tales.[16]

Significantly, young children also borrow phraseology from stories to serve as markers for their own tales. "Once upon a time" is commonly borrowed for a clearly-defined beginning and "they lived happily ever after" is used as a typical ending. According to Bernice E. Cullinan—editor-in-chief of Wordsong (the poetry imprint of Boyds Mills Press)—this borrowing indicates the extent to which children "have assimilated literature and dramatically illustrates the potential power of literature to affect language as well as cognitive and affective development."[17]

As children move through the various intellectual stages of maturity, they progressively interact more on an analytical basis with literature, until finally reaching the "formal operational mode" of thinking (late adolescence).[18] At this stage they are increasingly able to reason with abstractions, symbols and logic. Signs of the approaching mode can be seen in most children as early as fourth or fifth grade (nine to eleven years old). It is an age when children gain the ability to both identify with and emulate the traits of those characters in books with whom they can identify. This is why it is so crucial for parents to know the kinds of characters contained in the books their children are reading.

ME, MYSELF AND OTHERS

Literature can significantly affect a child's ability to interact socially. According to the late Northrop Frye, who was a widely respected literature professor at the University of Toronto, educating the imagination through literature directly influences the eventual depth of one's social vision.[19] Frye held the opinion that one of the main purposes of imagination is to produce a vision of a society we want to live in, as opposed to the one we have to live in—i.e., our ideal world versus our real world. In reference to Frye's perspective, Bernice Cullinan writes the following in *Literature and Your Child*:

> One world is around us, the other is a vision inside our minds, born and fostered by the imagination, yet real enough for us to try to make the world we see conform to its shape. Frye goes on to say that the quest of human beings is to discover their identities and their place within their societies, to discover who they are and where they belong. . . . Literature plays a strong role in helping children envision a world they do not see. E.B. White's *Charlotte's Web* . . . an ode to friendship, explores relationships in a fantasy world that have lasting meaning in the real world. Lloyd Alexander's The Book of Three series follows Taran's quest for his lost identity and celebrates an individual's joy of knowing who he or she is. Literature feeds the imagination; it helps us create a vision of society to work toward.[20]

Since the very future of our society is in the hands of our children—the next generation of adults who will control society—it seems perfectly reasonable that those children should have their imaginations educated and exercised. But when it comes to the literature that we allow them to read, there is a very crucial question parents must ask: What kind of "vision of society" is a particular book presenting? Answering this question alone may be enough for parents to know whether or a not a book is appropriate for their child. We must never underestimate the power that a certain piece of literature, or body of literature, can have over a generation. It could ultimately affect society in general on a very large scale in years to come.

In reference to even the simple fairy tale, Jane Yolen has correctly noted that they came out of society and then went back into society "changing the shape of that society in turn." Fairy tales "were part of the belief system of the class of people who listened to and learned from and believed in them. . . . Children today are that class." Yolen warns us all: "And so the modern mythmakers, knowing how powerful the tales can be, must not . . . bear this burden lightly."[21]

MAGICAL APPEAL

Regardless of their developmental level, there is something unique about how every child feels drawn toward all that is magical. The natural attraction begins anew each day as that child awakens to an as-yet unexplored world. Child education expert James E. Higgins writes,

> Today he may find it in the magic of an ice-cream-stick-boat caught up in the current of a gutter-river and racing rapids to disappear over the edge of a sewer-falls, down into the darkness of who-knows-where. . . . [I]t may come to him in the simple magic of waking up to the chatter of birds or to the quiet of a snowfall, he will capture glimpses of it at work and at play (which for the child are very often the same thing), at mealtime and at bedtime. It will always be there—the haunting mystery of his world.[22]

Literature, especially fantasy, can affect children so deeply that their reading experience is nothing less than a kind of spiritual event. To the child, the world is naturally met each day as a place where "the material and the spiritual are so intricately entwined that they are one and the same."[23] I have experienced this in my own life, and have seen it to be true in the lives of those children with whom I have interacted as an adult.

For example, many years ago I met a boy of about eight years old on a playground and asked him if he believed in God. He assured me he did. When I asked him why, he unabashedly declared that it was an obvious fact. As he pointed to all the trees that surrounded us, the birds, the sky and the sun, he rhetorically asked a question packed with theological significance: "Who else could have made all of this?"[24] My young friend effortlessly merged the physical with the spiritual. He was naturally open to the supernatural, the spiritual and the mystical.

Literature (particularly fantasy), like the mind and heart of a child, "integrates the spiritual and the material into a unified whole."[25] Professor James Higgins explains:

> Story offers the child another key to the understanding of the universe—a universe which stretches multi-light-years in time and distance beyond the reader's own experience. Literature accepts the imagination of the child as a legitimate vehicle for passing beyond the differences of appearance and into the unity of truth.... [T]here is something spiritual and mystifying about almost any good story written about children, and many good books written for children.[26]

C.S. Lewis (1898-1963), George MacDonald (1824-1905) and J.R.R. Tolkien (1892-1973) were especially adept at capturing the spiritual/mystical within the pages of their fantasy works. So too are several other contemporary authors such as Stephen Lawhead (b. 1950) and Lloyd Alexander (b. 1924). The spiritual undertones of their works are apparent to all who enter their created worlds. Renowned poet Richard Le Gallienne recognized the presence of such spirituality as an indispensable facet of good fantasy (or fairy tale), saying, "The earth cannot get along all by itself. It is always in need of help from the stars. This is one of the many morals of the fairy tale, which thus gives expression to the holy hunger of the human heart."[27]

The gifted fantasy writer Lloyd Alexander sees several benefits for readers of fantasy—young and old alike. First, there is the "sheer delight" of "let's pretend" and the "eager suspension of disbelief." To Alexander, "[t]here is an exuberance in good fantasy quite unlike the most exalted moments of realistic literature."[28]

Second, fantasy elicits our emotions as vividly as a dream. Alexander feels that the fantasy adventure "seems always on a larger scale, the deeds bolder, the people brighter." He adds, "In fantasy, we have more plausible scope for strong feelings. . . . [W]e can laugh harder, weep longer—and be a little corny."[29]

Third, fantasy can be wonderfully influential in the area of morality. The genre offers clear values, true heroes, ultimate justice, endless mercy and fierce courage. Alexander notes, "Fantasy, by its power to move us so deeply, to dramatize, even melodramatize, morality, can be one of the most effective means of establishing a capacity [in children] for adult values."[30]

Finally, fantasy, including science fiction (and to a degree even some types of horror), can offer hope, which Alexander describes as "one of the most precious human values."[31] It, in fact, is the essential thread of all fantasy genres. Award-winning fantasy/sci-fi author Terry Pratchett comments,

> The morality of fantasy and horror is, by and large, the strict morality of the fairy tale. The vampire is slain, the alien is blown out of the airlock, the evil Dark Lord is vanquished and, perhaps at some loss, the Good triumph—not because they are better armed, but because Providence is on their side. Let there be goblin hordes, let there be terrible environmental threats, let there be giant mutated slugs if you really must, but let there also be Hope.[32]

As Lloyd Alexander astutely observed in his essay "Wishful Thinking—or Hopeful Dreaming," "If we say, 'While there's life, there's hope,' we can also say, 'While there's hope, there's life.' "[33] With special regard to children, popular novelist G.K. Chesterton made an observation about fairy tales that is equally applicable to fantasy: "The objection to fairy stories is that they tell children there are dragons. But children have always known there are dragons. Fairy stories tell children that dragons can be killed."[34]

MAGIC VS. MAGICK

One consistent question raised by parents, especially those from within the religious community, has to do with the positive portrayal of "magic" in fantasy: Is it a danger? Magic, of course, is a common element not only in fantasy, but also in fairy tales, folktales, myths, fables, and legends. It serves as a convenient tool that can be used to propel the plot and characters forward.

Magic is as much a key element to fantasy as advanced technology is to science fiction because both magic and advanced technology allow for things to happen in their respective stories that otherwise could not happen. While few parents would have a problem with Captain Kirk's "communicator" and "phaser" or the starship *Enterprise*'s photon torpedoes in *Star Trek*, many parents are uncomfortable when it comes to "magic" in stories for children.

But "magic" in fantasy should never be confused with "magick"—i.e., real-world occult practices.[35] They are two altogether different things. Magic without a "k"—the kind found in most fantasy books and fairy tales—is imaginary. It bears little resemblance to widely recognized occult beliefs and practices in the real world. The only commonality that "magic" may have to our world are uses of age-old symbols that represent beliefs, hopes and fears that are common to all people.

Even the various objects associated with "magic" in a fantasy tend to be invented for the sake of that story, and if not wholly invented, then at least altered in some way (by use or appearance) from similar real-world objects. As Christian author J.R.R. Tolkien said, true fantasy is filled with images and imagery that "are not only 'not actually present,' but which are indeed not to be found in our primary world at all, or are generally believed not to be found there."[36] Even when certain objects or practices are not changed significantly enough for them to be completely unrecognizable, they still are usually found within the confines of an entirely different reality, thereby taking them away from any real-world context. Consequently, such objects or practices would still not be objectionable.

In The Chronicles of Narnia series, for instance, devout Christian C.S. Lewis positively speaks of a "stargazer," which in our world normally would refer to an astrologer. Such a reference completely contradicts Lewis' faith. Noteworthy, however, is the fact that Lewis' "stargazer" is not in our world. Hence, his passing reference might refer to someone who is more of an astronomer, or who fits some description Lewis had in his own mind that he applied to the Narnian world.

In fantasy, which commonly takes place in an alternate reality, different definitions, meanings and laws of existence apply. So parents must not automatically reject a fantasy book just because it may mention wizards, spells and/or magic. Such elements are not necessarily reflective of real occultism.

A lot of fantasy, for instance, leans heavily on magic and contains as lead characters some kind of magician (i.e., a wizard). But the classic "wizard" often serves as a symbol of benevolence and help, which is why wizards are found fighting evil. Of course, there are evil wizards, but these are almost always portrayed as having gone bad and are at war with good wizards. In either case, the "magic" they perform has little to do with any real-world occult practices and tying the two together would be a mistake.

Now, fantasy that closely mirrors magick—spelled with a "k"—could legitimately be objected to by parents because magick operates in a real way in our real world. Moreover, it often produces some seriously negative consequences (see Appendix A). Divination, spiritualism, necromancy, astrology, crystal-gazing, spells, witchcraft, sorcery and numerology all fall within the magick category. These and other occult practices, as well as their related beliefs, invade fantasy when they are too accurately presented by an author. In such instances, magic and magick become virtually the same thing.

This is in direct contrast to what J.R.R. Tolkien believed. To Tolkien, the "magic" in fantasy was so different from anything in our world that he thought perhaps the very word "magic" should not even be used in connection with fantasy. In *Tree and Leaf*, he explained that real magick "produces, or pretends to produce, an alteration in the Primary World [i.e., our world, as opposed to the Secondary World of fantasy]. . . . [I]t is not an art but a technique; its desire is power in this world, domination of things and wills."[37]

Today, however, there is an increase in the blending through fantasy of magick with magic; reality with alternate reality. It happens consistently in the Harry Potter series (see Part Three). This is problematic when it comes to children, because as we have seen, young people learn, grow and develop in some very specific and fragile ways. Just as children need food appropriate to their physical development, so they need literature appropriate to their intellectual, emotional, psychological and spiritual development.

In conclusion, it must be acknowledged that fantasy does have some pitfalls and parents need to be aware of them. At the same time, concerned parents should recognize that certain works of fantasy are ideal for children. Far from being a way of simply escaping reality, fantasy can be for them a path toward understanding it. In his essay titled "Sometimes Fairy Stories May Say Best What's to Be Said," C.S. Lewis commented:

> The Fantastic or Mythical is a Mode available at all ages. . . .
> At all ages if it is well used by the author and meets the right
> reader, it has the same power: to generalize while remaining
> concrete, to present in palpable form not concepts or even
> experiences but whole classes of experience. . . . But at its best
> it can do more; it can give us experiences we have never had
> and thus, instead of "commenting on life," can add to it.[38]

The danger, then, regarding magic in fiction/fantasy is when
"magick" is inserted into it. Such an insertion confuses the worlds
of fiction and reality, especially for younger children. Unfortunately, this is exactly what is happening today in certain forms of
"parallel world" fantasy, where authors heavily draw upon
real-world occultism in an effort to create works reflecting society's current fascination with the occult (see chapter 6). Moreover, there has been a marked downturn in the artistic quality of
fantasy, as well as in its psychological and spiritual merit. This disturbing trend in the literary community will be discussed in chapter 3.

THE FALL OF
FANTASY

3

[C]hildren's book publishing was rescued [in the 1980s] by the fast-growing chain bookstores to be found in malls. . . . This social space was different from the library in that the child or parent chose books without the advice or supervision of a librarian or teacher and without discussion of the book's merits. To attract children and adults as consumers of literature, the very nature of the book—its design and contents—began to change.

—Jack Zipes[1]
folklore expert, University of Minnesota

Children's books at one time were carefully chosen and published by editors committed to producing literature to inspire and elevate young minds. Today, consumerism drives the children's book industry, for the most part, and many publishing insiders have not hesitated to say so. For instance, Tom Engelhardt, a longtime editor at Pantheon, began years ago to decry the commercialization and exploitation of reading by conglomerates interested primarily in making money. According to Engelhardt, the publisher's goal is no longer to produce quality children's books, but to publish what will facilitate sales of expensive spin-offs such as tapes or CDs, clothing, movies and videos.

In the words of Margaret R. Marshall, former chairman of the Children's Libraries Section of the International Federation of Library Associations, publishing is now "in the hands of the financiers."[2] Hence, many children's book producers—most of which are tied in to food or toy companies—now do little more than create in kids an appetite for specific kinds of literature.

Then, to satisfy that appetite, they mass-market only those types of books. Advertised along with them, of course, are related and often costly products. University of Minnesota professor Jack Zipes observes: "Rather than opening new worlds to children, they [book publishers] invite them [children] to repeat certain predictable and comforting experiences that they can easily and affordably buy into."[3]

But there is more to this disturbing trend. Once the making of children's books became big business, publishers saw that the main money holders (parents) had to be motivated to lay down cash for whatever was being offered. So book producers, with the help of well-meaning librarians and teachers, began painting a frightening portrait of millions of illiterate children glued to a video game or the TV—all because they had not developed a reading habit. Fear quickly replaced critical thinking about children's literature.

This is not to say that their warnings about children's reading habits were inaccurate. As far back as 1983, for instance, "the average American adolescent had already in his or her lifetime watched 17,000 hours of television."[4] Reading statistics, on the other hand, were less than impressive.[5] Consider the following:

- A 1998 survey of teens (twelve to seventeen years old) found that on average they spend only 2.53 hours reading per week, as opposed to 6.18 hours talking on the phone, 8.58 hours just "hanging out" and 9.46 hours listening to music.[6]
- A 1999 survey revealed that on a daily basis, kids aged two to eighteen spend only about forty-four minutes reading for fun, in comparison to two hours forty-six minutes watching TV.[7]

- Between 1983 and 1999 more than 10 million Americans reached the twelfth grade without having learned to read at a basic level.[8]
- As of 2001, more than twenty percent of adults were reading at or below a fifth-grade level—far below the level needed to earn a living wage.[9]

There is obviously a problem of literacy in America. But it is nothing new. A survey by two Illinois professors revealed that adolescent reading habits have "changed little over time, from 1927 to 1992. Reading for pleasure has always been third on the list of leisure activities [after being with friends and playing sports]."[10]

The real problem today, then, may not be that kids are *not* reading, but rather, the substance of what they *are* reading. In a recent essay, Jim Viccaro—managing editor of *The Book & The Computer*—quoted the venerable U.S. literary quarterly, *Sewanee Review*, the editor of which stated,

> People are reading more and more trash and less and less serious literature. One of the odd situations facing the country is that we have too d*** many writers and not enough readers. I don't know what the answer to this dilemma is.[11]

The *Sewanee Review* points out a troubling truth traceable to corporate America's campaign to warn the public about juvenile illiteracy: Parents have accepted the highly flawed and perilous idea that *any* reading is better than *no* reading. Many parents now believe that reading is intrinsically good regardless of the quality of the material being read. In a hard-hitting 1991 *Harper's Magazine* article titled "Reading May Be Harmful to Your Kids," Engelhardt complained,

> That habit [of reading] was invoked with reverential seriousness by the people producing the flood of new books. To inculcate that habit in the young was, it seemed, not so much a vocation as a consummate challenge in a world where competitive distractions for children came ever

thicker and faster. In fact, the issue was increasingly not so much what you read but that you read at all.[12]

The result has been a steady stream of less than admirable, but profitable, so-called children's books flooding the marketplace. Moreover, anyone daring to defend the validity of using *moderate* discretion in connection to choosing what is child-appropriate literature is vehemently shouted down by panic-stricken adults worried about only one thing: getting kids to read again. Not only are people overlooking the actual content of these books, but they are not recognizing that the glut of volumes reflect "a calculated way of looking at children as consumers with a common denominator, and many of the products represent a dumbing down of children rather than a challenge to their creativity."[13]

As far back as 1987, award-winning fantasy writer Michael Moorcock saw on the horizon this commercialization of book publishing. In *Wizardry and Wild Romance*, he expressed his fear that the public would eventually be denied access to truly good writers "who have soldiered on regardless, ignoring the fluctuations of fashion and the commercial demands of a 'market' which half the time doesn't even have the slightest idea what the public wants or why."[14]

In reference not only to this ongoing problem, but also to the media's inundation of kids with gratuitous violence and overt sexuality, respected film critic David Denby wrote a scathing 1996 essay for *The New Yorker* titled "Buried Alive: Our Children and the Avalanche of Crud." It reads:

> The danger is not mere exposure to occasional violent or prurient images but the acceptance of a degraded environment that devalues everything—a shadow world in which our kids are breathing an awful lot of poison without knowing that there's clean air and sunshine elsewhere. They are shaped by the media as consumers before they've had a chance to develop their souls.[15]

Denby went on to lambaste pop culture in general, noting that it "consumes our children."[16] He then pointed his accusatory finger at parents, who in many cases have seemingly neglected their duty to raise their children to be individualists, rather than cookie-cutter victims of the mass market interests and materialism.[17] Sadly, what we find ourselves facing, particularly in America, is a money-making industry that has co-opted the institutional label "Children's Literature." And this corporate industry is force-feeding today's youth anything and everything, as long as it rings up dollar signs. Fantasy, thanks to media marketing strategies, has been at the center of this whole controversy.

HARRY, HARRY, HARRY

The most obvious example of consumerism's link to books for children is the ongoing hysteria over J.K. Rowling's Harry Potter series. In a July 2000 *New York Times* article, Janet Maslin insightfully noted,

> The frenzy that has greeted the fourth book in the series, *Harry Potter and the Goblet of Fire*, would seem to go beyond any reasonable response to fiction, no matter how genuinely delightful that fiction happens to be. Instead, the current wave of Harrymania brings the Potter series to a fever pitch better associated with movie hype, major sports events and hot new Christmas toys.[18]

Maslin's observation echoes the sentiments of professor Jack Zipes, who has been involved in the study and criticism of literature for more than twenty years:

> Phenomena such as the Harry Potter books are driven by commodity consumption that at the same time sets the parameters of reading and aesthetic taste. . . . What readers passionately devour and enjoy may be, like many a Disney film or Barbie doll, a phenomenal experience and have personal significance, but it is also an *induced* experience calcu-

lated to conform to a cultural convention of amusement and distraction.[19]

Zipes, a well-respected and highly knowledgeable children's literature specialist, additionally feels the Harry Potter books are not only formulaic, but also sexist. For publicly expressing such opinions he has been "aggressively attacked" during radio shows by callers accusing him of demeaning J.K. Rowling and her work. Such heated responses from Harry Potter fans have become the norm, rather than the exception. Literary critics, for example, who see Rowling's books as rather ordinary, and in many ways substandard when compared to other fiction, are loudly condemned as arrogant and/or jealous snobs too rigid to see the literary excellence of Harry Potter.

Into this category of despised individuals fall many well-respected and knowledgeable critics who have made commendable contributions to the world of literature, such as Oxford-educated Anthony Holden (an award-winning journalist and best-selling biographer), Roger Hutton (editor of *The Horn Book*, a seventy-five-year-old children's literary digest) and Harold Bloom (renowned literary critic and Yale scholar). Holden described Harry Potter as "not particularly well-written,"[20] while Sutton called it a "critically insignificant" series, adding that, as literature goes, Rowling's books are "nothing to get excited about."[21]

It was Bloom, however, who took off the proverbial gloves by writing a piece for the *Wall Street Journal* about Harry Potter titled "Can 35 Million Book Buyers Be Wrong? Yes."[22] On the PBS interview program, *Charlie Rose*, he candidly said of Rowling's books, "They're just an endless string of clichés. I cannot think that does anyone any good. That's not *Wind in the Willows*. That's not *Through the Looking Glass*. . . . It's really just slop."[23] Needless to say, Harry Potter fans were less than happy with these eminently qualified reviewers from the literary community.

Anyone daring to question the "child-appropriateness" of Rowling's books has fallen under even greater disdain, however; they have been called stupid, narrow-minded and ignorant. Harry Potter critics who also happen to express religiously oriented concerns about the books and the occultism they contain have been the most vilified. Many of the more strongly worded reactions have not been against the actual objections raised by critics, but against religion in general, with particularly vile sentiments being leveled at Christianity.[24]

This overly defensive attitude demonstrated by a vast number of Harry Potter fans additionally could be linked to the Harry Potter phenomenon itself. Once any "phenomenon" begins, especially one that is media-driven, people habitually lose the ability to reason and think objectively. Zipes explains:

> The ordinary becomes extraordinary, and we are so taken
> by the phenomenon that we admire, worship, and idolize it
> without grasping fully why we regard it with so much reverence and awe except to say that so many others regard it as a
> phenomenon and, therefore, it must be a phenomenon.[25]

Blind allegiance to anything—whether a piece of literature, a religion, a politician or an entertainment personality—certainly opens a doorway to a host of potentially detrimental and destructive consequences. But blind allegiance to something inherently negative surely presents a greater danger. Yet this is already occurring within our society as certain kinds of fantasy/fiction are being marketed to children. They are known as "shock fiction" books for children and are nothing short of reprehensible—morally, intellectually and spiritually.

THE HORROR OF FEAR STREET AND GOOSEBUMPS

In 1970, child education expert James E. Higgins rightly noted, "No one has to remind parents that a bad book can seduce."[26] Yet an alarming number of adults today seem to have forgotten that some books, though entertaining, might indeed be bad for children. All manner of reading material is now being introduced to young, impressionable minds, even though not too long ago their contents would have been deemed potentially harmful. The Fear Street and Goosebumps series by R.L. Stine typify—indeed, have served as a prototype for—such books.

Robert Lawrence Stine (b. 1943), who holds a B.A. in education from Ohio State University, first gained widespread notoriety in 1986 with the release of *Blind Date*, his first horror story for teenagers. It became an immediate best-seller. "It was a complete surprise for me," recalls Stine. "I realized I'd really struck a chord with kids. They liked scary books!"[27] Then in 1989 Parachute Press began publishing Stine's Fear Street series for preteens and teens (now numbering more than eighty books). These tales revolve around the gruesome events that happen to people who live on, or near, "Fear Street" in the town of Shadyside. Although the books are primarily marketed to preteens and teens, they are commonly read by children as young as nine or ten. Approximately 100 million copies have sold worldwide.

The ongoing series, which continues to sell at an astonishing rate, revolves around teenage characters who encounter mayhem, violence, brutality, murder and oftentimes, occult phenomena. The publisher's description for *Halloween Party* (1993), for instance, reads: "An invitation to a Halloween party hosted by the beautiful but mysterious Justine Cameron spells danger, terror, and murder for the guests." Other titles are equally revealing: *Spring Break: Sun, Fun . . . MURDER!* (1999); *The Best Friend: Sometimes Friendship Can Be Murder* (1992); *Dance Of Death* (1997); *Killer's Kiss* (1997); and *Who Killed the Homecoming Queen?* (1997).

Stine seems particularly obsessed with murder, especially the killing of young women. Such subject matter becomes all the more disturbing when one views his cover illustrations—they often depict attractive teenage girls in terrifying situations: being stalked, kidnaped or lying dead. Stine's plots are almost misogynistic in their incessant depiction of young women being victimized, both verbally and physically. Consider the following Fear Street volumes and the descriptions of them offered by the publisher:

- *Cheerleaders—The New Evil: Seasons Greetings . . . The Evil Is Back* (1992): "[T]he Shadyside cheerleaders are sure that the evil spirit is destroyed. Then Hannah is mysteriously thrown through the car window and Naomi is nearly burned to death."

- *Broken Hearts: Valentine's Day Can Be a Killer* (1993): "When Josie and Melissa receive threatening Valentine's Day messages, and then the girls of Shadyside High begin turning up dead, the two friends are certain that they will be the next victims."

- *Silent Night 2: Jingle Bells . . . Santa Kills* (1993): "Reva Dalby thinks that the world is hers for the taking—until a stalker wearing a Santa Claus suit decides to kidnap her."

- *Wrong Number 2: Call Waiting to Kill* (1995): " 'You're not safe anywhere. I'll get my revenge!' Can it really be Mr. Faberson on the line? He should still be locked up after trying to kill Deema and Jade last year. But Jade and Deema soon realize that someone is nearby, watching their every move, and waiting to kill them."

Fiction writer Diana West, in her 1995 *American Educator* article "The Horror of R.L. Stine," observed, "In this literary landscape, narrative exists solely to support a series of shocks occurring at absurdly frequent intervals. Push-button characters serve as disposable inserts to advance the narrative shock after shock."[28] One does no have to read very far into the Fear Street books for evidence supporting West's assertion.

In Stine's *Cheerleaders: The New Evil*, we find the character Corky letting out "a horrified wail" as she sees a "bright red gush of blood spurting from Rochelle's neck." A screwdriver has plunged into Rochelle's body after falling from high up in the gym bleachers: "The blood poured out over Rochelle. The hairbrush fell from her hand. She slumped forward until her head hit the floor" (Stine, p. 49).

Three pages later we read about a girl named Bobbi: "[She] had been trapped in the shower. . . . [S]he'd been locked inside. Then scalding hot water shot out of the showers. Unable to escape, Bobbi had suffocated in the boiling steam. Murdered" (Stine, p. 52). In *Broken Hearts* there is this disturbing scene described in lurid detail: "He stared at the bloody wound in her side. Stared at the puddle of blood at his feet. . . . The blood red swirls floated angrily in Dave's eyes. Blinding him. Suffocating him. So much blood. Such a big, red wound. And so much blood. Puddles and pools" (Stine, p. 141).

How have parents responded to these grotesque mockeries of literature? In an interview with the now-defunct *New York Newsday*, the mother of eleven-year-old Bill exclaimed, "I'm thrilled." She added, "He's literally reading a book a day. He always says, 'Just a few more pages.' . . . he devours [them]."[29] The mother of nine-year-old Tommy explained: "They just weren't my choice of subject matter. But I'm happy he's reading. If he wasn't reading this, he wouldn't be reading anything at all. Now he's at the point where he's constantly reading. He's fixated on horror."[30]

To complement his Fear Street series, Stine has produced another set of books known as the Fear Street Saga. This 1993 trilogy—*The Betrayal*, *The Secret* and *The Burning*—explains to fans of Fear Street why Shadyside is so filled with supernatural events, death and murder. According to the first book of this series, *The Betrayal*, the horrors all started 300 years earlier with the death of a young girl who was burned at the stake for witchcraft.

The story begins in the 1600s, when Susannah Goode falls in love with Edward Fier, the son of Governor Benjamin Fier. But when Benjamin learns that Edward wants to marry Susannah,

Benjamin falsely accuses her and her mother of practicing witch-craft because he believes Susannah is not a perfect match for Edward. Susannah and her mother are burned at the stake. They are innocent. But Susannah's father, who turns out to be a male witch, retaliates by putting a curse on the Fier family. Edward moves on, eventually marrying another woman—and her mother!

The Secret chronicles the continuing events surrounding members of the Fier family. Young Abigail Fier, for instance, is murdered by a ghost. Then, Delilah Goode, fiancée of Jonathan Fier, is shot and killed. A magical amulet linked to the curse is buried, but only for 100 years, until it is unearthed by Elizabeth Fier. Her sister, Kate, is subsequently murdered by Franklin Goode, who in turn is killed by Elizabeth's brother, Simon. The Fier family then changes their name to Fear, hoping to escape their curse.

Finally, *The Betrayal* brings us nearly up-to-date with the Fear family and their curse. An excellent summary of this book was posted at Amazon.com by a young fan of the series:

> From the moment Simon Fear saw Angelica Pierce at her Mardi Gras party, he knew he had to have her, even if that meant killing her two suitors. However, Angelica has a surprise of her own—she is just as eager to get rid of them as he is. She later reveals to Simon that she, too, is involved in the occult and wishes to manifest her "power through evil." Clearly, these two are a match made in hell, perfect for each other. Twenty years pass and Simon and Angelica Fear now live in Shadyside Village. . . . It seems as though Simon has finally fled his family curse. That is, until one horrible afternoon when two of his daughters are brutally murdered. . . . It's not until 35 years later, in 1900, that the final climax to the Fear-Goode saga occurs.[31]

For those too young for the Fear Street books, Stine has written a third series that is marketed specifically to children ages eight to twelve: Goosebumps. This series has sold a stag-

gering 220 million copies in more than sixteen languages since
1992. By 1994 it was already selling at an unprecedented rate of
1.25 million copies per month.[32] Stine was subsequently named
the number-one best-selling author in America by *USA Today*
from 1994 to 1996—three straight years.

The Goosebumps books, like the Fear Street volumes, are
packed with gruesome plots involving murder, revenge, violence, occultism and pure gore. One excerpt reads: "And then
the heads. Human heads. Hair caked with dirt. Skin loose,
hanging from their skulls. They stared at me with pleading eyes,
faces twisted, mouths hanging open in pain. 'Take me with
you,' one of them called in a dry whisper."[33]

Interestingly, the publisher of these grisly volumes is none
other than Scholastic, the U.S. publisher of Harry Potter. As
with the Fear Street series, the Goosebumps titles tell the whole
story: *Return to Horrorland: No Time to Scream*; *Welcome to
Dead House: It Will Just Kill You*; and *Piano Lessons Can Be
Murder*. Novelist Michael O'Brien, author of the best-selling
Father Elijah, makes these observations:

> For sheer perversity these tales rival anything that has been
> published to date. Each is brimming over with murder, gro-
> tesque scenes of horror, terror, mutilation (liberally sea-
> soned with gobbets and gobbets of blood and gore). Shock
> after shock pummels the reader's mind, and the child expe-
> riences them as both psychological and physical stimuli.
> These shocks are presented as ends in themselves, raw vio-
> lence as entertainment.[34]

In "Horror: To Gratify, Not Edify"—an article in *Language
Arts*, published by the National Council of Teachers of En-
glish—Randi Dickson highlighted a variety of perspectives on
Goosebumps, but concluded:

> My sampling of the series left me with little to admire. . . .
> One of the things I found most disturbing was the endings.

Each book ended in a completely unsatisfactory manner to me. . . . For example, at the end of *The Girl Who Cried Monster*, her parents invite Mr. Mortman to dinner and when he asks what's for dinner, they reply, "You!" They then grow fangs and eat him. At no point in the book was there any hint that the parents were "monsters" too. And then the book ends. (I kept looking for the missing pages.) . . . I wonder what expectations these children bring to literature or to the reading experience itself at this stage of their independent reading lives. . . . In *The Barking Ghost*, and in *Welcome to the Dead House*, there are siblings who do nothing but tease and torment one another. The parents in all cases are suspicious of their children and do little to help or support them. There is no character development, no satisfactory explanations to the dilemmas posed, and little, if anything, to be learned from their stories.[35]

It is no surprise that Stine's books have caused controversy in public schools. Some parents have gone so far as to call for a ban on the books in children's libraries, which in 1997 made the series number one on the American Library Association's list of Most Challenged Books.[36] But such protests usually have been drowned out by the now common argument, "At least the kids are reading." Librarian Shirley Emmert of the St. Paul-Minneapolis school district used this line of reasoning in 1997 during a regional debate over Goosebumps. When interviewed by KTCA-TV, she was asked: "[Y]our approach would be to get the kids to read?"

Emmert replied: "Yes."

"[N]o matter what they're reading, to begin with?" asked the KTCA newsman.

"Yes," she responded.

"[A]nd then worry about exactly what they read later on?"

"Yes, yes."[37]

This mind-set has been echoed again and again by parents, teachers and librarians.[38] Predictably, Stine himself unhesitatingly proclaims that kids should have virtually no restrictions placed on them when it comes to literature, saying, "I always think kids are the best judge of what they should read and not read. . . . I think kids are really smart, and I don't think they will read anything that is inappropriate for them. . . . I think everyone is glad that kids are reading."[39]

Even the Internet-based Learning Network Parent Channel, familyeducation.com, has capitulated to this sort of thinking. In a familyeducation.com online article for parents titled "Why Kids Love Goosebumps: An Interview with Fright-Meister R.L. Stine," Timothy Harper conceded,

> I have pretty much overcome my misgivings about his work. Yes, some of it is violent and scary. But Stine does something that most teachers and parents struggle with: He gets kids, especially boys, to read on their own. . . . Kids should be reading good stuff. But at least Stine gets them reading.[40]

Others, however, disagree. Fourth-grade teacher David Edholm, who was part of the 1997 St. Paul-Minneapolis controversy, stated, "For them to say at least the kids are reading, if they're reading a wrong message, their reading skill does not mean that much." He added, "The same argument could be used if middle school boys aren't reading, you know, do we put erotic novels in the middle school library so that they would read, and so we can do better. We can do better than these types of books."[41]

As for the children who have already grown up on Stine and are now young adults, they remember with fondness their experiences. A recent news story by former child readers of Stine wrote,

> Blood-curling shrieks, slow-motion accidents, and lots and many violent murders kept us on the edge of our seats [as children], shivering as we anxiously turned the pages to get to the end of the story. R.L. Stine was the reason we could

not sleep at night or go to the bathroom alone, fearing that someone with a knife might jump at us. But the thrills were exhilarating as we walked down Fear Street at night past the infamous cemetery where all the spirits roamed in unrest.[42]

Parents would do well to consider whether or not these kinds of memories are what they want stored in the minds of their children. And the need for making such a decision will not be going away any time soon. Stine is a highly prolific author who continues to churn out volume after volume. As of 2002, he had released more than 160 Fear Street/Goosebumps books for children, as well as twenty additional spine-chilling horror novels for young adults. He currently has plans for a TV mini-series, already has a Goosebumps kids show on television (FOX-TV), and is working on a Fear Street major motion picture tentatively titled *Scream, Jennifer, Scream*.

Unfortunately, Stine's success has prompted other writers to produce copycat volumes. Christopher Pike, for instance, has a line of "Spookesville" books, targeting children ages nine to twelve. They include titles like: *The Witches' Gift* and *Time Terror*. He also has written a number books in a series titled The Last Vampire. Diana West astutely surmises the most damaging aspect of such books, especially those written by Stine: They show an utter lack of respect for, and a dismissal of, the journey from childhood to adulthood.

> Stine's audience is being encouraged at a critical age to engage in literary pursuits devoid of content, crammed with shock. . . . Just as crimes against children still wound [us]. . . so too should shock fiction, for its role in desensitizing the very young, stunting the life of the mind before it has even begun.[13]

Author Steve Russo (*The Seduction of Our Children* and *The Devil's Playground*), an expert in the occult, also has expressed concerns. He admits that it would be extreme to say that all children who read Goosebumps are going to end up worshiping the devil or committing a heinous crime. He does, however, offer a word of caution, saying, "[T]hey will become desensitized to evil and violence. This type of desensitization is subtle and can affect the child long term." Russo further believes that Goosebumps also has the potential to become a gateway into the world of the occult. "Evil is enticing," says Russo. "And for some kids a hunger for more can easily develop, causing them to search down the wrong path to satisfy their appetites by dabbling in the darkness."[44]

GUARDING YOUR FAMILY

Reading fantasy can be a wonderful experience, in which a child (or adult) can live vicariously through the adventures of fictitious characters. Fantasy can also help us learn how others might handle certain situations and problems, which in turn could alter how we ourselves look at our own situations. Fantasy, then, is not intrinsically evil. But because it can send powerful messages to readers, great care ought to be taken when choosing material to read. Exactly how does one evaluate a children's book?

First, consider the book itself. Look at its appearance (size, front cover design, back cover information). Check for what you may consider any disturbing or child-inappropriate images. Read the description of the book on the inside cover flap (for hardbound) or on the back cover (soft cover). Take a moment to read about the author and see what other kinds of books he or she has written.

Second, know why you are buying the book for your child. Is it for private reading? Is it for classroom reading? Will you be reading it to your child or will your child be reading it unsupervised? What message, values or lessons do you want the book to present to him?

Third, take a moment to read a few chapters. Many bookstores now have a café where you can relax and peruse a volume before purchasing it. You might also want to use the Internet to look up some reviews of the book from sources you trust, making sure to read the comments of at least two or three different reviewers.

Additional suggestions on how to pick good books for children are found in *An Introduction to the World of Children's Literature* by Margaret R. Marshall. This volume counsels adults to select children's books that:

- Introduce children to their own cultural heritage.
- Enlarge the mind and the imagination.
- Offer experience in the creative and scientific inquiry process.
- Encourage an appreciation of beauty and human achievement, motivation and aspiration.
- Allow the discernment of good/bad, right/wrong.[45]

Regarding the current popularity of horror-related fantasy novels, it should be remembered that children can be affected in negative ways by scary images (visual or textual). Nicholas Tucker—an educational psychologist at the University of Sussex who has written extensively on children's literature—has stated that even for a child aware of the differences between fantasy and reality, "there are still some books that by the very force and vividness of their detail can overcome his defenses and make him dread the light going out and the bad dream."[46]

Tucker also has raised a cautionary flag over stories that "dwell on certain details with such lingering and even gloating effect that this too can become difficult for a child who is not yet ready for them." Consider, for instance, the following excerpts from *Harry Potter and the Goblet of Fire*:

> Wormtail was whimpering. He pulled a long, thin, shining silver dagger from inside his cloak. His voice broke into petrified sobs. . . .
>
> He stretched his right hand out in front of him—the hand with the missing finger. He gripped the dagger very tightly in his left hand and swung it upward.
>
> Harry realized what Wormtail was about to do a second

before it happened—he closed his eyes . . . but he could not
block the scream that pierced the night. . . . He heard something fall to the ground, heard Wormtail's anguished pant-
ing . . . as something was dropped into the cauldron.

. . . [Harry] saw the shining dagger shaking in Wormtail's
remaining hand. He felt its point penetrate the crook of his
right arm and blood seeping down the sleeve of his torn
robes. Wormtail . . . fumbled in his pocket for a glass vial
and held it to Harry's cut, so that a dribble of blood fell into
it. . . . [47]

Tucker, in discussing such gruesome imagery in children's
literature, describes them as scenes of "unnecessary nastiness."
He writes: "Although young children can take some horror,
there is a difference between a story containing a ghost and a
ghost story. One mentions fears, the other aggrandizes them."[48]
In *A Landscape with Dragons: The Battle for Your Child's Mind*,
Michael O'Brien addresses this same issue by comparing the
horror of Goosebumps with classic scary tales:

In sharp contrast [to Goosebumps], the momentary horrors that occur in classical tales always have a higher purpose; they are intended to underline the necessity of
courage, ingenuity, and character; the tales are about brave
young people struggling through adversity to moments of
illumination, truth, and maturity; they emphatically demonstrate that good is far more powerful than evil. Not so
with the new wave of shock-fiction. Its "heroes" and "hero-
ines" are usually rude, selfish, sometimes clever (but in no
way wise), and they never grow up.[49]

The morality in modern fantasy, or lack thereof, also may
present problems for young readers. Celebrated novelist and
short story writer Jan Mark (*The Ennead* and *Nothing to Be
Afraid Of*) has stated, "[I]n contemporary popular fiction, it's
sometimes very difficult, if you are not told, to decide which of

the main characters is the hero and which is the villain, because their behavior and attitudes are so morally dubious."[50]

In some cases, such as Harry Potter, for example, the "good" characters often indulge in the same kind of "bad" behavior manifested by the evil characters (see Part 3). This characteristic of some modern fantasy novels should not be forgotten by any parent seeking to find good literature for their children. Lillian Smith (1887-1983)—the first children's librarian in the British Empire—voiced an opinion many years ago that is still applicable today:

> We should put into their hands only books worthy of them, the books of honesty, integrity, and vision—the books on which they can grow. . . . They must have change and activity of both mind and body. Reading which does not stir the imaginations, which does not stretch their minds, not only wastes their time but will not hold children permanently.[51]

No one, especially a child, longs to read a boring book. Desiring that children read "appropriate" literature does not have to be the same as wanting children to be given sanitized, lifeless volumes that shy away from difficult issues, intense emotion or frightening scenes. Even mild violence may be an appropriate and necessary part of the story (e.g., the various battles in Tolkien's The Lord of the Rings series). Children want to be, and should be, helped to deal with real-world dangers and evils through literature. Fantasy is especially beneficial in this area because it provides what one might call "mock battles" that can "better prepare a child to live a pure life in a fallen world."[52]

But there is a proper way to deal with such issues because, as Lillian Smith noted many years ago, "The impressions of childhood are lasting, and the sum of its impressions are taken on by maturity. . . . Can we afford to be indifferent to the impressions that children receive from their reading?"[53]

Parents, of course, should undoubtedly be the final arbiter of what is and what is not proper reading for their children, especially when it comes to the horror-style of books so popular today. Only parents know their child well enough to make determinations concerning appropriate reading material.

What about censorship? This is a very sensitive issue because, as award-winning children's author Joan Aiken in 1980 explained, "[W]hat terrifies one child may seem merely comic to another, or may be completely ignored; one can't legislate fear."[54] At the same time, Aiken did not condemn censorship outright, saying,

> [I]f one is to exercise any kind of censorship whatever over children's reading matter, it seems to me that this kind of uncontrolled, almost sick, fantasy is a better candidate for the axe than, for instance, comics, the usual target for parental or educational disapproval.[55]

Interestingly, into her own personal category of works worthy of censorship, Aiken placed those written by Lewis Carroll (*Alice's Adventures in Wonderland* and *Through the Looking Glass*). There is obviously a great degree of subjectivity when it comes to literature. No one, therefore, should be too quick to condemn others for believing that certain works of literature are harmful to children. It is all a matter of perspective.

In conclusion, fantasy can be used either for good or for evil; to extol morality or glorify immorality; to terrify or to teach. There is no reason to reject outright the whole genre of fantasy just because some negative examples within that category exist. A little discernment and care can go a long way. Mary Sheehan Warren—English teacher, reading specialist and director of curriculum for Aquinas Academy in Maryland—writes,

> [A child's] undeveloped intellect is unable to objectively appraise the worth of what he digests, so that his malnutrition—even poisoning—may continue undetected. The life-supporting sustenance that the young mind seeks is what

a truly civilized society is composed upon, and what God calls His people to recognize and affirm: Truth, Goodness, and Beauty.[56]

Sheehan additionally gives some helpful counsel with regard to exactly what a parent needs to look for when evaluating children's literature:

> *TRUTH*: "A text should be examined for its presentation of the Truth. What are the underlying assumptions of the story? . . . Is the dignity of the human person properly addressed? . . . Does it laugh at what is considered to be sacred? Does it appropriately portray what is right? In examining the plot and the characters, the teacher or parent must check to see how the roles of men, women, adults, and children are portrayed in the story. Is there mutual respect, especially among the characters who might be considered to be 'ideal' by the reader? Are both fathers and mothers considered to be important?"
>
> *GOODNESS*: "Goodness can be offered to the child reader in two different ways: By affirming all things that are good; and by demonstrating what things are not good and why. . . . [M]ost of children's literature still seems to be a joyful recognition of the good that is found in this world. Unfortunately, the parent or teacher must first decide if Goodness is really what is being praised within a plot. Our culture today has developed a hideous tendency to describe vices as virtues."
>
> *BEAUTY*: "Children's literature presents conceptual, auditory, and visual beauty. Simplicity of plot, richness of description, and nobility of character not only expose the child to Beauty, but also help to expand his capacity to imagine and to create beauty himself. He can observe how language, when expertly crafted, can excite many feelings, and he can become inspired to invent such happy pretend worlds for himself."[57]

Despite today's Goosebumps-like books, many fantasy volumes are truly magical in their ability to capture the hearts and minds of all readers. These include such classics as *The Wind in the Willows*, *Gulliver's Travels*, *Charlotte's Web*, The Chronicles of Narnia and *Journey to the Center of the Earth*. But most fantasy lovers would say that none of them can compare in scope, majesty or poignancy to The Lord of the Rings trilogy by J.R.R. Tolkien—the subject of Part Two.

Part
Two

A Man Named
J.R.R. Tolkien
(1892-1973)

Three Rings for Elven-Kings under the sky,
Seven for Dwarf-lords in their halls of stone,
Nine for Mortal Men doomed to die,
One for the Dark Lord on his dark throne,
In the Land of Mordor where Shadows lie,
One Ring to rule them all, One Ring to find them,
One Ring to bring them all
   and in the darkness bind them,
In the Land of Mordor where the Shadows lie.

—*The Fellowship of the Ring* (Tolkien, p. 75)

MIDDLE-EARTH'S MAKER

Tolkien changed fantasy; he elevated it and redefined it, to such an extent that it will never be the same again.

—George R.R. Martin[1]
award-winning author, screenwriter

We are all deeply in J.R.R. Tolkien's debt, writers perhaps even more than readers. He gave us the greatest fantasy of our time, which also stands tall in the whole world of literature.

—Poul Anderson[2]
award-winning fantasy author

John Ronald Reuel Tolkien was born January 3, 1892, in South Africa to English parents, Arthur Tolkien and Mabel Suffield. Arthur was a banker who, before marrying Mabel, worked for Lloyds Bank of Birmingham in the West Midlands of England.[3] Mabel, an attractive and intelligent woman, had met her husband while still a teenager.[4] In fact, the two became engaged when she was just eighteen. Arthur was thirty-three.

Their age difference prompted Mabel's parents to forbid her marriage to Arthur until she was older. It was during this time of parentally enforced waiting that Arthur sought financial stability in South Africa, working for the Bank of Africa. But he had to leave behind a very distraught Mabel. The separation, however, lasted only until she turned twenty-one. By then, Arthur had obtained not only an excellent position at the bank as a manager, but also had purchased a house and hired several servants.

When Arthur wrote Mabel, asking that she join him in Africa to be his wife, she agreed. Her parents too consented. So in January 1891 she set sail for a new life in a new land. They married on April 16, 1891, in the large urban center of Cape Town. Their home would be 700 miles away in the small English outpost of Bloemfontein, a place not much to Mabel's liking.

In a letter to her family she summed up her opinion of her new home, calling it an " 'Owlin' Wilderness! Horrid Waste!"[5] The people were nice enough. Their house was moderately comfortable. But the environment was hostile and dangerous, complete with wild animals roaming nearby. Furthermore, there was little in Bloemfontein to occupy her time.

The outpost had no large stores, elegant restaurants or significant sources of amusement. The place could boast of only a couple churches, hospital, small library, tennis court, some shops and a park that amounted to "no more than about ten willows and a patch of water."[6] Intense, unrelenting heat and relatively few creature comforts only made things worse.

It was much too different from England for Mabel's taste and she wanted to go home. Nevertheless, she stayed and made the best of her situation. She and Arthur, after all, did love each other very much. Besides, she soon found herself pregnant. Nine months later, they welcomed into the world their first-born child—John Ronald Reuel.

OUT OF AFRICA

Life went well at first for the new Tolkien family, until Mabel and Arthur had another child in February 1894: Hilary Arthur Reuel. Soon, the strain of taking care of two boys in such a difficult clime began to take its toll on Mabel, who longed for the comforts of England. Arthur, unfortunately, consumed by his work, seemed to not notice Mabel's stress and provided only a modest degree of help with the children.

Making matters worse was J.R.R.'s health which, unlike his brother's, was not good. He suffered a bronchial infection, skin ailments and numerous eye diseases. He also endured a tarantula bite, which would have proved fatal had it not been for the swift response of a nanny who sucked the poison from J.R.R.'s wound before the deadly venom could take its toll.

Mabel had had enough and told Arthur she and the boys needed to return to England, at least temporarily, just to visit family. Arthur agreed, but explained with unwavering certainty that he himself could not afford such a luxury. Doing so might jeopardize his position at the bank. As he wrote to his father, "In these days of competition one does not like to leave one's business in the hands of others."[7]

So in April 1895, Mabel, J.R.R., Hilary and a hired nurse left Arthur, believing that they would see him again very soon. The plan was for Arthur to wait until a more convenient time to leave. In England, the weary travelers settled in with Mabel's parents in King's Heath. Arthur, they assumed, would join them within a month or so. He, however, was delayed after catching rheumatic fever in November, only a little more than six months after his family had departed. In a letter he wrote to them, Arthur promised that as soon as the weather turned better and the symptoms of his illness subsided, he would be on his way.

But by early 1896 Arthur was still fighting the fever. His trip was indefinitely postponed. After deciding that Arthur's illness was a sure sign that she should return immediately to South Africa, Mabel began in late January to make preparations for the trip. Before she could leave, however, a letter arrived in February, informing her that Arthur had died unexpectedly after suffering a hemorrhage.[8] J.R.R. was only four years old, and within a short time he would lose the few memories he still had of his father.

Eventually, Mabel found a home for herself and her boys in a "semi-detached brick cottage in the hamlet of Sarehole, a mile or so beyond the southern edge of Birmingham."[9] This new environment and the events that took place in it would provide J.R.R. with a rich collection of memories from which he would one day pull to write his fantasy tales.

For example, J.R.R.'s Aunt Jane lived nearby at a place called "Bag End." And "cotton-wool," known as "gamgee-tissue" in Sarehole, was named after a one-time local resident—Samson Gamgee—who had invented it. "Bag-End" and "Sam Gamgee" would be featured prominently in Tolkien's The Lord of the Rings.[10] There also was a local miller known as the "White Ogre" because he always appeared covered in flour. A farmer, who had once chased young J.R.R. for picking his mushrooms, was irreverently referred to as the "Black Ogre."

Other influences on Tolkien were the books he read with an appetite that never seemed satisfied. He adored fantasy: e.g., *Alice's Adventures in Wonderland*, the legends of King Arthur, selected works of George MacDonald, and perhaps most importantly, Andrew Lang's fairy books, which spoke of mystical places, noble knights and dragons.[11] Lang's *Red Fairy Book* in particular appealed to Tolkien. It included the legend of Sigurd, who slew the dragon Fafnir. Tolkien loved dragons, revealing many years later:

> I desired dragons with a profound desire. . . . [I] did not wish to have them in the neighbourhood. But the world that contained even the imagination of Fafnir was richer and more beautiful, at whatever cost of peril.[12]

By the age of seven J.R.R. already was trying his hand at writing fantasy. Some small inner voice was whispering for him to write tales about characters living in realms beyond his sight, but still very real. His first attempt to do so came in the form of a story about a dragon. In a 1955 letter to W.H. Auden, a reviewer for the *New York Times Book Review*, Tolkien recalled:

> I remember nothing about it except a philological fact. My mother said nothing about the dragon, but pointed out that one could not say "a green great dragon," but had to say "a great green dragon." I wondered why, and still do.[13]

Tolkien did not write again for many years, perhaps because his mind was distracted by other pursuits and by life's tribulations. His family's move in 1900 from the beautiful countryside surrounding Sarehole to the center of Birmingham, for example, was particularly disruptive. His family also was somewhat destitute, having been financially cut off by Mabel's parents because of her conversion in 1900 to Roman Catholicism. J.R.R.'s health too continued to be rather poor in general.

But most hurtful to Tolkien was his mother's diabetes-induced death in 1904 when he was only twelve. Fortunately, several years before dying at the age of thirty-four, J.R.R.'s mother had befriended a Roman Catholic priest—Father Francis Xavier Morgan. He had been a father figure to J.R.R., and once Mabel passed away, Morgan lovingly assumed the role of guardian over her sons. It was he who made sure the boys continued their education, and a morally upright lifestyle as well, as they grew into young men.

LOVE AND LIFE

After their mother's death, J.R.R. and Hilary moved in with an aunt, but after three years they relocated to the second-floor lodgings in the home of a Mrs. Faulkner. It was there that Tolkien met Edith Bratt, an attractive young woman who had lived most of her life in Handsworth near Birmingham. Her room was on the first floor. He was sixteen. She was nineteen. The two youths seemed made for each other and for a year spent ever-increasing time together.[14]

J.R.R. and Edith were certain that true love had found them. They had a great deal in common. They were orphans. They both embraced Christianity. They enjoyed a shared sense of humor. And both could appreciate in like ways the quiet splendor of a sunset. Most of all, they both relished having fun: "Edith and Ronald took to frequenting Birmingham teashops, especially one that had a balcony overlooking the pavement. There they would sit and throw sugarlumps into the hats of passers-by, moving to the next table when the sugar-bowl was empty."[15]

But the two starry-eyed teens ran into a problem—Father Morgan. Out of concern for the boy in his charge, he demanded that the relationship end immediately. If their feelings remained until J.R.R. had turned twenty-one, only then would the romance be allowed to blossom. To end the courtship, Tolkien and his brother were moved to another home nearby, and Edith was to be taken to live with family friends in faraway Cheltenham.[16]

Edith departed soon afterward, leaving Tolkien with no other choice but to pursue his studies. These eventually led him in 1911 to Oxford's famed Exeter College. The classes there that proved most influential on him were those involving philology—i.e., the science of words, the study of language and languages. It was a predictable turn of events.

Long before Oxford, Tolkien had already begun to manifest his predilection for language by inventing his own primitive mode of communicating that he called Nevbosh (i.e., the New Nonsense). He then created an even more complex language called Naffarin, which was loosely based on Spanish. Tolkien would in time come up with Quenya, built in part upon Finnish, wherein one word can be used for what would normally require a whole phrase in English. This language would be the one used predominantly as the language of Elves in his later works of fantasy.

Tolkien's college courses in language blended well with mythology, something else that dominated much of his spare time. He greatly enjoyed mythology and spent long hours perusing myths of Rome, Greece, Germany, Finland and the Norsemen. His only sadness was that there existed no similarly rich storehouse of English myths, only the Arthurian legends. He hoped that one day he might be able to remedy the situation.

Schoolwork kept him more than sufficiently occupied for several years, but it never so consumed him that he forgot about Edith. Finally, after endless days of pining for her, Tolkien turned twenty-one. The night before his birthday he stayed up until midnight, so he could with a clear conscience pen a letter to Edith. "How long will it be before we can be joined together before God and the world?" he asked.[17]

Tolkien mailed it the next day and Edith's reply came back within the week. But the words of her letter pierced his heart with more pain than he thought anyone could possibly feel. "No," she responded. "I can't. I'm sorry, but I'm engaged to marry someone else."[18] She apparently had agreed to marry a man named George Fields, the brother of a former schoolmate. Tolkien immediately left for Cheltenham to change her mind before it was too late.

In Cheltenham Edith met J.R.R. and the two spent long hours talking about the situation. Finally, she confided that her heart still belonged to him. Only out of family pressure had she said "yes" to George's proposal of marriage. But now Tolkien's presence changed everything. Edith gained a new resolve to follow her feelings, rather than her duty, and she agreed to marry the boy she had fallen in love with so many years earlier.

But the wedding was immediately threatened. Rumors of war already were spreading across Europe and it did not take long for a full scale conflagration to develop—World War I, the Great War, the "war to end all wars." Tolkien, like many brave men, enrolled in the army. Fortunately, he was able to benefit from a special program that allowed university students to train for military duty while completing their college courses. His work ended in June 1915, when he graduated with not only a B.A. degree, but also first-class honors.

This same month also brought Tolkien a telegram with orders that would lead him to the battle lines in France. Before leaving, however, on March 22, 1916, he and Edith were joined in marriage. Their joy lasted only as long as a week-long honeymoon in Somerset. Then there was a brief time spent relocating Edith to Staffordshire, near the army camp where J.R.R. had been posted. A few weeks later, Second Lieutenant Tolkien went off to war.

In France, Tolkien's 11th Battalion saw some of the heaviest action witnessed by troops. They were at the Battle of Somme, where the first day of engagement with the enemy ended only after 19,000 British soldiers had been killed by German machine-gun fire. Sixty thousand men had been injured. It was the largest single-day loss in the history of the British army. Tolkien survived because he had been held in reserve with the second wave of soldiers. Their turn to face the enemy came five days later, but even then, only "A Company" was ordered to battle. Tolkien was in "B Company."

Tolkien's company finally went forward a week later under cover of darkness. J.R.R. fought continuously for forty-eight hours, while watching his friends and fellow soldiers falling mortally wounded around him. He, however, miraculously sustained only a few cuts and scratches.[19] A brief lull occurred and Tolkien was able to rest for three hours, then he found himself fighting for another twelve-hour stretch before returning to his base camp at Bouzincourt.[20]

Waiting for him was a pile of letters. One of them from Oxford classmate G.B. Smith revealed that their close friend, Rob Gilson, had been killed during the first wave at Somme. "I am very sorry and most frightfully depressed at this worst news," the letter read. "O my dear John Ronald what ever are we going to do."[21] But there was no time to properly mourn. J.R.R. went back into the trenches day after day. These trenches gradually became little more than elongated pits of death. And with the onset of winter, they became "more mud-clogged than ever; sometimes the slurry ran waist deep, and always it was foul-smelling, diseased, and infested with rats."[22]

Finally, in November 1916, five months after Tolkien first went into battle, he contracted trench fever. This highly infectious disease was transmitted by the lice that lived on the countless soldiers forced to bear the filthy conditions of the battlefield. It so ravaged Tolkien's body that he was evacuated to a nearby hospital. When the illness did not abate, he was sent home to England.

Tolkien's recovery would take nearly a full year. But the sickness had undoubtedly saved his life, or at the very least, had rescued him from further torments of war. As it turned out, every member of Tolkien's entire battalion was eventually either killed or captured at Chemin des Dames.[23]

J.R.R.'s body was healing, but the bloody confrontations he had witnessed were not easily forgotten, and they often plagued his mind. Their images haunted him daily, until they gave birth to guilt over having left his fellow soldiers. As the months passed, he heard again and again about various Oxford companions, including G.B. Smith, who had escaped disease only to die in battle; in what Tolkien called "the 'animal horror' of trench warfare."[24] Many years later he remembered: "By 1918 all but one of my close friends were dead."[25]

THE CREATION OF MIDDLE-EARTH

It was while recovering in the hospital that Tolkien continued writing about his imaginary world called Middle-earth. This creative pastime began as early as 1914 in the form of a short poem titled "The Voyage of Earendel the Evening Star." It includes a passing reference to Westerland, which Tolkien would later define in his fantasy works as the land of the immortals in the distant West.[26]

A collection of related poems followed, until his writing was interrupted by WWI. The experiences in France would serve their own purpose by becoming a significant influence on him. Consid-

er Tolkien's first complete story, "The Fall of Gondolin," which
he began writing during his sick-leave toward the end of 1916. The
tale depicts a horrific battle in which the hero, Earendel, helps
elves fight against the ultimate evil: Morgoth.[27]

After composing "The Fall of Gondolin" Tolkien continued
authoring similar works including "The Lay of Beren and
Lúthien," a tragic romance about a mortal man, Beren, who falls
in love with an immortal elven maid after watching her dance.
Some of the inspiration for this story came from Edith, who often danced for Tolkien in a glade of hemlock flowers while he
convalesced. Her graceful movements and enchanting manner
found their way into the character Aragorn's song:

> The leaves were long, the grass was green,
> The hemlock-umbels tall and fair,
> And in the glade a light was seen
> Of stars in shadow shimmering.
> Tinúviel was dancing there
> To music of a pipe unseen,
> And light of stars was in her hair,
> And in her raiment glimmering.
>
> There Beren came from mountains cold
> And lost he wandered under leaves,
> And where the Elven-river rolled
> He walked alone and sorrowing.
> He peered between the hemlock-leaves
> And saw in wonder flowers of gold
> Upon her mantle and her sleeves,
> And her hair like shadow following.[28]

In 1917 Tolkien's first son—John Francis Reuel—was born.
Then, a year later the war ended and Tolkien was sent back to ci-
vilian life; back to Oxford, where he continued his work on languages. He had gained a position as an assistant lexicographer on
what would become the first edition of the *Oxford English Dictio-*

nary. Then, in 1920 J.R.R. and Edith had another son, Michael. Yet another baby boy, Christopher, joined their household in 1924. Their fourth child, this time a girl, was born in 1929. They named her Priscilla.

Meanwhile, Tolkien temporarily left Oxford for a position at the University at Leeds (1920-1924), but by 1925 he had returned to Oxford as the professor of Anglo-Saxon. Although his teaching responsibilities were taxing, he continued to find the time to author several mythic poems and interesting tales, all of which took place in Middle-earth, his own sub-creation: e.g., *The Tale of the Children of Húrin* (1925).

These stories eventually formed a lengthy yarn that Tolkien titled *The Book of Lost Tales.*[29] It would become *The Silmarillion*, a historic narrative tracing the events of Middle-earth. The narrative was never published during Tolkien's lifetime; in fact, he would never even finish the saga. That task, which ultimately fell to his son, Christopher, would not be completed and released to the public until 1977—four years after Tolkien's death.

Interestingly, none of Tolkien's first works significantly contributed to his notoriety. This is not to say that he failed to gain a wide reputation as an outstanding scholar in those early years. On the contrary, he gained a notable following as far back as 1925, thanks to his edition of the Middle English *Sir Gawain and the Green Knight* (Clarendon Press), coedited with E.V. Gordon. It was a major contribution to the study of medieval literature and it placed him in high regard among those who walked the hallowed halls of Oxford.

Yet Tolkien remained discontented in many ways. He consistently strove to find a balance between his dry university duties and those pursuits that were always more fulfilling for him—either writing mythic tales, painting/drawing or conversing about literature. To engage like-minded men, who were his intellectual equals, Tolkien formed a number of enriching associations, the most famous one being that of the "Inklings."[30]

COALBITERS AND INKLINGS

At some point around 1925 or 1926—no one knows precisely when—Tolkien and several of his peers at Oxford began meeting regularly to discuss what they were reading, writing and thinking. They called their private club the Coalbiters, after the Icelandic *kolbíter*, a lighthearted term used to describe people huddled "so close to a fire in winter that they could almost bite the coals."[31] The roster of members read like a "Who's Who" list of Oxford's most brilliant thinkers:

- Nevill Coghill, Exeter scholar of medieval literature
- Richard Dawkins, professor of Byzantine and modern Greek
- George Gordon, president of Magdalen College
- C.T. Onions, grammarian and editor of the *Oxford English Dictionary*

Word quickly spread concerning this small society of professors and soon others were interested in joining. But that honor came by invitation only. One person eventually invited was none other than Clive Staples Lewis (1898-1963), more commonly known as C.S. Lewis and fondly called "Jack" by his friends. He met Tolkien for the first time on May 11, 1926 at a meeting of the English department where Lewis had been made a professor (Merton College). In his diary, Lewis wrote: "He is a smooth, pale, fluent little chap. . . . Thinks all literature is written for the amusement of *men* between thirty and forty. . . . No harm in him: only needs a good smack or two."[32]

Tolkien never recorded his observations of the encounter, but history shows that they became the best of friends. As Tolkien wrote in an October 1933 diary entry: "[B]esides giving constant pleasure and comfort, [it] has done me much good from the contact with a man [i.e., Lewis] at once honest, brave, intellectual—a scholar, a poet, and a philosopher."[33]

It was an unlikely camaraderie. Tolkien swore allegiance to Roman Catholicism, while Lewis was a Church of England member.

Lewis, however, was not a Christian. In fact, he did not even believe in God. Lewis would not become a theist until 1929, after having had many conversations with Tolkien and others about God. Then, some two years later (c. 1931), due in part to his ongoing religious discussions with Tolkien, Lewis became a Christian.

But much to Tolkien's surprise and disappointment, Lewis remained an Irish Protestant—one that had been born and raised in anti-Catholic Northern Ireland. Such divergent paths of spirituality between friends was no small thing back in the 1930s, when religio-political biases, anti-Catholic sentiment and phobias concerning papal domination of the world abounded.

And Lewis, an Irishman from Belfast, admittedly harbored more than a trace of prejudice toward Romanism.[34] Nevertheless, the two men overcame their differences in favor of the satisfaction gained by matching their intellects. It was around this time that the Coalbiters began drifting apart, leading Tolkien and Lewis to form another by-invitation-only group: the Inklings.

From the 1930s through the 1940s Lewis and Tolkien, along with the rest of this "club," met Thursday evenings, usually in Lewis' rooms at Magdalen College. The meetings, often attended by anywhere from ten to fifteen men, normally lasted well into the night. At each gathering these men would sit around listening to each other read their literary works in progress.

Those present "would then give their comments, often not sparing the feelings of the poor soul who had just read out something he had been working on for months."[35] Besides Tolkien, C.S. Lewis and Lewis' brother, Warnie, the list of regular attendees included:

- Hugo Dyson, English literature professor at Reading University and a tutor at Merton College, Oxford;
- Colin Hardie, a tutor at Magdalen College and a one-time director of the British School in Rome;

- Charles Williams, the gifted author of numerous novels, including *War in Heaven*, *The Place of the Lion* and *All Hallows' Eve*.

Some members of the Inklings also met on Tuesday mornings at "The Eagle and the Child," an Oxford pub known to regulars as "The Bird and Baby." Although these daylight meetings were smaller and less formal than the official gatherings at night, they were still an enjoyable and useful way to spend free hours. They continued up through the early 1960s.[36] C.S. Lewis's brother, Warnie, recorded in his diary the oft-occurring scene:

> When half a dozen or so had arrived, tea would be produced, and then when the pipes were well alight Jack would say, "Well, has nobody got anything to read to us?" Out would come a manuscript, and we would settle down to sit in judgment upon it.[37]

It was in this environment that Tolkien shared bits and pieces of the many mythic poems and storylines associated with Middle-earth.[38] Obviously, these early writings that Tolkien read to friends in a pub contributed in many ways to perhaps his most famous tale, *The Lord of the Rings*. That story, however, would not see the light of day until well after the 1936 publication of yet another Tolkien volume, one that started taking shape around 1930.

It began unexpectedly while Tolkien was correcting School Certificate exams on a warm summer day. He turned over one of the exam papers, and found that the student had for some unknown reason left the page blank. Quite unthinkingly, a bored J.R.R. casually scrawled on it a single sentence that had mysteriously popped into his mind. It would forever change the fantasy genre. Tolkien's sentence read: "In a hole in the ground there lived a hobbit."[39]

THERE AND BACK AGAIN

J.R.R. had no idea what his sentence about a "hobbit" meant. It seemed to have come from nowhere in particular. In looking back at the incident, Tolkien admitted: "Eventually I thought I'd better find out what hobbits were like."[40] After much thought he concluded that hobbits were small people having little or no magic about them at all. He also discovered:

> They are inclined to be fat in the stomach; they dress in bright colours (chiefly green and yellow); wear no shoes, because their feet grow natural leathery soles and thick warm brown hair like the stuff on their heads (which is curly); have long, clever brown fingers, good-natured faces, and laugh deep fruity laughs (especially after dinner, which they have twice a day when they can get it).[41]

As Tolkien further explored the nature, character and habits of hobbits, he wove a tale that would become his first published book about Middle-earth: *The Hobbit, or There and Back Again*. It is the story of Bilbo Baggins, a respectable hobbit. His adventures begin with a visit from a powerful wizard named Gandalf, who reveals that Bilbo's destiny is to travel with a group of thirteen dwarves to a mountain where Smaug, an evil dragon, dwells. The group's goal is nothing less than death-defying—i.e., slay the dragon and steal his treasure, which rightfully belongs to the dwarves.

But the dwarves are unsure of Gandalf's choice of Bilbo, who in the words of one doubting dwarf, "looks more like a grocer than a burglar!"[42] Bilbo has his own reservations about the journey, especially after hearing Thorin Oakenshield—leader of the dwarves— detail how many dangers will be encountered along the way.

Despite his fears, Bilbo ultimately end ups traveling far from home with the dwarves to Lonely Mountain, where Smaug dwells in his lair on mounds of the stolen wealth. During the quest Bilbo and his companions face numerous hardships (storms, hunger, fatigue, etc.) and dangers (e.g., trolls, goblins, evil wolves and giant spiders). Additionally, when Bilbo becomes separated from the group, he confronts a particularly vile creature named Gollum.

Eventually, Bilbo escapes Gollum, reunites with the dwarves and Smaug is slain. Bilbo returns home with various treasures: gold and silver, a coat of elven-made mail, a sword that glows if goblins are near and a magic ring with which anyone can become invisible:

> His gold and silver was largely spent in presents, both useful and extravagant—which to a certain extent accounts for the affection of his nephews and his nieces. His magic ring he kept secret, for he chiefly used it when unpleasant callers came. . . . [T]hough few believed any of his tales, he remained very happy to the end of his days, and those were extraordinarily long.[43]

C.S. Lewis, in a review of *The Hobbit*, wrote: "[It] will be funniest to its youngest readers, and only years later, at a tenth or a twentieth reading, will they begin to realize what deft scholarship and profound reflection have gone to make everything in it so ripe, so friendly, and in its own way so true. . . . *The Hobbit* may well prove a classic."[44]

SUCCESS AT LAST

Contrary to what many people may believe, Tolkien did not expend a great deal of effort pursuing a publisher for *The Hobbit*. His story just happened to be seen in an unfinished form by a former student, Elaine Griffiths, who mentioned it to another Oxford graduate, Susan Dagnall. She at that time was employed by Allen and Unwin publishers (London). Curiosity prompted her to contact Tolkien and ask for a copy of the story, which he gladly submitted.

Dagnall was so enthralled by the incomplete manuscript that she asked Tolkien if he would finish it and send her a copy. He again complied. She in turn passed the pages along to Stanley Unwin, her firm's chairman. Unwin too found *The Hobbit* engaging. But to confirm what seemed to be the obvious, he gave it to his ten-year-old son, Rayner. Stanley paid the boy a shilling to read the book and write a report.[45]

After young Rayner gave his father a "thumbs up" concerning the story's appeal to children, *The Hobbit* was published in 1937. Its first printing sold out within three months of being released. A second printing began flying off bookstore shelves shortly thereafter, which not only pleased Tolkien, but surprised him. His tale, after all, was nothing more than a straightforward children's story. *The Hobbit*, however, in retrospect, struck deep emotional chords with readers young and old throughout the late 1930s and early 1940s.

The tale was seen as a story of a quest—one of the oldest of universal themes. Moreover, it took place in a faraway land, where heroes fought; where good was rewarded; where evil's form was discernable. In Middle-earth, moral abstractions were made concrete. Such a work held great appeal in 1937. Hitler had already begun reversing the Treaty of Versailles by rebuilding his army and moving troops into the Rhineland. He also had tried to unite Germany and Austria. War was imminent—again. People could feel it and longed to escape.

Clearly, there needed to be a sequel to *The Hobbit*. But in response to Stanley Unwin's request for a new book, Tolkien only forwarded a bundle of incomplete and disordered papers with no clearly continuous section—except a poem. He called this haphazard collection *The Silmarillion*. When the lone poem was passed to the publisher's reader, it did not receive a favorable review. Unwin wrote to Tolkien, tactfully declining the lengthy manuscript.[46]

Tolkien immediately started to write something else. The first thing he realized was that his link between the stories had to be the ring Bilbo had obtained from Gollum in *The Hobbit*. Then Tolkien began to understand just how important hobbits were to Middle-earth. In fact, their courage, perseverance and integrity would ultimately prove to be the salvation of J.R.R.'s entire sub-creation. Surprisingly, the plot of this new book began taking a decidedly darker turn than anything he had intended. Warfare, evil, death, betrayal, doom, destruction, danger—all these issues quickly worked their way into the storyline, which concerned Tolkien.

In October 1938 he wrote Unwin, saying that his sequel was "becoming more terrifying than *The Hobbit*" and he wanted to make sure he did not forget the children. Gradually, though, his fears abated and he proceeded so that by the end of 1938 he had titled his new tale The Lord of the Rings. By 1939 he had written several chapters, which indicated that a different hero would be featured—Frodo Baggins—Bilbo's nephew.

At this point, Tolkien also began seeing that what he was creating would be epic in scope; something that would, as he put it, fill "a large canvas."[47] What he did not know was that it would take him another dozen years to complete (c. 1949), followed by almost another five years before it would see publication.

THE LORE OF
THE RINGS

[The Lord of the Rings] is a work of art. . . . It has invention, fancy, and imagination. . . . It is a profound parable of man's everlasting struggle against evil.

—Book review, *Country Life*[1]
August 26, 1954

Stanley Unwin hoped that Tolkien would finish his new book within two years or so of *The Hobbit*. But such hopes were in vain. First, World War II erupted in 1939. Next, Tolkien took a year-long hiatus in 1940. Then, by 1943, after having written only about one half of what would eventually be volume one of The Lord of the Rings, Tolkien found himself "dead stuck," with no clear direction for the story.[2] Part of the problem was Tolkien's perfectionism. In *J.R.R. Tolkien: A Biography*, Humphrey Carpenter explains:

> [H]e felt he must ensure that every single detail fitted satisfactorily into the total pattern. Geography, chronology, and nomenclature all had to be entirely consistent. . . . [H]e made endless calculations of time and distance, drawing up elaborate charts concerning events in the story, showing dates, the days of the week, the hours, and sometimes even the direction of the wind and the phase of the moon. . . . Long afterwards he said: "I wanted people simply to get inside this story

and take it (in a sense) as actual history!" Name-making also involved much of his attention, as was inevitable, for the invented languages from which the names were constructed were both the mainspring of his mythology and in themselves a central activity of his intellect. . . . Moreover he had reached a point where the story divided into several independent and in themselves complicated chains of events.[3]

As of early 1944, The Lord of the Rings had gone untouched by Tolkien for many months. New inspiration, however, came from his old friend C.S. Lewis, who urged J.R.R. to keep forging ahead.[4] So in April 1944, the process began again, with Tolkien writing feverishly for days on end, often late into the night.[5]

But this burst of creativity ended in June, and he wrote nothing more for the remainder of that year, nor did he write anything during 1945. In 1946 Tolkien promised his publishers that The Lord of the Rings was nearly complete. Nevertheless, that year, along with 1947 and 1948, came and went without a completed manuscript being delivered. Everyone kept asking themselves and others: "What is Tolkien doing?"[6]

Finally, in the autumn of 1949, after a good deal of revising and re-editing, Tolkien completed The Lord of the Rings. He sent a copy to C.S. Lewis, who responded with hearty approval, writing back the following comments:

I have drained the rich cup and satisfied a long thirst. . . . [T]he steady upward slope of grandeur and terror . . . is almost unequalled in the whole range of narrative art known to me. . . . I congratulate you. All the long years you have spent on it are justified.[7]

Tolkien was nearly sixty years old by this time. For more than a dozen years he had poured his heart and soul into the book. As he said in 1947 when it was nearing completion, "It is written in my life-blood."[8]

But because of several more publishing delays, it was not until April 1953 that Tolkien's lengthy manuscript went to press. Not until 1954 did the first book of The Lord of the Rings (*The Fellowship of the Ring*) get released. The next two volumes, *The Two Towers* and *The Return of the King*, were released the following year. C.S. Lewis wrote one of the first public reviews of *The Fellowship of the Ring*, saying: "This book is like lightning from a clear sky. . . . To say that in it heroic romance, gorgeous, eloquent, and unashamed, has suddenly returned . . . is inadequate."[9]

A TRILOGY IS BORN

The Lord of the Rings trilogy fits well with *The Hobbit* by beginning sixty years after the end of that tale. Bilbo is making preparations for his 111th birthday party. He plans on using the occasion to leave his home in the Shire. All of his possessions, including his house, will go to his nephew, Frodo. Bilbo's hope is to do some peaceful traveling and visit the mountains one last time before he dies.

At the conclusion of his party, Bilbo slips on the magic ring and disappears before everyone's eyes. He quickly returns to his hobbit hole, packs a few last items as planned, then quietly departs the Shire. He, however, leaves behind his magic ring—but only at the insistence of his friend, Gandalf the wizard, who is visiting Hobbiton.

Frodo soon moves into Bilbo's home and among his inherited possessions is the left-behind magic ring, which Gandalf now suspects to be a very dangerous item. Gandalf leaves, but returns many years later, having discovered that the ring, which now belongs to Frodo, actually is one of three rings created in the distant past. In fact, it is the most powerful one, originally owned by the Dark Lord, Sauron, who had tried to conquer all of Middle-earth.

Sauron vanished for a time after being defeated by armies of Men and Elves, but in *The Fellowship of the Ring* he has risen again and is seeking the ring in order to fully restore his powers.

If he succeeds he will be virtually invincible. The only way dwellers of Middle-earth will ever defeat Sauron is if someone (i.e., Frodo) destroys the ring by throwing it into the volcanic fires of the Crack of Doom in which it was forged; in the depths of Orodruin, beneath the Fire Mountain.

Frodo, however, has a number of enemies with which to deal. There are nine Black Riders, or Ringwraiths, also known as the Nazgûl. These terrifying specters were formerly human kings who, because they succumbed to the power of magic rings they wore in life, were corrupted and transformed by Sauron into "undead" servants. Their invisible forms, clothed in dark robes and armor, ride black horses throughout the countryside, hunting for the One Ring. Nothing can stand in their way.

Another foe of Frodo is Gollum, the creature in *The Hobbit*, from whom Bilbo originally acquired the ring. Most interesting is the fact that at one point in *The Hobbit*, Bilbo had an opportunity to kill Gollum, but out of mercy he let him live. Early in The Lord of the Rings, Frodo laments: "What a pity Bilbo did not stab the vile creature when he had a chance!"[10]

Gandalf corrects Frodo, saying: "Pity? It was Pity that stayed his hand. Pity and Mercy: not to strike without need." Gandalf adds a profound observation: "Many that live deserve death. And some that die deserve life. Can you give it to them? . . . [D]o not be too eager to deal out death in judgment. For even the very wise cannot see all ends."[11]

The tale continues as Frodo and his three hobbit companions— Sam, Merry and Pippin—continue their mission to destroy the ring. Along the way, however, they are separated and must face dire perils, while at the same time avoiding enemies seeking to capture them. Meanwhile, it is discovered that Saruman, once thought to be a good wizard, has turned toward evil and is himself seeking the ring of power.

Additionally, Frodo must fight the psychological and emotional strains caused by the ring itself. The ring seeks to take over

Frodo's will; seeks to consume him just as it had consumed Gollum. The struggle against the power is so overwhelming that by the time Frodo reaches the Crack of Doom, he cannot follow through with destroying the ring and decides to keep it for himself. Fortunately, Gollum is nearby and attacks, biting off Frodo's finger to reclaim the ring. But Gollum loses his balance and falls, along with the ring, into the Crack of Doom.

Meanwhile, Sauron's evil hordes are converging on the last stronghold of Middle-earth's defenders. The Armageddon-like battle that is raging seems destined to be won by Sauron's armies. But just as the last shreds of hope begin vanishing, the ring's destruction by Gollum breaks Sauron's power. The forces of good triumph and Middle-earth is saved from the Dark Lord's tyranny.

Yet it is a bittersweet victory. Although Sauron has been defeated, the destruction of the ring marks the beginning of the end of Middle-earth, for its allotted time has passed. The world of hobbits, dwarves and elves must give way to the time of men. Middle-earth must be replaced by another kind of Earth, one where magic will be all but nonexistent. And so the trilogy ends with the ring-bearers (Bilbo and Frodo) sailing west across the sea, out of Middle-earth.

Tolkien's Legacy

The Lord of the Rings probably has inspired more commentary and creativity than any other modern-day work of literature. For nearly half a century nothing less than an obsession with Tolkien's work has consumed legions of fans. It began almost immediately after the trilogy was published. As early as 1956 graffiti proclaiming "Frodo Lives!" was appearing on New York subway trains. Pranksters then started decorating walls of college campuses with messages reading: "J.R.R. Tolkien is hobbit forming."

The trilogy quickly became a college craze as students everywhere started wearing buttons that said, "Frodo Lives" and "Gandalf for President." By the mid-1960s Tolkien had developed

a huge following, particularly among that era's "flower children."
This turn of events was so surprising that it prompted extensive
media coverage, including a short 1966 article in *Time*.[12]

Few members of the younger generation were immune to
Tolkien. In 1967, for instance, Micky Dolenz of the chart-topping
TV band The Monkees, placed a "Frodo Lives!" button on the
hippie-style poncho he wore to shoot a television episode. The
gesture only further popularized the trilogy. Tolkien's works even
inspired actor Leonard Nimoy (Spock of *Star Trek* fame) to release a recording of "The Song of Bilbo Baggins."

Gradually, fan clubs appeared across the globe like mushrooms
in the Shire, people wrote each other letters in Elvish and automobile bumper stickers declared (in a variety of ways) the glory of
Tolkien. Then, in England, fantasy-author Vera Chapman officially founded the Tolkien Society.

By the 1970s "hobbit clubs" were prevalent in high schools,
where some members took nicknames from Tolkien's books:
e.g., Meriadoc, Aragorn and Pippin. Also in full swing was the
hype and hysteria surrounding Dungeons & Dragons, a new
role-playing game indirectly inspired by The Lord of the Rings.

In late 1996 Tolkien was voted author of the century. This jolt
to the literary world resulted when the popular British bookshop
chain, Waterstone's, decided to take a poll to determine the five
books people considered "the greatest of the century." Of the
25,000 or so readers who replied, more than 5,000 gave their first
place vote to The Lord of the Rings trilogy.[13] Professional critics,
literature experts and journalists were stunned.

England's *Daily Telegraph* responded by conducting its own
survey. Again, Tolkien's trilogy came out on top.[14] But some
literary critics could not, indeed would not, accept these results
as valid. Some of them went so far as to write articles denounc-
ing not only the findings, but also Tolkien's work, saying it was
wholly unworthy of such an honor. Rebuttals to such bitter at-

tacks against The Lord of the Rings came swiftly. One of them came from Professor Jeffrey Richards of Lancaster University:

> The Lord of the Rings is a work of unique power, scope and imagination. Tolkien's language is rich and allusive, his vocabulary extensive and varied. His descriptive writing is wonderful. His evocation of such invaluable virtues as loyalty, service, comradeship and idealism is inspiring. Above all, he creates a universe of myth, magic, and archetype that resonates in the deepest recesses of the memory and the imagination. . . . The more children, indeed the more people of all ages, who read The Lord of the Rings, the better it will be not only for the literary level of this country but for its spiritual health.[15]

Officials of the highly esteemed Folio Society of Britain decided to do their own study. Their 50,000 members, all "serious readers, connoisseurs of fine literature, and not likely to respond to mere fashion," were polled in July 1997.[16] Finishing ahead of the pack, which included such great works of literature as Jane Austen's *Pride and Prejudice* and Charles Dickens's *David Copperfield*, was Tolkien and The Lord of the Rings.[17]

One can see why Tolkien's masterpieces have remained in print for nearly fifty years and have sold more than 100 million copies. The greatness of The Lord of the Rings, however, has less to do with its popularity and much more to do with its content. It is more than just a children's story. As one 2000 article in the *Baltimore City Paper* observed: "The Lord of the Rings is a completely adult tragedy with profound moral and religious implications."[18] These themes sprang from Tolkien's devout faith in not only a personal God, but in the death, burial and resurrection of Jesus, whom Tolkien unabashedly proclaimed as his Lord and Savior.

THE SPIRITUALITY OF MIDDLE-EARTH

Nowhere in The Lord of the Rings can be found any explicit mention of "God," churches, prayers or sacred devotion. Yet

Tolkien's story is a spiritual work through and through. He himself admitted that his mythology was a religious volume—a Christian one, in fact, with Roman Catholic underpinnings. Although
this aspect of Middle-earth and The Lord of the Rings is not
clearly visible, it is easily adduced from various segments of *The
Silmarillion*.

Additional information about the spirituality of Middle-earth
can be gleaned from numerous letters Tolkien wrote to his fans.
From his correspondence, for example, we learn that Middle-
earth's "wizards," contrary to popular belief, are not human. Each
of them, including Gandalf, is "Maia"—i.e., angelic-like beings
that have taken on human form.[19] Even Sauron, the evil wizard in
The Lord of the Rings, is a Maia, albeit a fallen one. According to
Tolkien, these Maiar (plural of Maia) were sent into Middle-earth
to render assistance to Elves and Men.[20]

Gandalf and Sauron, along with the other wizards in Middle-
earth (e.g., the treacherous Saruman) are, in essence, illustrations
of good angels and evil angels (i.e., demons). Their powers are not
supernatural or related to the occult in any way, but are natural aspects of their race.[21] In a late 1951 letter, Tolkien clarified his intentions to never link them to occultism, saying:

> Their name, as related to Wise, is an Englishing of their Elvish
> name, and is used throughout as *utterly distinct* from Sorcerer
> or Magician [emphasis added]. . . . [T]hey were as one might
> say the near equivalent in the mode of these tales of Angels,
> guardian Angels. Their powers are directed primarily to the
> encouragement of the enemies of evil, to cause them to use
> their own wits and valor, to unite and endure.[22]

Tolkien also revealed that he did not necessarily want to use the
word "wizard," but was forced to do so by the limitations of English. He viewed "wizard" as a translation from the Elven-tongue
that unfortunately was "perhaps not suitable," but necessary.[23] He
ran into the same problem with his concept of dwarves. J.R.R.
wrote:

"[W]izards" are not in any sense or degree "shady." Not mine. I am under the difficulty of finding English names for mythological creatures with other names, since people would not "take" a string of Elvish names, and I would rather they took my legendary creatures even with the false associations of the "translation" than not at all. Even the dwarfs are not really Germanic "dwarfs" . . . and I call them "dwarves" to mark that. They are not naturally evil, not necessarily hostile, and not a kind of maggot-folk bred in stone; but a variety of incarnate rational creature.[24]

In this same letter he spoke further not only of "wizards," but also of another race named the Valar:

The *istari* are translated "wizards" because of the connexion of "wizard" with *wise*. . . . They are actually emissaries from the True West, and so mediately from God, sent precisely to strengthen the resistance of the "good," when the Valar become aware that the shadow of Sauron is taking shape again.[25]

As this statement explains, the Istari (the "wizards") were sent to Middle-earth by the Valar, who, according to *The Silmarillion*, are an even higher order of spiritual beings. One example of a Vala (singular of Valar) is the Dark Lord Morgoth—perhaps the most powerful of the Valar—a satanic character who tried to subjugate Middle-earth.[26] His wickedness resulted from direct rebellion against the divine authority presiding over everything—i.e, the Creator of all, *Eru*, also known as *Ilúvatar*. This entity is the supreme deity; the One God worshiped by any Middle-earth races engaged in religious activity.

Tolkien unreservedly said that "religion" in any pagan sense (e.g., polytheism) was false worship in Middle-earth. The Númenóreans, for example—the most honorable men throughout Tolkien's sub-creation—originally were monotheists before their loss of integrity as a nation. In a 1956 letter, J.R.R. stated:

"[Middle-earth] is a 'monotheistic but sub-creational mythology.' "[27] In starker terms, a subsequent letter read: "There are no 'Gods,' properly so-called, in the mythological background of my stories."[28] Again, in 1954, Tolkien wrote: "There is only one 'god,' *Eru Ilúvatar*."[29]

The influence of *Ilúvatar* over the affairs of Middle-earth is plainly seen in one segment of *The Fellowship of the Ring*, where Gandalf is speaking to Frodo about the ring. Their dialogue suggests that some supreme power, far beyond the confines of Middle-earth, is in absolute control of all that is happening. We learn that the seemingly random series of events that led to Frodo's dire situation is far from random. Frodo himself acknowledges that he was, in some cosmic way, "chosen" to complete the mission. He is not pleased.

But Gandalf gives him a word of encouragement that shows his faith in the sovereign entity—i.e., *Ilúvatar*—who is watching Middle-earth's events unfold according to his plan. Sauron's schemes are but part of a much larger, unknown plan, one held in place by *Ilúvatar*:

> "I wish it need not have happened in my time," said Frodo.
>
> "So do I," said Gandalf, "and so do all who live to see such times. But that is not for them to decide. All we have to decide is what to do with the time that is given us. . . . It was not Gollum, Frodo, but the Ring itself that decided things. The Ring left *him*."
>
> "What, just in time to meet Bilbo?" said Frodo.
>
> ". . . It was the strangest event in the whole history of the Ring so far: Bilbo's arrival just at that time, and putting his hand on it, blindly, in the dark. There was more than one power at work, Frodo. . . . [T]here was something else at work, beyond the design of the Ring-maker [i.e., Sauron]. I can put it no plainer than by saying that Bilbo was meant to find the Ring, and not by its maker. In which case you also

were meant to have it. And that may be an encouraging thought."[30]

This passage, and others from The Lord of the Rings, brought Willis B. Glover—emeritus professor of history at Mercer University—to a significant conclusion. In his 1971 essay "The Christian Character of Tolkien's Invented World," Glover stated that the sense of history in Tolkien's fantasy is far more biblical than that of other modern novels because it suggests the existence of an "unnamed authority" to whom the "actors are responsible and who works in history in ways inscrutable to finite creatures."[31]

In addition to a sovereign God presiding over Middle-earth, Tolkien also wove into his mythology a sort of heaven—i.e., Valinor—where the Valar dwell. One story relating to Valinor that is particularly interesting involves the form of Middle-earth, which according to The Silmarillion, originally was a flat world. Valinor, or heaven, was connected to Middle-earth and could be reached via sailing-ships. Unfortunately, the Númenóreans, who lived in the land of Númenór, were deceived by Sauron into attacking Valinor.[32]

The reason for their assault is reminiscent of the Bible's story of Adam and Eve, who were not content with their original state. Adam and Eve disobeyed God and by doing so caused death to enter the world. They also lost intimate contact with God. These penalties closely resemble what happened to the Númenóreans. Despite having been granted longer life than other humans (a triple span), they envied the immortality of the Elves. It became an obsession, which in turn caused their spans of life to wane even more.

Finally, near the end of the Second Age in Middle-earth, the Númenóreans, led by King Ar-Pharazon, attacked Valinor, thinking that they would achieve immortality by controlling the heavenly realm. Their plan to conquer Valinor, of course, failed. In fact, a great chasm opened in the sea into which Númenór sank (a

clear reflection of the age-old Atlantis legend). Tolkien explained
that their delusion was initiated by a "Satanic lie."[33]

This tragic event changed the whole structure of Middle-earth.
It not only became a round world, but its physical connection
with heaven was severed forever.[34] From that point onward, no
real worship or religion existed in Middle-earth, until after
Sauron's defeat in The Lord of the Rings. In a 1954 letter to Peter
Hastings, J.R.R. himself detailed the spirituality of Middle-earth,
as found in *The Silmarillion*:

> There are thus no temples or "churches" or fanes in this
> "world" among "good" peoples. They had little or no "reli-
> gion" in the sense of worship. For help they may call on a
> Vala (as *Elbereth*), as a Catholic might on a Saint, though no
> doubt knowing . . . that the power of the Vala was limited
> and derivative. But this is a "primitive age": and these folk
> may be said to view the Valar as children view their parents
> or immediate adult superiors. . . . I do not think Hobbits
> practiced any form of worship or prayer (unless through
> exceptional contact with Elves). The Númenóreans (and
> others of that branch of Humanity, that fought against
> Morgoth, even if they elected to remain in Middle-earth
> and did not go to Númenór such as the Rohirrim) were
> pure monotheists. But there was no temple in Númenór
> (until Sauron introduced the cult of Morgoth). The top of
> the Mountain, the Meneltarma or Pillar of Heaven, was
> dedicated to Eru, the One, and there at any time privately,
> and at certain times publicly, God was invoked, praised, and
> adored: an imitation of the Valar and the Mountain of
> Aman. But Númenór fell and was destroyed and the Moun-
> tain engulfed, and there was no substitute.[35]

Equally stunning parallels between Tolkien's Middle-earth
mythology and Christianity have been catalogued by professor
Tom Shippey, Tolkien's successor at Oxford University. He

made a number of insightful observations in *J.R.R. Tolkien: Author of the Century*:

> *The Silmarillion* bears a kind of relationship to Christian myth [i.e., a traditional tale, not necessarily untrue]. The rebellion of Melkor [Morgoth], and his subordinate spirits, is analogous to the Fall of Lucifer and the rebel angels. Lucifer is by tradition *princeps huius mundi*, "the prince of this world," and Melkor calls himself, perhaps truthfully, "Master of the fates of Arda." The origin of the fall is also the same in both cases, for the sin of Lucifer was (according to C.S. Lewis) the urge to put his own purposes before those of God, and that of Melkor was "to interweave matters of his own imagining" with the "theme of Ilúvatar [the Creator]." This "fall of the angels" also leads in both mythologies to a second fall: the Fall of Man and the exile from the Garden of Eden in the Book of Genesis, the loss of elvish innocence and the emigration from Aman (which becomes an exile) in *The Silmarillion*. . . . [H]e also built in, or rather left a space for, the traditional story of the Fall of Man. . . . [W]hen the humans do enter Middle-earth from the east all that is known about them to the elves . . . is that something dreadful had happened to them already, a "darkness" which "lay upon the hearts of Men" and which was connected with an unknown expedition of Morgoth: one could believe that Morgoth here is identical with Satan, and his expedition was to lure humanity into their "original sin."[36]

In The Lord of the Rings itself can be found Christian symbolism, albeit somewhat obscured. For example, we see Sauron and Morgoth as demonic figures. Gandalf fulfills the role of a prophet. The Elven way-bread, *lembas*, might even represent the Roman Catholic sacrament of holy communion.[37] And certain characteristics of the Elf queen Galadriel mirror aspects of the Roman Catholic concept of the Virgin Mary.

94 FANTASY AND YOUR FAMILY

This latter observation about Galadriel was first submitted to Tolkien in a letter by his friend Father Murray. In his reply, "Tolkien thanked the priest for his perceptive interpretations and agreed that he indeed had placed many of his views concerning Mary into the character of Galadriel."[38] Perhaps even more fascinating are two time reckonings in his trilogy that certainly must have been deliberate insertions:

> In Appendix B of The Lord of the Rings we are told that the fellowship leaves Rivendell to begin its mission on December 25 [i.e., Christmas]. Frodo and Sam destroy the ring by throwing it into the Crack of Doom. This heralds the new era on, according to the Gondorian reckoning, March 25. . . . [I]n the old English tradition (a subject about which Tolkien was quite familiar), March 25 was the date of the first Good Friday, the date of Christ's crucifixion. This means that the main events in the story of how the ring is destroyed and Sauron is defeated are played out during the mythic period between Christ's birth on December 25 and his death on March 25.[39]

Tolkien's narrative also contains a plethora of events that advocate many Christian values and virtues: self-sacrifice, steadfast devotion and faith. Also featured in the tale are distinctly religious topics such as temptation, sin, betrayal, mercy and forgiveness. In Tolkien's Ordinary Virtues, Mark Eddy Smith lists and expounds on several more Christian-related subjects in The Lord of the Rings: Simplicity, Generosity, Friendship, Hospitality, Faith, Atonement, Suffering, Resurrection, Humility, Trust, Trustworthiness, Wisdom, Hope, Imagination, Submission, Stewardship, Courage, Mirth, Foolishness, Perseverance, Celebration, Justice and Love.[40]

This is not to say that Tolkien consciously dealt with all these issues so that his work could be read as some sort of extended essay on Christian teachings. The underlying Christianity of The Lord of the Rings more likely found its way into the text simply as a result of it being so imprinted on Tolkien's psyche.

As Kurt Bruner and Jim Ware say in *Finding God in The Lord of the Rings*: "What Tolkien believed was part of him, and that belief became part of what he created."[41]

J.R.R. was a devout Christian, who "habitually referred to Jesus as 'our Lord' and possessed an unshakeable conviction in the power of prayer."[42] Tolkien's son, John, who became a Roman Catholic priest, maintained that faith "pervaded all [his father's] thinking, beliefs and everything else."[43] Indeed, Tolkien unreservedly declared his love for God and the centrality of the Creator to the very meaning of life, as he explained in a 1969 letter:

> [T]he chief purpose of life, for any one of us, is to increase according to our capacity our knowledge of God by all the means we have, and to be moved by it to praise and thanks. To do as we say in the Gloria in Excelsis . . . "We praise you, we call you holy, we worship you, we proclaim your glory, we thank you for the greatness of your splendour."[44]

Understandable, then, is Tolkien's 1953 admission that "*The Lord of the Rings* is of course a fundamentally religious and Catholic work; unconsciously so at first, but consciously in the revision."[45] In 1965, he wrote to W.H. Auden, plainly stating, "With regard to *The Lord of the Rings*. . . . I actually intended it to be consonant with Christian thought and belief."[46]

Closely associated with Tolkien's spirituality and its influence on Middle-earth's mythology was J.R.R.'s view of our human ability to create fantasy worlds—i.e., sub-creations. Fantasy-making, according to Tolkien, is a primal urge that is inescapable because it is part of our human nature. It is a reflection of our having been made in the image of God (Genesis 1-2): "[W]e make in our measure and in our derivative mode, because we are made: and not only made, but made in the image and likeness of a Maker."[47]

To Tolkien, being a sub-creator (the "Primary" creator being God) of a Secondary World was nothing less than a spiritual act that reflected God's creativity. J.R.R. saw Middle-earth as an expression of the talent God had given him to be a sub-creator, a master of a Secondary World. All humans are endowed with this same ability, albeit some to a greater extent than others. He believed that each individual actually is implanted with not only the desire to be a sub-creator, but also with a sort of natural attraction toward fairy tales, fiction, mythology and fantasy.[48]

Moreover, J.R.R. believed that all mythology in various ways ultimately pointed to Christianity. He stated: "I believe that legends and myths are largely made of 'truth,' and indeed present aspects of it that can only be received in this mode; and long ago certain truths and modes of this kind were discovered and must always reappear."[49] Humphrey Carpenter, who wrote the authorized biography of Tolkien, summarized J.R.R.'s views as follows:

> We have come from God, and inevitably the myths woven by us, though they contain error, will also reflect a splintered fragment of the true light, the eternal truth that is with God. Indeed, only by myth-making, only by becoming a "sub-creator" and inventing stories, can Man aspire to the state of perfection that he knew before the Fall. Our myths may be misguided, but they steer however shakily towards the true harbor.[50]

Both Tolkien and C.S. Lewis, in fact, maintained that the gospel stories of the Bible present the greatest of all myths, but one that became fact. Lewis said that the story of Christ was a "true myth, a myth that works on us in the same way as the others, but a myth that *really happened*."[51] For Tolkien, "the Gospel story constitutes the perfect fairy-tale by the most potent of all authors—God himself."[52] In *Tree and Leaf*, J.R.R. wrote about the Gospels:

> [They contain] many marvels—peculiarly artistic, beautiful, and moving: "mythical" in their perfect, self-contained significance. . . . There is no tale ever told that men would rather find was true, and none which so many skeptical men have accepted as true on its own merits. For the Art of it has the su-

premely convincing tone of Primary Art, that is, of Creation.[53]

During his 1939 lecture "On Fairie Stories," Tolkien neatly summarized his view of the Jesus "myth," saying: "[T]his story is supreme; and it is true. Art has been verified. God is the Lord, of angels, and of men—and of elves. Legend and History have met and fused [in the Gospels]."[54] In a letter to his son, he further stated, "Of course I do not mean the Gospels tell what is only a fairy-story; but I do mean very strongly that they do tell a fairy-story: the greatest."[55]

J.R.R. went on to explain to his son that humanity, as a story-telling race, would have to be redeemed "in a manner consonant with that nature: by a moving story. *But* since the author of it is the supreme Artist and the Author of Reality, this one was also made to Be, to be true on the Primary Plane [i.e., in the real world]."[56]

A Tale of Good vs. Evil

One of the most interesting aspects of The Lord of the Rings is the philosophy of good and evil it contains: "Nothing is evil in the beginning."[57] This perspective, expressed by Tolkien through the voice of Elrond at the Council in Rivendell, again echoes Christian thought. As a Roman Catholic, Tolkien believed, as the Bible's book of Genesis states, that God created everything good. In other words, evil does not have an independent existence. It came into our world, just as it entered Middle-earth: by a perversion, a twisting or corruption of a good thing.[58]

In Christianity, even Lucifer himself began life as a mighty angel, but he became Satan, the devil, only after rebelling in pride and selfish ambition against God. So too we hear from Elrond that Sauron (like Lucifer) was not initially evil, but became so through self-seeking. This leads to yet another facet of Tolkien's concept of good and evil: the tendency for power to corrupt. Elrond explains:

We cannot use the Ruling Ring.... It belongs to Sauron and
was made by him alone. . . . [It] is too great for anyone to
wield at will, save only those who have already a great power
of their own. But for them it holds an even deadlier peril.
The very desire of it corrupts the heart. . . . If any of the
Wise should with this Ring overthrow the Lord of Mordor,
using his own arts, he would then set himself on Sauron's
throne, and yet another Dark Lord would appear. And that
is another reason why the Ring should be destroyed: as long
as it is in the world it will be a danger even to the Wise.[59]

The ring will always destroy the one who bears it. Tolkien's
story perfectly illustrates the observation made by British historian Lord Acton (1834-1902), who wrote, "Power tends to
corrupt and absolute power corrupts absolutely."[60] At the same
time, however, Tolkien is careful to demonstrate that evil also is
always self-destructive. The end of evil will be judgment—a
theme intrinsic to the Bible's teachings (see Psalm 1:4-6, 9:5-6,
11:6; Proverbs 10:24-25; Galatians 6:7-8).

In "Christian Elements and Symbols in Tolkien's *The Lord of
the Rings*," Dan Graves points out another concept the trilogy illuminates: "Evil is self-blinded, too. That which it does in malice,
that which seems to be its greatest victory, proves to be its own
undoing."[61] This concept is revealed as Tolkien gradually exposes
Sauron's shortcomings, which include overconfidence, desperation and delusions of superiority. His own fears, coupled with a
blind assumption that all individuals, like him, will seek the power
of the ring, is what leads to his final undoing.[62]

Of particular interest is Tolkien's allusions to a kind of hell
that awaits Sauron, Saruman, the Nazgûl and all evil beings.
Their destiny is referred to as absolute nothingness—total loss
of being. In *Master of Middle-earth*, the late Paul H. Kocher (d.
1999), professor of English at Stanford University, wrote:

[Consider] Gandalf's stern command to Angmar when he
confronts the Nazgûl at the gates of Gondor: "Go back to

the abyss prepared for you! Go back! Fall into the nothing-ness that awaits you and your Master." Over and over Tolkien's own words connect Sauron and his servants with a nothingness that is the philosophical opposite of Being. Add, finally, the outer and inner decay of Saruman who "was great once, of a noble kind." . . . His death finishes the downward plunge. The spirit rising from his shrunken body is dissipated by a wind from the West, "and with a sigh dissolved into nothing." That word *nothing* is a repeated knell for the pass-ing of the lords of wickedness in *The Lord of the Rings*. Tolkien is careful never to say anything explicit about that nothingness to which they go, doubly careful never to call it hell, but it shares with hell the distinguishing feature of total estrangement from ultimate Being.[63]

Despite these and many more examples of Christian symbol-ism in Tolkien's works, many Christian fundamentalists have taken a decidedly negative view of The Lord of the Rings. Their concerns are primarily based on the belief that Tolkien's trilogy contains occult imagery and practices, particularly "magic" and "wizards."

TOLKIEN ON TRIAL

When closely examined, the concerns most often expressed by Christians regarding The Lord of the Rings are without merit. Their objections commonly rest on several misunderstandings of the text. For example, as previously stated, Tolkien's wizards are not the kind of wizards condemned in the Bible. They are, for all intents and purposes, angels.

Readers of The Lord of the Rings must never for a moment think that his reference to "wizards" suggests they have some connection to "wizards" as found in occult literature. Concerning the "magic" these wizards (i.e., angels) use, there is a distinct dif-ference between it and the occult-based/contemporary pagan "magick" found in our Primary World (see chapter 2).

Tolkien thoroughly disliked having to use the word "magic," but was forced to do so because he could find no other word closer to the meaning he intended.[64] As far back as 1939 he had expressed regret for having inserted the word "magic" into his story. He thought it brought to mind images of the occult "Magician" of our real world, which was something he did not want to do. As a result, "use of magic in his stories is quite sparing," according to philosophy professor Richard Purtill, an expert on Tolkien.[65]

J.R.R. also attempted to alleviate the problems associated with the word "magic" by placing strict limitations on it, including who possessed it, how it was used and why it was used. In various letters, Tolkien made it clear that "magic" in the context of Middle-earth is connected in no way to supernatural power. It is a natural ability, one which was *not* given to humans. For the Elves, "magic" is as natural as singing or drawing. Tolkien actually described "magic" as "art" without human limitations. He goes so far as to say that Elves are "primarily artists."[66] The source of their artistry (i.e., magic) rests within their own natures. It depends on no external power, nor can it be learned or enhanced.[67]

Richard Purtill observes: "In some ways, therefore, magic in Tolkien's stories is being used as a metaphor for art and technology."[68] Of great significance is how the very term "magic" in The Lord of the Rings is perplexing to Elves, who hear it being used by mortals to describe their abilities. This is apparent when Galadriel (Elven "Lady of Lorien") shows Frodo her "magic" mirror, saying: "For this is what your folk would call magic, I believe; though I do not understand clearly what they mean. . . . But this, if you will, is the magic of Galadriel."[69] Tolkien explained:

> [T]he Elven-queen Galadriel is obliged to remonstrate with the Hobbits on their confused use of the word both for the devices and operations of the Enemy, and for those of the Elves. . . . [T]he Elves are there (in my tales) to demonstrate the difference. Their "magic" is Art, delivered from many of its human limitations: more effortless, more quick, more

complete. . . . And its object is Art not Power, sub-creation not domination.[70]

Even though Tolkien took great pains to make such distinctions, he often lamented his use of the word "magic." It failed miserably to adequately or accurately explain its meaning in the context of his story:

> [Magic] is for them [i.e., Elves] a form of Art, and distinct from Wizardry or Magic, properly so called. . . . We need a word for this Elvish craft, but all the words that have been applied to it have been blurred and confused with other things. Magic is ready to hand, and I have used it above, but I should not have done so: Magic should be reserved for the operations of the Magician [practitioner of magick]. . . . Magic [occult magick in the Primary World] produces, or pretends to produce, an alteration in the Primary World. It does not matter by whom it is said to be practiced . . . it is not an art but a technique; its desire is power in this world, domination of things and wills.[71]

Like Tolkien's Elves, the Maiar and Valar are simply exercising their God-given (i.e., *Eru*-given) abilities when they practice "magic," either for good or evil.[72] No other race, including Orcs, Trolls, Dwarves, Hobbits, and others, has magical capabilities. Tolkien explained: "[I]t is in an inherent power not possessed or attainable by Men as such."[73] Interestingly, drastic and negative consequences always result in Middle-earth when its nonmagical residents get too close to magic. The Nazgûl, for example, were nine Men who, because of their magical rings, became servants of the evil Sauron.

Gollum likewise was corrupted by possessing a magic ring. Bilbo too began to be changed for the worse by the ring. Even Frodo, after his long journey with the ring, is never physically or psychologically the same. He tells Gandalf he has been forever "wounded" by the ordeal.[74] Every year on the anniversary of the ring's destruction, he becomes bed-ridden with nausea.[75]

In Middle-earth all who dabble in powers not meant for them are ensnared by those powers. The character Elrond emphasizes this message, saying, "It is perilous to study too deeply the arts of the Enemy, for good or for ill."[76] Obviously, the properties of "magic" in Middle-earth are very different from "magick" in our real world.

It can be argued that The Lord of the Rings is a Christian classic, rather than a work derived from paganism. Literature scholars from diverse fields of specialty are in agreement on this issue. Patrick Grant, for instance, a specialist in Renaissance literature who teaches English at the University of Victoria, British Columbia, writes,

> *The Lord of the Rings* embodies an "inherent morality," as Tolkien calls it, which derives largely from the traditions of Christian and epic poetry. . . . First, and most important, is the concept of Christian heroism, a spiritual quality which depends on obedience rather than prowess or personal power. Second, heroism is basic to the meaning of love. Third, charity, or love, is the foundation of faith and hope. And last, Providence directs the affairs of the world. . . . We find the morality of the story not in doctrinal formulations which are the staples of allegory, but in the traditional and implicit motifs of Christian heroism, obedience, charity, and providence. Just as, historically, the simmering stock in the cauldron of the story is substantially flavored by the Christian ingredient, so are the archetypes in *The Lord of the Rings.*[77]

Joseph Pearce—author of *Tolkien: Man and Myth*—agrees with Grant. In an interview with the Zenit News Agency, Pearce commented,

> *The Lord of the Rings* is a profoundly Christian myth. . . .
> The values that emerge in *The Lord of the Rings* are the values
> that emerge in the Gospels. In the characterization of the
> Hobbits, the most reluctant and the most unlikely of heroes,
> we see the exaltation of the humble. In the figure of Gandalf
> we see the archetype of an Old Testament patriarch, his staff
> apparently having the same power as that possessed by Mo-
> ses. In his apparent "death" and "resurrection" we see him
> emerge as a Christ-like figure. His "resurrection" results in
> his transfiguration. . . . The character of Gollum is debased by
> his attachment to the Ring, the symbol of the sin of pride. . . .
> Ultimately, the bearing of the Ring by Frodo, and his heroic
> struggle to resist the temptation to succumb to its evil pow-
> ers, is akin to the Carrying of the Cross, the supreme act of
> selflessness. Throughout the whole of *The Lord of the Rings*
> the forces of evil are seen as powerful but not all-powerful.
> There is always the sense that divine providence is on the side
> of the Fellowship and that, ultimately, it will prevail against
> all the odds. As Tolkien put it succinctly, "Above all shadows
> rides the Sun."[78]

Surprisingly, despite such learned opinions, The Lord of the
Rings continues to be interpreted by some individuals as a kind of
promotional volume for occultism.[79] This may be due in part to
their unfamiliarity with the work. A more significant cause, however, may be contemporary society's obsession with occultism in
general and the explosive growth of occult-based belief systems
such as neo-paganism and Wicca. These issues will be the subject
of Part Three.

Part
Three

WELCOME TO THE AGE
OF ABRACADABRA

Our superstitions provide answers to things we
do not understand and cannot explain. Even today, when we know so much, we turn for answers
to astrology and to the occult; and like our ances-
tors, we continue to cross our fingers, wish on
stars, and knock on wood.

—Alvin Schwartz
author, *Scary Stories to Tell in the Dark*
("Children, Humor, and Folklore," in
Paul Heins, ed., *Crosscurrents of Criticism:
Horn Book Essays* 1968-1977, p. 215)

TWENTY-FIRST-CENTURY MAGICK

The phenomenal interest aroused by the Harry Potter books, written by J.K. Rowling, indicates a burning desire on the part of young and old to enter the enticing world of magic.

—The Gnostic Society (August 4, 2000)[1]
"True Magical Practices and Harry Potter"

Spirituality has engulfed America.[2] As far back as 1993, God was "in" and atheism/agnosticism was "out." As church historian and University of Chicago professor Martin Marty observed in November of that year, "[S]pirituality is back, almost with a vengeance. . . . [I see] concern for spirituality as an event of our era."[3] Marty's assertion repeatedly found confirmation in 1994 through multiple news stories bearing titles such as "In Search of the Sacred," "The New Spin Is Spirituality," and "Desperately Seeking Spirituality."[4]

More telling were figures from a 1994 *Newsweek* poll, which showed that fifty-eight percent of Americans felt "the need to experience spiritual growth."[5] By 2000, more than eighty percent desired spiritual growth.[6] During this same year fifty-four percent of U.S. residents were calling themselves religious, while thirty percent were viewing themselves as "spiritual."[7]

Given such findings, it is no surprise that the production of books on religion/spirituality rose 112 percent from 1991 to 1996.[8] By 1999, religious book sales had hit an all-time high of $2.15 billion (sixteen percent of *all* books sold), which made religious volumes the second biggest book category after general fiction. The Book Industry Study Group, an organization that tracks publishing trends, has predicted that sales of spirituality-related books will likely climb to $2.74 billion by 2004.[9]

IN THE GODDESS WE TRUST

Americans evidently are seeking answers to humanity's perennial questions: What is the meaning of life? Is there consciousness after death? Does God exist? Interestingly, many of today's truth-seekers are not searching for spiritual relief in mainstream churches. They are looking instead to non-traditional and/or non-Western groups, beliefs and rituals, such as transcendental meditation, Hinduism, Buddhism and Shamanism.

According to nationally syndicated columnist Terry Mattingly—associate professor of media and religion at Palm Beach Atlantic College—people currently pursuing spirituality are not committed to the doctrines of any one particular faith, and they are *especially* reticent to embrace Christianity.[10] It no longer seems to be an appealing choice for many people. Indeed, the overall picture of America's landscape suggests there has been a kind of mass exodus away from the Christian church and its teachings.[11]

But if people are no longer seeking solace for their souls in the arms of Christianity (allegedly "America's religion"), then where is the public looking for religious fulfillment? According to the Gallup Organization newsletter, *Emerging Trends*, there has been a substantial increase in acceptance of "psychic, paranormal and occult phenomena over the past decade."[12] Consider how dramatically American views have changed over the last several decades regarding the following occult subjects:

Which if any of the following do you believe at least to some degree?[13]		
BELIEF	1976	1997
Spiritualism (i.e., communication with the dead)	12%	52%
Astrology	17%	37%
Reincarnation	9%	25%
Fortune-Telling	4%	14%

Table 6.1

These findings suggest that today's most popular forms of spirituality are those associated in some way with the occult, neopaganism and witchcraft. Renowned scholar Mircea Eliade foresaw with great clarity such a trend as far back as 1976, writing:

> As a historian of religions, I cannot fail but be impressed by the amazing popularity of witchcraft in modern Western culture and its subcultures. However, the contemporary interest in witchcraft is only part and parcel of a larger trend, namely, the vogue of the occult and the esoteric.[14]

Eliade could not have spoken truer words. The number of individuals embracing occult practices, neopagan beliefs and principles of Witchcraft (capitalized to designate a religious system, a.k.a. Wicca) has grown exponentially since the 1970s. Although no one knows exactly how many neopagans and Wiccans are in America, recent estimates place the U.S. Wiccan population between 250,000 to 400,000.[15] Perhaps the most accurate guess comes from Helen Berger, associate professor of sociology at West Chester University of Pennsylvania. She surveyed more than 2,000 Wiccans and estimates America's Witch population to be near 150,000 to 200,000.[16]

Whichever figure one accepts, there is no doubt that the number of persons following Wicca and neopaganism is rising. But what exactly is neopaganism? What do Wiccans/Witches believe? How do Wiccans differ from neopagans? What practices fall under the heading of occultism? These questions are answered incorrectly far too often. Consequently, a general overview of these subjects is necessary.

THE OCCULT AND NEOPAGANISM

The word "occult" derives from the Latin word *occulere* ("to hide"), a term originally used in reference to the knowledge held by initiates of various "mystery religions" and secret societies of long ago. Occultism dates back thousands of years to when people believed that "deviations from natural law involved mysterious and miraculous 'supernatural' or occult laws, deriving from gods, invisible entities or the souls of the dead."[17]

Hoping to access the laws of power, individuals and cultures developed "magick" rituals. These rituals gave rise to witch doctors and shamans, who claimed a heightened ability to perform magick. An indispensable part of their activities often included some form of necromancy—i.e., communication with spirits of the dead. Thus began humanity's quest to control an uncontrollable world through the alteration, manipulation or suspension of various laws of nature.

The occult, then, is a vast system of religious studies, theories, practices and beliefs that allegedly enable participants to obtain knowledge by which they can control, or at least influence, the world around them—e.g., change the future, attract a mate, heal the sick, secure sudden wealth, evolve to a higher spiritual level.

The occult label is applicable to an endless list of practices, such as astrology, alchemy, channeling, crystal gazing, dowsing, dream interpretation, extrasensory perception (ESP), fortune-telling, numerology, Ouija boards, out-of-body travel (astral projection), palm reading, psychic healing, pyramidology, tarot cards, mediumship, voodoo and witchcraft.

Occultism also may encompass unusual phenomena such as UFO abductions, ghosts and unexplained creatures. Paranormal events that seem to contradict natural explanation (psychic visions, premonitions, etc.) fall within occultism as well. This makes discussing occultism a daunting task. In *The Occult: Secrets of the Hidden World*, Julien Tondriau explains:

> Occult belief comprises traditions both of immense antiquity and great complexity in which it is nearly impossible to find any degree of uniformity and consistency, and the followers of occultism are themselves notoriously given to mystification so that their own accounts of an [sic] subject are full of strange pseudo-scientific jargon and merely add to the confusion.[18]

Because the majority of occultists tend to be eclectic in their views, not all occultists can be easily categorized.[19] But of those who do fall into some sort of classification, the largest number are neopagans. Neopaganism, according to the most commonly held view, is a modernization of certain prehistoric sets of religious beliefs that thrived until they were suppressed by Christianity.

The word "paganism" comes from the Latin word *paganus*, meaning "country dweller." It is a term that refers to primitive peoples who developed religion as a means of explaining the world around them. Their belief system was allegedly based on the worship of: 1) a Mother Goddess who represented creation, birth, food-gathering, agricultural plenty and the summer; and 2) the Horned God, male consort of the Mother Goddess, who represented the hunt, death and the winter months.[20]

To these two primary deities, cultures added other gods and goddesses until a pantheon of deities were available for worship: Isis, Balder, Pan, Osiris, Odin, Diana, Astaroth, Brighid, Aphrodite, Athena, Cerridwen, Ceres, Hecate, Kali and Cybele. The Mother Goddess, by far the deity most commonly worshiped by Wiccans, is accepted in many forms: e.g., the Greek goddesses Artemis, Gaia and Sophia, as well as any one of the Celtic or Norse goddesses. Today these same deities are being by revered by a new generation of pagans (i.e., neopagans). In fact, the Internet's "Book of Deities" Web site lists more than 1,700 gods/goddesses invoked by followers of the supposed "old ways."[21]

But beyond recognizing pagan acceptance of multiple deities, it is difficult to solidify any rigid set of beliefs. Each neopagan essentially defines his or her own brand of paganism based on what "feels" right to him or her. As one popular Web site puts it, "Pagans pursue their own vision of the Divine as a direct and personal experience."[22] Nevertheless, a generalized summation of what *most* neopagans believe can be deduced from their literature:

> Neopagans hold a reverence for the Earth and all its creatures, generally see all life as interconnected, and tend to strive to attune one's self to the manifestation of this belief as seen in the cycles of nature. Pagans are usually polytheistic (believing in more than one god), and they usually believe in immanence, or the concept of divinity residing in all things. Many pagans, though polytheistic, see all things as being part of one Great Mystery. The apparent contradiction of being both polytheistic and monotheistic can be resolved by seeing the God/[Goddesses] as masks worn by the Great Mystery. Other pagans are simply monotheistic or polytheistic, and still others are atheistic.[23]

In addition to these views, neopagans may identify with one or more of several religious traditions (e.g., Greek, Egyptian, Norse, Celtic, Roman). Of the many different traditions of paganism that exist, none is more popular or influential today than Wicca, also known as either Witchcraft or simply the Craft.

A WICCAN WORLD[24]

Wicca is one of the most misunderstood religions of society. Mere mention of the word "witch" conjures up images of old hags, who at Satan's beck and call, boil magickal brews in cauldrons and fly overhead on broomsticks. In reality, however, contemporary Witches tend to be peace-loving, nature-honoring individuals who take somewhat of a "you-leave-me-alone-and-I'll-leave-you-alone" approach to life.[25]

As with paganism, Witchcraft has many strains: Gardnerian, Algard, Alexandrian, Cymry, Dianic, Corelliam and Guyddon, to name a few. The most common elements binding these and other forms of Witchcraft are as follows:

- Exaltation of experience over any set of dogmatic beliefs.
- Acceptance of diversity of beliefs as healthy and essential to humanity's well-being.
- Denial of absolute truth. No single religion or morality is objectively right. "True is what is true for you; right is what is right for you. . . .Your path may not be my own, but both are equally viable trails of truth and spirituality."
- Adherence to the Wiccan ethical code, or rede: "If ye harm none, do what ye will."
- Working of magick and various divination techniques.
- Development of personal psychic abilities.[26]

Witchcraft is particularly attractive today for various reasons, as Ronald Hutton observes in his 1991 book *The Pagan Religions of the Ancient British Isles* (1991):

> The advantage of the label "witch" is that it has all the exciting connotations of a figure who flouts conventions of normal society and is possessed of powers unavailable to it, at once feared and persecuted. It is a marvelous rallying-point for a counter-culture and also one of the few images of independent female power in early modern European civilization.[27]

Even more alluring is Wiccan morality, or rather, the lack of it. Wiccans adhere to their "own path" of right and wrong, which ultimately amounts to a denial of any standard definition for good or evil. As Wiccan priestess Vivianne Crowley admits: "In the circle there are no absolutes—no rights and wrongs."[28]

In other words, Wiccans simply follow their own personal self-interests. They judge what is "moral" by their own subjective determination of whether or not a particular behavior may be harmful to someone else. This follows the Wiccan rede: "If it harm none, do what you will."

Such a broad code of conduct obviously leaves room for a plethora of activities that may range from sexual promiscuity, to use of illegal drugs, to stealing, to lying—as long as a Witch feels that he or she is not hurting anyone. Such a determination, of course, is based entirely on subjective feelings rather than any objective standard of measure. Moral relativism is the result.

The moral inexactness of the Rede has caused a considerable amount of controversy regarding Wiccan sexuality in relation to children. Wicca's moral atmosphere is so sexually permissive that no consensus exists within that religion about where the line between appropriate and inappropriate behavior should be drawn. Helen Berger notes:

> [T]he Neo-Pagan community is on the whole sexually permissive—accepting open sexuality, homosexuality, bisexuality . . . group marriages and open marriages. Witches exalt both homosexuality and heterosexuality as magical arts.[29]

A danger to children is posed because Wicca basically advocates little more than the pursuit of one's selfish desires. No self-interest is out-of-bounds, as long as Wiccans can convince themselves that what they are doing is not harmful. As Starhawk, founder of the Covenant of the Goddess, plainly states, "In witchcraft, we do not fight self-interest, we follow it."[30]

Phillip Davis—author of *The Goddess Unmasked* and professor of religion at the University of Prince Edward Island, Canada—says Wiccan reasoning is naive at best. "Encouraging people to think they are divine is very dangerous," says Davis. "It takes the limits off and doesn't leave any moral restraints."[31] Tal Brooke, director of the Spiritual Counterfeits Project and one-time practitioner of Eastern mysticism, likewise warns that Wicca is "narcissistic, amoral and pleasure-seeking—the perfect postmodern religion for the nineties."[32]

Even the most sympathetic researchers of Wicca agree that the morality inherent to Witchcraft is confusing at best. Anthropologist Susan Greenwood, a research fellow in the Department of Sociology and Anthropology at Goldsmiths College, University of London, reached this conclusion after studying Wicca extensively. She, in fact, was a participant-observer within British magical and Wiccan communities for several years in both "high magic" and witchcraft groups. In her 2000 book *Magic, Witchcraft, and the Otherworld*, she specifically addresses Wiccan morality, saying:

> [T]he Wiccan Rede is a rather vague moral maxim to follow. It repudiates dogma in the name of individual freedom; but this often means that it becomes dogmatic in its anti-dogma, resulting in the fact that it is difficult for witches to have any sense of communal ethics. . . . [T]he Wiccan Rede is a problematic basis for the creation of morality in everyday life; it is difficult to interpret practically. . . . [D]iscussions on how to follow "An' it harm none" remain scarce. . . . [T]he passive nature and broad interpretation fail to provide an adequate ethical structure for Paganism as a community. . . . [Some] would view racism and sexism as harmful, but others might not. They might limit the Rede to physical or magical harm, and see verbal disrespect as ethically acceptable.[33]

Because Wicca fits under the umbrella category of neopaganism, all Witches are pagans. Not all pagans, however, are Witches.[34] Consequently, while maintaining distinctiveness, the two religious systems share numerous beliefs. Both are anti-dogmatic, anti-authoritarian, usually polytheistic, find divinity in nature, love/worship nature to some extent, believe in humanity's inherent divinity and cultivate psychic abilities.[35] Another key component of both Witchcraft and neopaganism is occult magick, which is defined as follows:

> [T]he attempt to control, manipulate, bend, shape, twist, turn, or direct reality for one's own ends or goals. This is

supposedly accomplished by invoking or employing spirits
or extra-dimensional entities or beings, or mysteries, unknown or relatively unknown, or seldom used powers,
forces, rules, guidelines, and/or laws [of nature].[36]

Magick normally is accomplished through spells or incantations. These usually consist of physical rituals and highly evoca-
tive imagery expressed through repetitive phrases and/or power
words designed to bring forth either natural external forces or
the inner powers of the self. *The Encyclopedia of Occultism and
Parapsychology* defines a spell as a "written or spoken formula
of words supposed to be capable of magical effects."[37]

The theory behind spellcasting comes from the notion that
there exists an intimate connection between words and whatever
objects or persons they signify. It is believed that under the right
circumstances a Witch can cause an event to occur by either
chanting about, or describing, the event desired, while simultaneously relating those actions to the objects/people/spirits involved.[38]

The essence of magick has yet to be precisely defined, but
many occultists (especially Witches) see it as something natural, rather than supernatural. In *Witchcraft: The Old Religion*,
Leo Martello remarks, "I make no claims as a Witch to 'supernatural powers,' but I totally believe in the *super* powers that reside in the *natural*."[39] Wiccan Scott Cunningham agrees: "Folk
magic cannot and could not be construed as a supernatural, oth-
erworldly process. . . . It's a perfectly natural process that most
of us simply haven't used."[40]

Cunningham additionally writes: "Folk magicians don't use supernatural powers. . . . They simply sense and utilize natural energies which have not yet been quantified, codified and accepted
into the hallowed halls of science."[41] In other words, magick is
merely a way of harnessing natural forces not yet discovered by
science. As the infamous Aleister Crowley (1875-1947), who
popularized the spelling of "magick" with a "k," said, "Magick is

the Science and Art of causing Change to occur in conformity with Will."[42]

It is this alleged ability to cause change in conformity with one's own will that undoubtedly has contributed to the widespread popularity of Witchcraft. Wicca is now so prevalent that some commentators have labeled it "the fastest-growing religion in America."[43] Witchcraft's acceptability can be seen and felt everywhere. "Proud to Be a Witch" bumper stickers are seen on cars. Web sites extolling the virtues of Wicca, magick and paganism abound. Bookstore shelves dedicated to paganism, Wicca and occultism continue to expand as more volumes on these subjects are released each year.

According to Jo Pearson, organizer for England's "The Development of Paganism" conference in 2001, the Wiccan revival has spread not only throughout the U.S., but Canada, Australia, New Zealand, Germany, the Netherlands and Scandinavia.[44] Neopaganism and Wicca have even penetrated mainstream Christian churches—both Roman Catholic and Protestant. A 1999 issue of *Insight* magazine noted, "Feminist proponents of Wicca, or modern-day witchcraft, now can be found within the clergy promoting the cult of the Goddess in many mainline Christian denominations" (see Appendix B).[45]

MARKETING MAGICK TO MINORS

Perhaps as many as 10 million book-buyers in America regularly purchase neopagan literature.[46] Interestingly, according to buying patterns, several surveys and various research reports, a significant percentage of individuals buying the material are children and teens. Wicca in particular seems to be the subject in which most of them are interested. This phenomena has been noticed and informally tracked by various journalists, religion scholars and organizations devoted to the study of cults/occultism.

Danny Aguirre of the Spiritual Counterfeits Project, for instance, recently reported, "In the last six months, I have received

more inquiries about Wicca than any other religion in the 10 years
I have worked here . . . all teen-age girls."[47] A similar observation
has been made by B.A. Robinson of the Ontario Consultants on
Religious Tolerance:

> [I have] noticed an increase in recent years of: The percentage
> of small bookstores carrying Wiccan and other Neopagan
> books[;] The percentage of Wiccan books in bookstores'
> New Age section[;] The numbers of Emails received by this
> website from teenagers with questions about Wicca[;] Media
> reports of the number of conflicts between Wiccan students
> in public high schools and their school boards over the wear-
> ing of pentacles.[48]

Book publishers many years ago saw the lucrative appeal of this
occult-youth market. Consequently, since the early 1990s, major
publishers have released a steady stream of occult-glamorizing fiction volumes targeting children and teens. In 1994, for instance,
Dial Books for Young Readers produced *The War of the Wizards*
(ages four to eight), which displayed a pentagram inside its front
cover. In 1999, Magic Carpet Books released *Wizard's Hall* (ages
nine to twelve), a novel about a young boy at a school for wizards.

Even more widely read has been Diane Duane's "young
adult" wizard series, which follows the adventures of a teenage
girl witch and her wizard boyfriend: *So You Want to Be a Wizard* (1996), *Deep Wizardry* (1996), *High Wizardry* (1997) and *A
Wizard Abroad* (1999). These volumes helped initiate what has
become a near obsession among teenage girls—i.e., the female
teen witch character.[49]

As of mid-2001 four publishers had launched a new paperback
fiction series revolving around teenage girls' involvement in
witchcraft. The first three—Sweep (Penguin Putnam) by Cate
Tiernan; Circle of Three (Avon) by Isobel Bird; and the Daughters of the Moon (Volo, an imprint of Hyperion) by Lynne Ew-
ing—target teenagers. The fourth, T*Witches (Scholastic) by
H.B. Gilmour and Randi Reisfeld, is aimed at preteens.

According to Jean Feiwel, editor-in-chief at Scholastic, the new volumes have merely tapped into an increased teen interest in witches. "It's almost gotten—dare I say it—acceptable," Feiwel said in a 2001 news story.[50] This same article also revealed: "Practicing witches are amused by this trend in teen books." Publishers report that "the books are selling so well that the writers have been given contracts to write more volumes."[51] The most popular additions to this growing body of literature have been the Sweep books and the T*Witches series.

Sweep—a fourteen-volume series with titles such as *The Coven*, *Blood Witch* and *Dark Magick*—follows the adventures of sixteen-year-old Morgan Rowlands.[52] Volume I, *Book of Shadows*, introduces Morgan as a drab and shy teenager who falls for a handsome high school heartthrob named Cal. Morgan would love to attract him, but she is nothing but a plain-looking, Catholic girl, embarrassed to still be a virgin. Cal is "gorgeous." He also is a Wiccan, as is his mother (a high priestess). Morgan soon discovers that she has an exceptional sensitivity to natural energies and is unusually adept at magick, especially when it comes to channeling occult power.[53]

The story continues with Morgan joining Cal's new coven and learning from him how to perform Wiccan rituals, complete with chants of "Blessed Be" as well as praises to "the Goddess" and "the God."[54] Morgan and her friends are enthralled by the Wiccan rituals. Week after week Cal teaches his young followers more about Wiccan history, rituals, spells, paraphernalia and powers.[55] "Our group was starting to listen to him like he was an apostle, teaching us," Morgan rejoices.[56] The occult bookstore quickly becomes her favorite hangout and resource center for occult literature and supplies.[57]

The remainder of Book I follows Morgan as she begins casting spells and starts listening to her inner witch voice, which causes several episodes of psychic phenomena.[58] Wicca is exalted as the most exciting, fulfilling and rewarding of all religious belief systems. And with the help of magick, Morgan blossoms into a strong, confident and powerful young woman. As it turns out, she is a "blood witch"—a descendant in a long line of powerful witches that can be traced back to members of the original covens of centuries ago.[59] In subsequent volumes Morgan, along with other good witches, end up battling evil forces and discovering her family's magickal history.

Tiernan's series effectively doubles as a virtual training manual for teens on how to start their own covens. As one Web site by a Sweep fan stated, "The books have to do with a religion called, Wicca."[60] The volumes also take a variety of unnecessary swipes at Christianity. For example, the author misrepresents and ridicules the concept of the Trinity when Morgan's parents object to her choice of Wicca's multiple gods over monotheistic Christianity. Morgan snaps: "I thought we believed in the Father, the Son, and the Holy Ghost. That's three" (Tiernan, p. 103).

The Sweep series is little more than thinly veiled publicity tool extolling the virtues of Wicca. Not only does it exalt Wicca and denigrate Christianity (the religion in which Morgan was raised by her adoptive parents), but it puts forth several highly dubious yet oft-repeated claims, including the assertion that Wicca is based on prehistoric beliefs and ancient Celtic traditions.[61]

In reality, *modern* Wicca has little to do with the ancient Celts or any other pagan culture. At best it is loosely based on a few ancient traditions that have been significantly altered. Charlotte Allen, in her enlightening article on Wicca that appeared in *The Atlantic Monthly*, writes:

> Historically speaking, the "ancient" rituals of the Goddess movement are almost certainly bunk. . . . In all probability, not a single element of the Wiccan story is true. The evidence is overwhelming that Wicca is a distinctly new religion, a 1950s concoction influenced by such things as Masonic ritual and a late-nineteenth-century fascination with the esoteric and the occult, and that various assumptions informing the

Wiccan view of history are deeply flawed. Furthermore, scholars generally agree that there is no indication, either archaeological or in the written record, that any ancient people ever worshipped a single, archetypal goddess—a conclusion that strikes at the heart of Wiccan belief. . . . In the 1950s [Gerald] Gardner introduced a religion he called (and spelled) Wica. Although Gardner claimed to have learned Wiccan lore from a centuries-old coven of witches who also belonged to the Fellowship of Crotona . . . no one had been able to locate the coven and [it is said] that Gardner had invented the rites he trumpeted, borrowing from rituals created early in the twentieth century by the notorious British occultist Aleister Crowley, among others.[62]

Despite such information, Sweep has lulled untold numbers of teens into thinking that Wicca is something that it is not.

Similarly crafted to make Wicca appear attractive are the T∗Witch books by Scholastic, the same publisher that produces the Harry Potter series. The T∗Witch volumes (advertised for ages nine to twelve) are about identical twins, Camryn Barnes and Alexandra Fielding, who were separated at birth. They are the daughters of two powerful witches and are imbued with tremendous abilities. Camryn can foresee the future and Alexandra can read people's minds. Both are reunited as teens and begin sharing adventures in the wonderful world of Wicca.

Scholastic has devoted an entire "Kids-Fun-Online" Web site to the T∗Witch series, where children can go and answer a series of questions to find out which T∗Witch they most resemble.[63] The Web site also includes a "Magick Tip" Archive, where information is given to assist children in their "own private spell-binding."[64] In this archive the word "magick" is consistently spelled in its occult form, using a "k." The following sample texts taken from the Web site present authentic occult, Wiccan and neopagan teachings:

- *Rhyming Power*: Herbs, candles, moonlight, they're all good for spells. But the secret to a truly powerful spell . . . is the RHYME.

- *Powerful Places*: Some spells need atmosphere. . . . Get outside and work with Mother Nature to make some magick under the sun or the stars, near trees or water. The energy of all living things will add their power to yours.

- *Creature Companions*: . . . Cats, dogs, and many small creatures understand how magick works better than us humans. They can help by adding their energy to yours and helping you focus.

- *Timing Is Everything*: Don't waste your time with untimely spells. Do you need a full moon? . . . Timing matters as much as the words you recite and the candles you light! Be patient and powerful and you will succeed!

There is even a place at this Web site called the "Spellbook," which lists numerous spells submitted by *children* who practice magick.[65] The following incantations represent only a small sampling of posts by children wanting to help their peers learn and use various spells. Although juvenile in content, they accurately reflect Wiccan or neopagan procedures for casting spells:[66]

RHYMING SPELLS

Katie, Age 12—Whirl whirl twist and twirl, magic mother of thy pearl. Twist and mix with beach at bay, every mother's secret day. Sound of light and sight of day, come together, make a ray.

Hannah, Age 11, FL—Howling winds; Listen twins; Winds that frighten; Let your hearts lighten; The rain that falls; And the simple squalls; Put your powers together; Let them be gone forever!

LOVE SPELLS

Katherine, Age 13—Pluck some flowers . . . and go to some water (a lake at the full moon works best, but you can use a bowl of water in a pinch). Throw the flowers in the water, thinking about the person you desire, and saying: "I place my enchantment with all my might, May it come true this very night!"

Erin, Age 11, IL—Glorious sunlight please set me free, From the darkness that clings to me. Please give to me my heart's one need, That hatred and death cannot succeed.

Gigi, Age 11, MA—We are fifteen, on Halloween. Make us light, To bring sight of what we need, we have grown from such a little seed. Let us outgrow, please show!

Kendall, Age 12, FL—On a night with a full moon go to a lake or the sea and say this while sprinkling rose petals in the water: "True in power, what we seek, make sure our eyes will always meet. Power of moon, never sour, make him/her think of me every hour. Power of sun, our love will burn, to someone else he/she shall never turn. Hold our love forever and ever, from great Cupid's bow and quiver."

Table 6.2

MISCELLANEOUS SPELLS

Rain Spell - Jaron, Age 13, IN—"Air, Water, Earth, Flame. Give us storm. Bring us rain. My/our power, magick, help our deed, let us have what we need."

Energy Spell - Jaclyn, Age 12, PA—Take one part of a ginseng plant and rub it on your hands and feet. Make a circle with it only big enough to stand in. Repeat these words, while standing in the circle: "Let me find the energy and power. So that my body will not sour."

Find Lost Item Spell - Jennifer, Age 16, MD—"Keeper of what disappears. Hear me now, open your ears. Find for me what I now seek. By moon, sun, wind , fire, earth, and sea." Concentrate on what you have lost while saying these words."

Against Being Grounded By Parents Spell - Falynn, Age 12, PA—Spin a frisbee counter-clockwise on your finger and say: "Let me loose, let me out. Swing around and turn about. Sentence lifted, Spirit gifted. Grounding over without a doubt!"

Summoning Spell - Aaron, Age 12, AL—Make a circle on the floor/ground, and place rocks on the North, South, East, and West points. Sit in the center of the circle, facing East, and chant: "Be (s)he far or be (s)he near, Bring [name] to me here."

Truth Revealing Spell - Paula, Age 9, CT—On the night of the full
moon, sit in a clearing with a bowl half-filled with water. Add to the
bowl a handful of cyclamen blossoms. Drizzle a little jasmine oil on
top. Staring into the bowl (make sure the moon is reflected in the
water), concentrate on your question. After a few minutes, repeat
the following words: "Moon of night, at its peak, Provide me with
the truth I seek."

Table 6.3

Such Web sites demonstrate how books can effectively promote religious ideas to children. Wiccans and neopagans understand as much and have begun publishing not only fiction works
lauding their religion, but *non*fiction volumes on occultism.[67]
These volumes boldly teach Witchcraft to children/teens. Popular
titles include: *Spells for Teenage Witches* by Marina Baker, who describes her treatise as a "a self-help book for young people"; *The
Young Witches Handbook* by Kate West, vice president of the Pagan Federation—it contains spells for passing school exams or at-
tracting a partner[68]; and Silver Ravenwolf's *To Ride a Silver
Broomstick: New Generation Witchcraft* (more than 170,000 copies sold), which is touted as "the definitive Wicca 101 book."[69]

Perhaps the most prominent Wicca indoctrination tool continues to be another Ravenwolf volume—*Teen Witch: Wicca for a
New Generation*. This book, with a cover illustration depicting
five provocatively dressed adolescents (four girls and one boy)
standing in sexually suggestive poses, is aimed directly at young
audiences. An advertisement for this "how-to" manual reads:

> Be a Witch 24/7. *Teen Witch!* is the book you've been waiting
> for! Written for teens between the ages of 13 and 18, this ter-
> rific book is designed "just for you." Complete with serious
> explanations on techniques used by today's practicing
> Wiccans, this innovative book is packed with useful spells and
> rituals to help any teenage Witch spread his or her wings into
> the world of magick. From cell phone magick to learning
> how to work enchantments with your friends—you'll love
> this down-to-earth book.[70]

Teen Witch is produced by Llewellyn Publications, which specializes in Wiccan, neopagan, occult and magick books. According to Llewellyn publicist Jamie Schumacher, *Teen Witch* has sold more copies than any other book in the company's ninety-five-year history.[71] The text begins with a section directed to parents who have learned that their child is interested in Wicca. It also contains a section on how a teen can practice Wicca even though his or her parents have forbidden him or her to do so.

THE MAGICK OF MEDIA

Witchcraft is being propagated even more potently via Hollywood movies and television shows. For many years now directors and producers have been releasing a steady stream of movies that portray occultism in a positive way (e.g., *Ghost* [1990] and *Phenomenon* [1996]). Some films have specifically targeted younger audiences. Columbia Pictures' *The Craft* (1996), for instance, tells the tale of four attractive high school girls who mischievously use witchcraft in order to achieve their every desire.

Most people think such films are innocent fun, but occultists and knowledgeable observers of America's religious landscape understand the proselytizing value of these movies. In an article on Wicca produced by the Ontario Consultants on Religious Tolerance, for instance, author B.A. Robinson stated that *The Craft* "probably generated a great deal of interest in Wicca (a.k.a. The Craft) among teenagers."[72]

Before Robinson ever made this observation, the publication *New Worlds of Mind and Spirit* (produced by Wiccans/neopagans) had already declared as much. An issue distributed soon after *The Craft* hit theaters read:

> Whether you loved it or hated it, *The Craft* created a surge
> of interest in magick, the occult, and Witchcraft. New students and interested seekers are flocking to bookstores,
> people are looking for or establishing covens. There is an
> intense interest in Wicca reminiscent of the late sixties.[73]

Several occult-based programs also have enjoyed immense popularity, no doubt contributing to the current interest in occultism and witchcraft: *PSI Factor: Chronicles of the Paranormal* (CBS); *Poltergeist: The Legacy* (SCI-FI); *The X-Files* (FOX TV); *Charmed* (WBN); *Sabrina, the Teenage Witch* (ABC) and *Buffy: The Vampire Slayer* (UPN). These last two programs have been the most successful shows by far.

In the fall of 1997, *Sabrina* was watched weekly by nearly 8 million households, and the week of November 30-December 6, 1998, saw *Buffy* receive a 3.7 Nielsen rating (approx. 3,677,800 households). Both shows continue to grow steadily in popularity, especially through the Internet where nearly 15,000 Web sites are dedicated to *Sabrina*, while some 71,000 Web sites are devoted to *Buffy*.

The TV/film industry, in addition to the book publishing industry, have undoubtedly persuaded countless young people to delve into occultism. Celebrated witch Phyllis Curott comments:

> I think Hollywood is very sensitive to where the audience is. They're creating product that reflects what's happening at the grassroots level—they're responding to the market. They know there's an audience. And, in fact, ratings are huge. Teenage girls and young women who are a big part of this market share have found the Goddess! And that is very empowering and liberating. . . . [T]hese shows (*Charmed*, *Sabrina*, *Buffy the Vampire Slayer* and *Practical Magic*) are showing witches as good, strong and independent young women who use their power to help people—who show them working together. All of those are steps in the right direction.[74]

This turn of events within the younger community has prompted a number of news articles. Consider, for example, the recent story titled "Wicca Casts Spell on Teen-Age Girls" (*Insight*). It reveals:

As teens begin to ask questions about life and religion, they are turning in surprising numbers to Wicca or Witchcraft for the answers. . . . The Covenant of the Goddess, one of the largest Witchcraft associations in the country, offers five pages on its Web site with links to other sites for a "new generation of Witches" complete with recommended reading lists for youth and children and ways to join the organization.[75]

Another recent article by London's CNS News Agency was titled "Paganism Finds Growing Interest Among UK Children" (August 2000). It noted that more than 100 young people, mostly girls, "approach the Pagan Federation in the UK each month for advice on witchcraft, the interest of many of them stirred by children's television programs and books relating to the subject."[76] Philip Davis (author of *The Goddess Unmasked*) concurs:

[Today's younger generation] has grown up with magic and the occult. Their cartoons feature ghosts and monsters, they have the Internet Web sites and prime-time TV is Buffy and Sabrina. All this stuff makes Wicca seem natural to them.[77]

A recent *New York Times* news article on Wicca in America supports Davis' assertion, saying that Witchcraft is "gaining an ardent following among teenagers, mostly girls, who are in part captivated by the glossy new image of witches portrayed on television shows and in the movies."[78]

Additional evidence suggests that an incalculable degree of influence is also being exerted on children by popular magazines and books like the T*Witch and Sweep volumes. For example, after the teen magazine *Bliss* published a report that included contact information for The Pagan Federation, the organization "received more than one thousand letters in one month."[79] Andy Norfolk, spokesperson for The Pagan Federation, had this to say about the surge of inquiries and its relation to current occult literature:

> I am sure that some of the increase in interest is because
> some of the films and books show young, glamorous
> women using magic to beat evil. These fantasies provide a
> role model for some young women who would like to emu-
> late their heroines, and so, [they] start to find out about
> contemporary paganism.[80]

Obviously, the positive presentation of occultism by the entertainment and publishing industries is having a profound effect on
young people. Perhaps even more significant, however, are the
findings of a 1997 Purdue University study that suggest many
adults are having their religious views influenced by the media as
well. This study discovered that "exposure to paranormal phenomena on television affected belief in such things as unidentified
flying objects, ghosts, devils and extrasensory perception."[81]

According to Glenn Sparks, professor of communication, television may explain ten percent of the belief in the paranormal.
"We are hoping to draw attention to the ways in which people ar-
rive at their beliefs about the nature of the world," Sparks said.[82]
He additionally noted that allegations about the media not exercising enough caution in disseminating information about paranormal events may be justified if it continues to be proven that the
media wields undue influence in shaping society's beliefs. Particularly susceptible would be persons with no prior personal experiences with the paranormal (e.g., children).[83]

Such findings coincide with some interesting observations by
University of Houston philosophy professor Cynthia A.
Freeland (author of *The Naked and the Undead: Evil and the Appeal of Horror*). Her research indicates that "films about the supernatural—an ever-growing genre in Hollywood—are almost
exclusively watched by teenagers and young adults."[84] In other
words, the media may at the very least be desensitizing the public
—particularly youths—to the very real dangers of occultism, especially as it is presented in connection to fashionable religious
belief systems such as Witchcraft and neopaganism.

This is not to say that all young girls are likely to convert to Wicca just by watching *Buffy* or *The Craft*. Such forms of entertainment, however, could become one significant factor among many that will in time draw some children in that direction. Even for less susceptible viewers—i.e., stable children, mature adults and/or teenagers who would never "believe in" magic or dabble in it—exposure to the barrage of occult-glamorizing films, books and magazines might reinforce the idea that magick and occultism are harmless forms of entertainment unworthy of serious moral objections.[85]

LURE OF THE OCCULT

It is undeniable that children, teens and young adults are turning to occultism with increasing frequency. But what is the attraction? In *Principalities and Powers*, author W. Elwyn Davies identifies the types of individuals consistently interested in occultism:

- The curious, who experiments with demonic forces without having a fully formed system of religious beliefs. A number of teenagers, for example, get involved in the occult due to nothing more than curiosity.
- The dissatisfied, "whose religious experience has left him unfulfilled and skeptical."
- The bereaved, "whose bereavement inclines him towards anything that offers knowledge of the dead."
- The psychically inclined, "who wants to develop suspected latent powers."
- The rebellious, "who recoils from the status quo in the church and in society, and seeks a viable alternative elsewhere."
- The credulous, who are ready to believe just about anything and everything.
- The conformist, who looks around at his or her peers and says, "'Everyone does it,' and then decides "to be another who 'does it.'"

- The children of practicing occultists, "who are conditioned from childhood."[86]

Radical feminist and Wiccan high priestess Phyllis Curott cites her own reasons for Wicca's popularity, believing that its growth among young girls is inevitable. To her it is the next logical step after feminism since Wicca strikes against the alleged last "bastion of misogyny—religion."[87] According to Curott, teenage girls are turning to Wicca because of its focus on feminine deity, nature worship and self-empowerment.

Best-selling fiction author Michael O'Brien takes a more comprehensive view of why so many young people are seeking spiritual fulfillment through occultism/Wicca:

> I think this is symptomatic of a generation—really a whole era—in which, as man loses his sense of the sacred and the transcendent, he senses a void opening up within himself. He is searching beyond his own limited world—the material world—for hints of, or avenues to, a higher meaning. The supernatural, and especially the occult, offers him access into what is supposedly a much bigger universe. The extraordinary rise of fascination with, and devotion to, fantasy in Western culture is really the innate hunger in man's nature for transcendence—for something more than just basic material existence on earth.[88]

Wicca, neopaganism and the occult also tend to eradicate feelings of powerlessness—something that most children/teens struggle with daily. It is a normal burden all young people must bear until they mature into adults, at which time they gain complete personal control over their lives. Herein lies both the danger and the draw of occultism: Its practices and philosophy promise power—power allegedly accessible by adults and children alike.

A magick spell, incantation, rite or ritual can be performed simply by knowing how to execute a formula. Most attractive to children is how these occult techniques can be done in complete privacy and without having to obtain approval from authority figures. Whether or not the expected results actually materialize is inconsequential. The sheer promise of a result, coupled with the personal feeling of power received from occult involvement, is enough to form a bond between a youth and occult activity. Wielding power—even the mere *hope* of wielding it—can be a very tantalizing thing.

Obviously, fantasy movies and books wherein children are portrayed as already being autonomous via magick are going to have great appeal to youths. Such stories offer children a kind of entertaining outlet for their unmet desires to experience freedom from parents, teachers and other authority figures. These types of stories, however, pose a risk if by their content they suggest that children in the real world can indeed seize personal power over their own lives and the lives of others.

It cannot be legitimately argued that fiction does not affect to some degree the way we think, feel and respond to the world around us. Certainly, the extent to which this happens varies from person to person. Most susceptible, however, are children, who are in their formative years.

Books, of course, have an extremely profound influence on children. According to children's education specialist James E. Higgins, a young reader of fantasy and realistic fiction can even confuse "the terrain of the author's world with that of his own."[89] The more realistic a book, the higher the probability that a child will mistake it for reality. Higgins notes:

> [T]he child who accepts the world of serial fiction (Nancy Drew and The Hardy Boys) as his own, is truly dealing with fantasy in the clinical sense. When the young reader identifies himself with the hero of such a story, he violently distorts the image he has of his own world, and his reading results in nothing more than a daydream.[90]

One series of "realistic fiction" books that is taking on a particularly important role in the lives of children is Harry Potter,

which coincidentally, fits very well into society's current preoccupation with Wicca and occultism. This series continues to be
touted as nothing but pure fantasy akin to Tolkien's The Lord
of the Rings. Nothing could be further from the truth.

HARRY POTTER: MAGICK AND MORALITY

It is good to see that the best selling series of books in the western world is such a positive tale about witches and wizards.

—The Children of Artemis[1]
Wicca/Neopagan Web site

[A] storyteller's moral sense will inform a story. A writer will not choose to tell a story that makes the author uncomfortable.

—Jane Yolen[2]
renowned children's book author

J.K. Rowling's Harry Potter novels are about an orphaned boy-wizard, Harry Potter, and his struggles against an evil sorcerer, Lord Voldemort. Potter fans say it is a classic "good versus evil" tale, complete with lessons that exalt courage, loyalty and selflessness. Rowling herself declares: "[T]he theme running through all of these books is the fight between good and evil."[3]

The series begins with Harry arriving as an infant at the home of his aunt and uncle (Petunia and Vernon Dursley), whose son, Dudley, is the epitome of a spoiled brat. Harry is placed in their care because his parents, James and Lily, were murdered by Voldemort. Unfortunately, Vernon and Petunia are hardly fitting replacements for Harry's mother and father, both of whom were beloved by their fellow witches and wizards.

The Dursleys, who are "muggles" (i.e., non-magical people), are an utterly detestable threesome. They abhor and fear magic so much that they conceal from Harry his true identity as a wizard. The Dursleys do not even tell him how his parents were really killed, instead making up the story that they died in an automobile accident.

Harry lives a miserable life year after year, completely oblivious to the world of magic. But then he begins receiving mysterious letters as his eleventh birthday approaches. These turn out to be from Hogwarts School of Witchcraft and Wizardry, the school his parents attended. He has been officially invited to become a wizard-in-training at the institution, which as one character explains, is "the finest school of witchcraft and wizardry in the world."[4]

The remainder of Book 1 (*Harry Potter and the Sorcerer's Stone*) follows Harry as he goes off to Hogwarts and begins learning how to hone his magical skills. Book 1 also brings into focus more information about the story's villain, Lord Voldemort, explaining that this vicious character's goal is threefold: 1) recover power he lost by attacking the Potters; 2) kill Harry; and 3) draw unto himself a band of followers through whom he can rule the world.

Subsequent volumes in the series—*Harry Potter and the Chamber of Secrets* (Book 2), *Harry Potter and the Prisoner of Azkaban* (Book 3), and *Harry Potter and the Goblet of Fire* (Book 4)—detail Harry's yearly activities. Each book covers another school season wherein Harry finds himself in various predicaments with mysteries to solve and dangers to avoid (usually due to the nefarious schemes of Voldemort). Meanwhile, of course, he and his classmates are learning how to be more powerful and competent witches and wizards.

The Magick Keeps Rowling Along

According to renowned children's book author Jane Yolen, modern tales reflect the society from which they emerge. Yolen also notes that such stories say a great deal about the individual who writes them. She asserts that it "would be naive to think otherwise."[5] Her observations are illustrated very well by Harry Potter, which indeed shows society's obsession—as well as Rowling's lifelong fascination—with occultism.

Rowling admits to having "always been interested in it."[6] In fact, she has for many years enjoyed a kind of hobby-like attraction to witchcraft, occultism and magick. Ian Potter and his sister, Vikki, who were childhood friends of hers, recall that Rowling always liked dressing up as a witch when she was a little girl and loved making potions.[7]

Although Rowling now claims to not necessarily accept the full efficacy of witchcraft, she readily states: "I know quite a lot about it."[8] She has even expressed sympathy for at least a few occult/magick notions. For example, she believes that the number seven has magical associations. As she says, it is "a magical number, a mystical number."[9] Her views on "seven" have been confirmed by several persons with whom she has spoken.[10]

This belief in the mystical powers of "seven" is consistent with occult teaching. One of the most vocal proponents of "seven" as a vehicle of power was the well-known occultist Helena Petrovna Blavatsky (1831-1891),[11] founder of Theosophy, an occult blend of Eastern philosophy, metaphysical thought, mental healing, spiritualism and pseudo-science. Interestingly, Rowling placed a veiled reference to Blavatsky in *Harry Potter and the Prisoner of Azkaban* (Rowling, p. 53). She first turned Blavatsky's name into an anagram (i.e., Vablatsky). Then it was used for a character, Cassandra Vablatsky, the author of a divination volume mentioned in Book 3 titled *Unfogging the Future*

Equally interesting is a word of encouragement Rowling gave to children as she began touring her book: "It's important to remember that we all have magic inside us."[12] She does not appear just to be talking here about some inner creativity or innate ability to change our lives and control our destinies. Interview questions on this issue suggest that Rowling is referring to some type of occult-like power—a kind of natural magickal ability that may simply need to be harnessed to be useful.

On one occasion, for example, Rowling was asked if everyone had magic inside them *similar to how her witches/wizards had internal magic*. She responded: "I think we do (outside the books)."[13] Compare this idea to the words of renowned witch Doreen Valiente: "[T]he powers of witchcraft, magic, shamanism, or whatever one likes to call it, are latent in everyone."[14] Valiente goes on to say that the only thing any of us have to do is properly train our abilities via "techniques which will bring them out and develop them."[15]

Also very telling is a 1999 comment by Rowling about the artwork for her books: "[T]he Scholastic cover looks the most like the way I had fantasized," she said excitedly. "It looks like a spell book because of the colors and the style of illustrations."[16] This remark reveals her deep knowledge of occultism, since it alludes to a common piece of witchcraft paraphernalia: a "spell book," also known as a Grimoire.

Grimoires, which take many forms, are books containing instructions on divination, spiritism and magick; this includes both published volumes and private journals.[17] A personalized Grimoire (i.e., one holding private thoughts, poetry, magickal experiences, dreams, divination experiments) would be a "Book of Shadows." Because these spiritual diaries usually contain spells, they often are called "spell books." A legitimate question is, Why would Rowling be so overjoyed that her books closely resemble real occult spell books?

Rowling maintains she is not a witch.[18] Yet questions remain because of her unwillingness to discuss at length her spiritual beliefs (see endnote for a discussion of Rowling's faith).[19] Occultists too have noticed her hesitation to detail her religious views. For example, a Wiccan named Okelle, who wrote an article for about.com, remarked: "The published material about Rowling says surprisingly little about her religious persuasion."[20]

Whenever she is asked if she believes in witchcraft/magick, Rowling often avoids answering with an unqualified no, and instead tends to leave room for belief in *some* sort of magick, albeit not the kind found in storybooks.[21] Adding to the confusion have been statements wherein she has expressed the oft-repeated view held by Wiccans that condemning magick outright is not prudent when one considers the ever-expanding list of scientific discoveries.[22] A 1999 news article reads:

> Rowling said she had always been interested in reading about folklore and legends of supernatural beings and experiences. "Although I don't believe in it myself, we shouldn't be too arrogant. Some of the stuff we believe in today will be considered rubbish in years to come, and things we think of as rubbish now will be considered true." After she began writing the Harry Potter books, Rowling researched wizardry more thoroughly, she said.[23]

Moreover, Rowling has presented information in her books that is not commonly known by persons other than occultists or scholars of religion and occultism. She displays a highly developed, vast and intricate knowledge of occultism, its history and nuances. The accuracy with which her books present such issues has caused many people to conclude that Rowling must be an occultist or, at least, a sympathetic observer of the occult: i.e., one who accepts *some* of its tenets.[24] During a July 2000 Canadian Broadcasting interview, for example, Rowling said Wiccans feel her books show that she is "wholeheartedly on their side."[25] She also has lamented: "Practicing wiccans think I'm also a witch."[26]

HARRY POTTER AND REAL-WORLD OCCULTISM

The fact that Wiccans think Rowling is a witch indicates that her books must contain a fairly accurate representation of *some* of their views. Yet she continues to dismiss as absurd all non-Wiccan concerns over the occultism in Harry Potter. At one public appearance, for instance, she was asked: "How do you feel when people try to censor your books because of their religious beliefs about witchcraft?" Rowling responded: "I just think they need psychiatric help. I think honestly. . . . [Here's] an interesting question: Can they read!"[27]

But such belittling remarks fail to address the issue. They only avoid the reality that her novels borrow heavily from occult lore, history, beliefs, legends and practices. According to Duke University's Thomas Robisheaux, an associate history professor who teaches a course on magick/witchcraft, "Rowling discusses alchemy and the whole range of occult arts—including natural, or 'good' magic, and divination—so well known in the Renaissance."[28]

This aspect of Harry Potter is obvious to any unbiased reader. Rowling herself admits that studying the occult has provided a wellspring of knowledge upon which she draws in order to write. During a 1999 interview with Barnes and Noble, J.K. stated: "[Y]es I have done research on witchcraft and wizardry, but I tend only to use things when they fit my plot."[29] During another 1999 interview, Rowling again discussed her research:

> [W]here I'm mentioning a creature, or a spell that people used to believe genuinely worked—of course, it didn't . . . then, I will find out exactly what the words were, and I will find out exactly what the characteristics of that creature or ghost was supposed to be.[30]

Rowling went on to say during this interview that one-third of the occult-related ideas in her books "are things that people genuinely used to believe in Britain."[31] On another occasion she said: "In the books you have a mixture of things that people used to believe. . . . I'd say about a third of it is based in historic accounts, and two-thirds of it I've just invented."[32] But what Rowling has consistently failed to mention is that a significant portion of material in her books is also based on things that people (i.e., occultists) *still* believe.

Moreover, after objections concerning the amount of real occultism in her books began creating serious controversy, Rowling started contradicting her "one-third" statements, claiming instead that she made up "at least 95 percent of it . . . just out of nowhere."[33] She further altered previous claims by saying "there's a *small percentage* of the stuff in books that is my *modification* of what people used to believe was true" (emphasis added).[34] In another interview she declared: "[T]he material is almost all from my imagination."[35]

Rowling's one-third estimation, however, is a much more accurate measure of how much material in Harry Potter has been borrowed from real witchcraft and occultism. Her books are so densely packed with occult-related material that cataloguing it has filled two lengthy volumes: *The Magical Worlds of Harry Potter* by David Colbert and *The Sorcerer's Companion* by Allan Zola Kronzek and Elizabeth Kronzek. Both books were produced by Rowling fans. The back of the latter work reads: "[W]ith *The Sorcerer's Companion*, those without access to the Hogwarts library can school themselves in the fascinating reality behind J.K. Rowling's world of magic."[36]

And yet Rowling's novels do not teach Witchcraft *per se*. They nowhere present or promote Wiccan doctrines, nor do they "deal with the philosophical precepts of Wicca."[37] This must be emphasized—Harry Potter does not outline the *technical* teachings of Witchcraft, nor do the books instruct children to study Wicca. But this does not mean Harry Potter does not contain witchcraft. How is such an apparent inconsistency possible?

It all involves terminology. As stated, Harry Potter does not explicitly teach the religious doctrines of Wicca, which is one category of occultism. Nevertheless, Rowling's series does present practices *used* by Wiccans, as well as related symbols, lore and subjects inseparable from Wicca and the occult, which is a second category. These two categories of "witchcraft" are often differentiated by Wiccans/neopagans by use of a capital and lower case "w." As one witch has explained:

- *Witchcraft*, spelled with a capital "W"—A religion recognizing the divine in nature and following the seasonal changes and moons.
- *witchcraft*, spelled with a small "w"—A magickal system which may or may not be used within a religious framework.[38]

Wren Walker—a practicing Wiccan and cofounder of The Witches' Voice (an umbrella organization for Wiccans worldwide)—admits,

> [Harry Potter books] really don't have anything to do with a "capital w" witchcraft as practiced by a large number of people. It's something more to do with a "small w" witchcraft, which can be done by any other religion.[39]

In other words, Rowling presents *witchcraft*, while simultaneously avoiding *Witchcraft*. She gives a generalized portrait of real magick/occultism, rather than a narrowly defined religious belief system (i.e., Wicca). This was highlighted in a 2001 news article wherein prominent neopagans Lisa Braun and Michael Sichmeller said the Harry Potter movie, although containing some exaggerations, represented their beliefs respectfully and accurately overall.[40] They further said, "Rowling clearly has done her research." Journalist Colin Covert reported that the neopagans were "particularly impressed with the characters' use of wands, which wiccans believe 'can direct energy.' "[41]

A similar comment appeared on the "Pagan Perspectives" message board at witchvox.com. Neopagan Moon Pixie stated that although magickal spells are not cast simply by the flick of a wand, "[t]he overall depiction of magick and witchcraft, though, is as accurate a reflection of our knowledge of them as could be asked for."[42] She added, "[T]he lessons about proper use of magick, etc., are realistic and perfectly placed in the story."[43] Starling, another Wiccan, posted a more detailed explanation:

> [The Harry Potter series], both as books and in the movie form, are a wonderful metaphor of how we, as Witches/ Wiccans/Pagans/Magickal people, perceive our own spirituality/work/studies, and our vision of the world. The symbolism is strong, and I have found myself reacting so many times, by reading between the lines and looking beyond the exaggerated way their magical acts and spells is [sic] depicted, and reacting positively, mostly thinking, "This is SO right!" Even, as, I think Quirrell himself has said it so plainly, although he was serving as host for Lord Voldemort, "There is no good and evil, there is only power, and those too weak to seek it." . . . This might actually offend some, but it hides one of the great truths of Witchcraft, that there is no White or Black Magick, there is only Magick, and it is the use we make of it that defines its purpose, although we usually see a dark use of Magick as weakness, rather than strength.[44]

Not surprisingly, Rowling's works are listed on the "Wicce Woman" Web site, which only features texts relating to Wicca, neopaganism, occultism, and magick. Persons listed with Rowling include many renowned neopagans and witches.[45] Similarly, Harry Potter is prominently featured at "The Inner Sanctum of Wicca and Witchcraft" Web site, which offers a plethora of neopagan works. The materials cover Wicca, magick technique, Wiccan rituals, spells, tools of witchcraft, information on divination and occult books.[46]

Noteworthy is yet another Web site, "The Harry Potter Witchcraft Spellbook," which is designed by a Harry Potter fan, whose screen-name is IO. The Web site is subtitled "Wherein is Explained Old Magical Secrets the Likes of Which J.K. Rowling's Book Series Was Based Upon." IO explains:

Yes. J.K. Rowling has done her homework. Her hidden references are so numerous, and her knowledge so deep, that I'm
certain she has done much research on the subject of real sorcery. Many of her characters are named after famous occultists of the past, many of her fantastic spells actually exist, and
her magical creatures are straight out of ancient mythology.
She is writing about the same witchcraft that I study at home,
far away from Hogwarts! . . . I recognise much of J.K.
Rowling's work from Middle Age grimoires I've read. These
charms and spells are more than just mere fantasy! They have
a historical basis. And I will be more than happy to share it
with you, here, on my Web site.[47]

IO then lists several Harry Potter elements and explains their
historical ties to real occultism: Invisibility Cloak, Magic Mirror, Sorcerer's Stone, Mandrake Root, Magic Wand, Hand of
Glory, Basilisk, Broomstick.[48] Such close associations between
Harry Potter and witchcraft may be why celebrated witch Phyllis Curott, in referring to her own Wiccan volume, *Book of
Shadows*, said, "I wouldn't mind subtitling my book *Harry Potter for Adults*."[49]

PRACTICAL MAGICK

Rowling's use of occult symbolism has resulted in some striking parallels to real-world magick. The school supplies for
Hogwarts' students match what most neopagans use, such as
cauldrons and magick wands.[50] The pets owned by Rowling's
characters hearken back to medieval associations between witches
and animals, and highlight the value of animals in modern Wicca.[51]

Harry Potter also contains the neopagan concept of magick
(i.e., "Magic is magic—it is neither good nor bad, it just is!").[52]
This belief, articulated by many occultists, including the infamous
Church of Satan founder, Anton LaVey, can be found in the
words of one of Voldemort's followers: "There is no good and
evil, there is only power and those too weak to seek it."[53]

Even the names of books read by Rowling's characters closely match books circulating throughout the neopagan/Wiccan community (see Table 7.1). Additionally, Hogwarts classes mirror courses offered by some occult groups like London's Ordo Anno Mundi (see Table 7.2).

The demarcation between our world and Rowling's "fantasy" realm fades even more due to the many historical persons/occult figures openly referenced in her books. These include: Cliodna, a Druidic goddess worshiped today by many neopagans; Adalbert Waffling, an apparent reference to Adalbert of Magdeburg, who was convicted of sorcery (744/45 A.D.); and Heinrich Cornelius Agrippa (1486-1535), a very important occultist whose writings on magic (e.g., *On Occult Philosophy*) "influenced generations of thinkers that followed and became part of the heritage of folk magic practiced by witches. . . . [He] embraced astrology, divination, numerology and the power of gems and stones. . . . It was said that he practiced necromancy [i.e., conjuring spirits of the dead] for divination."[54]

HARRY POTTER FANTASY[55]	REAL WORLD OCCULTISM
The Standard Book of Spells	*Book of Spells* (1997) by Arthur Edward Waite
A History of Magic	*The History of Magic* (1997) by Eliphas Levi
One Thousand Magical Herbs and Fungi	*Encyclopedia of Magical Herbs* (1985) by Scott Cunningham
Magical Drafts and Potions	*Magick Potions: How to Prepare and Use Homemade Oils, Aphrodisiacs, Brews and Much More* (1998) by Gurina Dunwich

Table 7.1

ORDO ANNO MUNDI[56]	HOGWARTS SCHOOL
"Divination"/"Spellcasting" (1st Degree)	"We will be covering the basic methods of Divination this year" (*Prisoner of Azkaban*, p. 103). "All students should have a copy of each of the following: *The Standard Book of Spells* (Grade 1)" (*Sorcerer's Stone*, p. 66).
"Werewolf" "Animal Transformation" [Transfiguration (4th Degree)]	"Transfiguration is some of the most complex and dangerous magic you will learn at Hogwarts" (*Sorcerer's Stone*, p. 134) "My transformations in those days— were terrible. It is very painful to turn into a werewolf. . . . [My friends] became Animagi. . . . They could each turn into a different animal at will" (*Prisoner of Azkaban*, pp. 353-354).
"Magical Lore" [History of Magic] (5th Degree)	"Their very last exam was History of Magic" (*Sorcerer's Stone*, p. 263).

Table 7.2

In short, Harry Potter depicts a wide array of occult subjects: divination, clairvoyance, magick, herbology, potions, spirit channeling and necromancy (i.e., communication with the dead).[57] As the *Encyclopedia of Wicca & Witchcraft* states: "The arts of Witchcraft include herbalism, divination, magick, ceremonial ritual, healing, potions, and spirit-world contact."[58] One Wiccan stated as much on a Web site for pagans:

> There are things in Harry's world that are "accurate" representations of what we believe. . . . Animals are seen as valuable magical beings and partners. Study is encouraged;

magic does not come easy and the principles must be learned. And, from the first book, an important lesson that I have taken to including in my teaching: one should call all things by their real name, for fear of a name increases fear of the thing named. So, yes, there are some good parallels.[59]

The Sorcerer's Companion emphasizes that Rowling's saga was fashioned partly using "the vast collective lore of magic from around the world."[60] This pro-Potter volume lists many occult entries relating to Harry Potter, including: amulets, arithmancy, astrology, charms, crystal balls, divination, magick (e.g., ritual, natural, high, low), mandrakes, palmistry, poltergeist, talismans and sexual demons (female) called veela.[61] One of Rowling's more blatant ties to real-world occultism involves the premise of *Harry Potter and the Sorcerer's Stone*, originally titled *Harry Potter and the Philosopher's Stone*.

THE PHILOSOPHER'S STONE AND ALCHEMY

In the *Encyclopedia of Occultism and Parapsychology*, the Philosopher's Stone is described as a legendary substance that supposedly enabled medieval alchemists to turn base metals into gold or silver.[62] But contrary to what is commonly believed by the general public, alchemists were far more than just metal-workers. They were spiritually minded individuals who pursued their brand of science as a means of purifying their souls and achieving an unclouded understanding of their own divine nature.

Transmuting base metals into gold was the external representation of an internal process through which they were seeking to transform themselves and obtain the "fifth element"—i.e., God's "creative power" by which all things receive life.[63] Alchemists also believed that creating the Philosopher's Stone brought forth a sort of natural by-product: the Elixir of Life. Rowling accurately says in Book I: "The stone will transform any metal into pure gold. It also produces the Elixir of Life, which will make the drinker immortal."[64]

Helene Vachet—retired Los Angeles School District assistant principal, a third-generation theosophist, and a past president of the Besant Lodge in Hollywood, California—writes:

> The title of the first Potter book . . . was *Harry Potter and the Philosopher's Stone*. To a student of the Kabbalah, Jungian psychology, or alchemy, the significance is obvious. The philosopher's stone was understood by the uninitiated as merely a device to turn base metals into gold and to make an elixir that gave everlasting life. However, to a student of alchemy, the philosopher's stone is a metaphor for turning our base, physical natures into our more spiritual selves. In other words, it is a tool for self-actualization, union with the Higher Self.[65]

This is not the only parallel between Rowling's stone and the one sought by medieval alchemists. In Book I, Harry and his friends learn that the Philosopher's Stone was created by a wizard named Nicholas Flamel.[66] Nicholas Flamel, as it turns out, really existed. He was a French alchemist who allegedly succeeded in making the Philosopher's Stone in the late 1300s.

According to historical documents/occult tradition, Flamel learned how to make the stone via the esoteric *Book of Abraham the Jew*. This text, supposedly written by the Jewish patriarch, contained various hieroglyphics. Alchemists throughout the centuries have believed that after deciphering these drawings, Flamel created the Philosopher's Stone, and by doing so, never died.[67]

Book I goes so far as to add some of Flamel's religious beliefs about death. Toward the book's conclusion, after Nicholas knows he will die, Dumbledore tells Harry that Nicholas is not afraid because to him dying will simply be "like going to bed after a very, very long day."[68] Dumbledore continues: "After all, to the well-organized mind, death is but the next great adventure." The book *Magicians, Seers, and Mystics* reports that Flamel, in fact, felt this way: "Flamel, after his discovery of the Philosopher's Stone, would have had no temptation to evade death; for he regarded death merely as the transition to a better state."[69]

SPELLS AND INCANTATIONS

According to Starhawk, an influential witch, spellcasting is a very important facet of Wicca.[70] The training of witches includes not only lessons on what spells can do, but the proper way to cast them. These particular tenets of Witchcraft permeate Harry Potter. They are discernible where Harry and his friends learn and use spells to cause change according to their wills (e.g., opening a door, levitating an object, immobilizing someone).

The seemingly nonsensical words used in Harry Potter (e.g., *Alomohora!*, *Finite Incantatem!*, *Expelliarmus!*, *Rictusempra!*) are assumed to be not from the occult, but mere Latinized babble that imparts a sense of mysticality to Rowling's books. As Rowling has said, "Most of the magic in the books is invented by me."[71] Such an explanation has alleviated many fears that Harry Potter portrays the proper mode of casting a spell. Francis Bridger, principal of Trinity College (Bristol, England), for instance, has declared, "The magic in Potterworld is make-believe nonsense, right down to the mock Latin. It is a fun fictional device."[72]

Noteworthy, however, is that sorcerers of the Middle Ages and ancient Egypt also used gibberish terms.[73] Secret words and phrases have always been indispensable to those practicing magick. According to the *Encyclopedia of Occultism and Parapsychology*, "The power of the spoken word was implicitly believed in by all primitive peoples, especially . . . if it be in a language or dialect unknown to ordinary people."[74]

What Bridger and others do not seem to understand is that inventing spells, even spells that are apparently "nonsense," is precisely how spellcasting is practiced. There exists no book of spells that all Wiccans use. Spells are very individual and normally are invented by neopagans/Wiccans. Moreover, a spell's words can either be accurate translations from another language, or be nothing but nonsense syllables, as is explained in *The Sorcerer's Companion*:

> [T]he Latin-sounding words taught at Hogwarts mean exactly what they seem to say. *Petrfiicus totalus* totally petrifies its victim, and *riddikulus* makes a formerly frightening boggart look, well, ridiculous. But magic words don't have to mean anything. A medieval spell book tells us that the nonsense words *saritap pernisox ottarim*, for example, will open any lock, while *onaim peranties rasonastos* will guide you to buried treasure and *agidem margidem sturgidem* will cure a toothache if said seven times on a Tuesday or a Thursday. Where these particular words came from and why they were believed to work is almost anybody's guess. Some were no doubt invented by practicing magicians to impress their clients. . . . Yet even without evident meaning, words were thought to have tremendous power, and could bring into being the intentions of the magician.[75]

In other words, Rowling has blended innocent-looking fantasy with real principles of magick, going so far as to invent spells that actually can be translated to a certain extent. Even the death curse Voldemort uses (*Avada Kedavra*) is an Aramaic phrase that means "may the thing be destroyed."[76] And the most common spell in the Harry Potter books—*lumos*, which lights the end of a wizard's wand—comes from the Latin word for "light."

Uttering such phrases obviously will not kill anyone or light up a stick, but the translations show that Rowling has successfully blurred the line dividing fantasy and fiction. Clearly, she has merged her "fantasy" magic with actual occultism (i.e., magick). She even portrays spells as lasting until an antidote potion or a counter-spell is provided.[77] Occultists believe their magick works in a like manner: "The power of the spell remained until such time as it was broken by an antidote or exorcism. Therefore, it was not a transient thing."[78]

Harry's training, too, is very akin to how occultists become adept at speaking magickal phrases. The *Encyclopedia of Occultism and Parapsychology* casts light on the issue, stating, "[N]ot only were the formulas [i.e., exact wording] of spells well fixed, but *the exact tone of voice* in which they were to be pronounced was specially taught" [emphasis added].[79]

This is precisely what Harry and others learn at Hogwarts. In one scene where Ron and Harry are incorrectly casting a spell, Hermione explains that they are saying the appropriate magic words, but are not putting the emphasis in the correct place:

> Professor Flitwick [reminded them] . . . "And saying the magic words properly is very important, too" . . . . "*Wingardium Leviosa!*" he [Ron] shouted . . . . "You're saying it wrong," Harry heard Hermione snap. "It's 'Wing-*gar*-dium Levi-*o*-sa,' make the 'gar' nice and long."[80]

Rowling, as we see, has on many levels accurately depicted spellcasting, right down to the process that students go through to learn appropriate terms and magick phrases. The realism is not difficult to spot. Of course, not all of Rowling's parallels to occultism are blatant. Some, in fact, are so obscure that they might only be noticed by an occultist or a researcher of magick.

In Harry Potter, for example, can be found passages about living portraits at Hogwarts.[81] But Rowling cannot be credited with inventing portraits that move and speak. Such imagery appeared in *The Chemical Wedding of Christian Rosenkreutz* (published in 1616).[82] This occult text details the inner transformation of the soul, according to the principles of Rosicrucianism—an occult sect built on astrology, reincarnation, trance meditation, mental telepathy, hypnotism, pyramidology, aura reading and alchemy.

An astonishing coincidence is that Rowling's alchemist character, Nicholas Flamel, was a Rosicrucianist in real life.[83] Moreover, *The Chemical Wedding* is an allegorical tale of the alchemic process.[84] Obviously, Rowling has aptly used her in-depth knowledge of occultism to slip into her stories some rather intricate pieces of occult-related lore and symbolism.

ACCORDING TO THE WITCHES

In a CNN interview, Rowling stated, "I absolutely did not start writing these books to encourage any child into witchcraft." She continued, "I'm laughing slightly because to me, the idea is absurd."[85] But since the series, after all, does contain beliefs and practices associated with witchcraft, neopaganism and occultism, it is neither absurd, nor laughable, to suppose that the Harry Potter books might lead *some* children, and even some adults, into occultism. The potential for this kind of influence is revealed in a February 2002 BBC news story titled "Potter Prompts Course in Witchcraft":

> A growing interest in sorcery and witchcraft generated by the Harry Potter stories has prompted an Australian university [Adelaide University] to launch a special course. . . . [that] will explore the witchdoctors of Africa, shamans . . . witches . . . and others who practise magic rituals.[86]

If adults are gaining an interest in occultism via the series, it is hardly paranoid to suggest that *some* children reading Harry Potter might grow curious about occult teachings and paraphernalia—especially with the release of the Harry Potter movie. The media can (and does) reshape individual and societal consciousness, particularly in the youth culture.

Recent proof of the media's influence on young people was seen on MTV's "Ultra Sound: Social History of the Mosh Pit." This report covered the origin, rise and progress of the "mosh pit" at punk music concerts and how it became a mainstay rock music phenomenon. The activity, which entails concert-goers thrashing violently near the music stage, existed underground for years until being seen on a 1981 Halloween episode of *Saturday Night Live* [*SNL*].[87] Afterward, young people everywhere in America sought to experience what they had seen on *SNL*.

Other examples of children copying activities first experienced through entertainment are numerous. In January 2001, for example, thirteen-year-old Jason Lind was admitted to a Boston hospital in critical condition with severe burns to his body. According to police, the boy was trying to mimic what he had seen on the popular MTV show "Jackass," which on more than one occasion featured the host setting himself on fire (while wearing a special suit). Investigators labeled it a "copycat stunt." Neighbor Arthur Shaw commented: "They've got to have more brains than that. . . . I don't understand why the kids would do that, but, you know, young lads today are influenced by that TV."[88] Lind is not alone. As of May 2001, half a dozen youngsters had suffered "serious injuries" by repeating stunts from this same MTV program.[89]

Other children have caused serious injury to themselves and others by copying the antics of wrestlers appearing in World Wrestling Federation (WWF) programming. In one incident, a seven-year-old boy accidentally killed his younger brother with a "clothesline" move that the *Dallas Morning News* reported "he had seen his wrestling heroes perform on TV." In Hudson County, Georgia, a four-year-old "jumped up and down on a 15-month-old baby while watching a WWF video the babysitter put on as he slipped out for cigarettes." And Jason Whala, a twelve-year-old from Yakima, Washington, killed his nineteen-month-old cousin with a "Jack-knife Power Bomb," a move that involved holding the baby over his head and slamming him to the ground.[90]

What about Harry Potter? Could it influence children in a similar way (albeit to different behaviors)? Apparently so. According to a 1999 BBC news story, interest in boarding schools has increased because of Harry Potter. Britain's Boarding Education Alliance (BEA) said the books "have helped to re-invent the image of boarding schools."[91] Ann Williamson, BEA campaign director, noted: "The books have probably done more for boarding than anything else we could have imagined."[92] This article, titled "Harry Potter Makes Boarding Fashionable," noted, "[T]he Harry Potter books have helped to project an image of choosing to go to boarding school as 'fun.' "[93]

Even more relevant was a 2002 news article titled "Siberian Potter Fans Drink Poisonous Potion." It detailed events surrounding the hospital admission of twenty-three children "poisoned after drinking a 'magic potion' inspired by the series of books about a boy wizard."[94] The story goes on to detail the incident:

> Local police suspect that older children stole copper sulphate from a school laboratory and fed it to younger children in a Potteresque initiation ceremony. . . . A reporter from Moscow's Komsomolskaya Pravda newspaper who went to the school, said children told him they had been inventing potions and ceremonies. "He [an older classmate] said there would be some initiation, so we came to the classroom and tried it," Sergey Ivanov, one of the pupils, told Russian NTV television.[95]

The fact is that children and teens emulate behavior if they feel that what they are seeing or reading about is "cool," radically new (at least to them) or extremely entertaining—even harmful or dangerous activities. This is common knowledge, as evidenced by the June 2002 warning issued nationwide regarding the movie *Like Mike*, starring basketball great, Michael Jordan.

The public statement (released by the U.S. electric utility Progress Energy, Inc.) warned youngsters not to mimic the film's fourteen-year-old protagonist, who climbs onto a roof to retrieve sneakers hanging from a power line. As his hand reaches the shoes, lightning strikes a power pole, throwing him to the ground and "energizing" the shoes. "The actions depicted in the movie's make-believe scene are extremely dangerous and if replicated would most likely result in severe electrical shock or death," the company said. Progress Energy, Inc.

spokesman Aaron Perlut added, "[Y]oung people are very impressionable. Very often, art is imitated in life."[96]

The problem, according to pediatricians and psychologists, is that children cannot properly filter media images. A 2001 ABC News story revealed: "Most children are unable to sift through the images presented in media, psychologists say, and are particularly vulnerable to the suggestions in images that are close to their own lives."[97] Child development experts say the tendency to copy observed behaviors is linked to the way children view and interact with the world:

> Not only are images much more compelling than words to children, but youngsters' brains have not developed the capacity to weigh the potential of long-term consequences of an action, even when those consequences are spelled out. . . . Over the last 40 years, an extensive body of research has accumulated, drawing a strong connection between exposure to images of violence in media—from cartoons to music videos and video games—and aggressive, violent behavior in children and teenagers. . . . While few psychologists say that exposure to violence in media alone will create a violent individual, most agree that when children also see violence in their home or community and have little close interaction with a parent or other adult, it increases their tendency to resort to violence themselves. . . . "There is an overwhelming amount of evidence that violence portrayed in media has an effect on teenage violence," said Dr. Michael Delahunt, a child psychologist. "I don't think it would cause someone who doesn't have a tendency to be violent to be violent, but it can fan the flames." Children learn by imitating what they see around them, trying things out that look interesting and adapting them to fit themselves. And that includes violence and idiotic stunts.[98]

With regard to Harry Potter, the books and movie are especially appealing to children because they so perfectly portray several aspects of their own lives: a school environment, childhood friendships, feelings of powerlessness, school rivalry. Young people are already dressing up like Rowling's characters at bookstore-hosted Harry Potter parties and "wizard breakfasts."

This may seem fun and innocent. But where will the fascination and emulation end? With playing dress up? With wanting to go to a boarding school? With experimenting with "fun" practices like the divination or spellcasting at Hogwarts? With taking college classes on occultism? As Harry Potter fans mature, will they desire to delve deeper into occultism?

Rowling's books could ultimately desensitize millions of children to the dangers of occultism (see Appendix A), which in turn could create in them a general apathy toward it. The release of the Harry Potter movies has made Rowling's fantasy even more influential. Peter Smith, a spokesperson for England's Association of Teachers and Lecturers, believes the Harry Potter movie "will lead to a whole new generation of youngsters discovering witchcraft and wizardry."[99] He adds,

> Children, particularly girls on the cusp of puberty, have always been interested in magic and in parallel worlds. Casting spells gives them a feeling of control over an increasingly confusing world at a time when many youngsters feel powerless. . . . Children must be protected from the more extreme influences of the occult and be taught in a responsible and positive way the risks of journeying into the unknown.[100]

Equally well-reasoned and thoughtful concerns have been expressed by a variety of persons observing the Harry Potter phenomenon:

- John Andrew Murray: "[It is] the world of witchcraft found in Harry Potter that is the greatest threat of all. This world—which will soon be marketed to our nation's children on a massive scale—is presenting occult practices in a way that is attractive and fun. And while few students are seeking to become witches or wizards, the desensitization to witchcraft that is occurring in America cannot help but have a detrimental effect."[101]

- Elizabeth A. Wittman: "An ardent reader of the Harry Potter books becomes familiar with terms such as divination, casting spells, omens, portents, and the weirdness of the occult is softened. . . . [A] child seeing a fortuneteller or palm reader sign will have a sense of recognition rather than suspicion."[102]

- Steven D. Greydanus: "The taste for such things, once awakened, may find titillation in play with Ouija boards, Tarot cards, or similar paraphernalia. . . . [S]ome may wish to go further, turning to the Internet or their local library for readily available information on Wiccan rituals or other forms of contemporary magical practice."[103]

- Michael O'Brien: "The most obvious problem, of course, is the author's use of the symbol-world of the occult as her primary metaphor, and occult activities as the dramatic engine of the plots. It presents these to the child reader through attractive role models, such as Harry and Hermione, who are students of witchcraft and sorcery. . . . Rationally, children know that the fantasy element in the books is not 'real.' But emotionally and subconsciously the young reader absorbs it as real. This is further complicated by the fact that in the world around us there are many opportunities for young people to enter the occult subcultures, where some of Harry's powers are indeed offered as real."[104]

Many neopagans/Wiccans have themselves theorized that untold numbers of children, teens and adults probably will be influenced by Harry Potter to at least take a look at occultism or magick—perhaps to join the Wiccan fold. Note these comments posted on an occult Web site:

- "Harry Potter happens to be one of the best things for witchcraft, and the understanding of it."[105]

- "I saw Harry Potter. . . . And, yes I do think it will get young people to look to the occult for answers to that particular type of magic(k)."[106]
- "Will it [Harry Potter] draw people to the craft, it will probably make some people very curious and therefore more open."[107]
- "Yes, I think that more people will start exploring witchcraft because of the movie [Harry Potter]."[108]
- "As to whether Harry Potter generates interest in Paganism, of course it does! Many people will explore Paganism because of Harry Potter."[109]
- "I think the movie will bring more attention to Paganism and the study of Magick. . . . [T]he open-minded people will go out and buy a few 'Wicca 101' books to learn more about witchcraft in the real world, and those who feel touched, may cross over and find a new path."[110]

An equally interesting disclosure appeared in the *Journal of Eclectic Magick*. Its 2001 article titled "Magick or Madness" reads:

> [H]ow long will it be until your Coven, Circle or Group is being inundated with the want-to-be wizards and witches, whose only exposure to magick is Harry Potter? . . . [A]s a Pagan parent, is there any value to the Harry Potter movie (or books)? . . . On the magickal side, there were a few "truths" slipped into the movie. The one that jumps to mind is "the wand selects the wizard." Over the years, it has been my experience that the tools that have served me the best, for the most part have selected me. In some cases I was not even looking at the time that I found them. . . . I personally feel that there is no true harm in the "Harry Potter" fad, and on a deeper level it points to the fact that our culture craves a touch of magick in their diet.[111]

But is there any evidence that children are indeed venturing toward occultism due to Rowling's material? Yes. And the evidence is continuing to mount as Rowling's books spread from country to country.

THE PROOF IS IN THE PAGANISM

According to James Woudhuysen, director of forecasting at international product designers Seymour Powell (London) and professor of innovation at De Montfort University (Leicester), "[T]he Harry Potter series of adult-read children's books has helped fuel a revival of British interest in the occult."[112] Additionally, in the August 4, 2000, article titled "Potter Fans Turning to Witchcraft," which appeared in the British publication *This Is London*, Pagan Federation officer Andy Norfolk explained,

> In response to increased inquiries coming from youngsters we established a youth officer . . . . It is quite probably linked to things like Harry Potter, *Sabrina the Teenage Witch*, and *Buffy the Vampire Slayer*. Every time an article on witchcraft or paganism appears, we had a huge surge in calls, mostly from young girls.[113]

Additional evidence comes from *The Sorcerer's Companion* by Allan and Elizabeth Kronzek. These authors state that when they asked child readers of Harry Potter which topics most interested them, a significant number of respondents asked for more information on "spells, charms, and curses."[114] Many bookstores are now displaying real occult volumes next to Harry Potter novels. And I personally have received dozens of contacts from parents whose children, after reading Harry Potter, became interested in Wicca/occultism.

Harry Potter also is motivating children to buy books that teach real witchcraft packaged after the courses offered at Hogwarts. One such book is *The Witch and Wizard Guide* (2001) by well-known Wiccan Sirona Knight, who has written extensively on neopaganism.[115] An advertisement for her volume, which targets children and teens, brazenly uses the popularity of Harry Potter to lure young buyers:

A complete guide to doing the magic in Harry Potter using modern Wiccan Techniques. Learn divining techniques such as tarot, runes, "witching," and crystal scrying. In addition this guide contains a history of witches and wizards, how to make potions, and defense against the dark arts.[116]

Knight covers subjects directly taken from Harry Potter, capitalizing on its phraseology. The guide's back cover, for instance, reads: "For anyone who has ever wanted to be a Witch or a Wizard and to make real magic."[117] Knight openly explains her desire to attract young fans of Harry Potter:

[W]ith the unparalleled popularity of the Harry Potter books by J.K. Rowling, a whole new generation—both young and old—are adventuring into the magical world of witches and wizards. . . . As you read through the pages of this book and go through the training methods, you will enter a world that up until now may have seemed like only a fantasy. . . . Transforming what seems like fiction into nonfiction can look like a difficult task, but it isn't.[118]

At Amazon.com, one young reader of Knight's book wrote the following review, which clearly notes occult subjects reminiscent of Hogwarts:

I would recommend it to anyone who wants to be a Witch or Wizard. . . . [Knight] gave a lot of thorough information on many magical topics such as Spellcasting, Potions, Divination, Animal Magic, and Defense Against the Dark Arts. . . . Also there are many spells to start you off. I was very impressed with how you are taught how to make many of your own magical tools. The divination part is great and gives a description of all of the runes and how to cast your fate using them.[119]

Two additional Amazon.com reviews posted by fans of Rowling favorably commented that *The Witch and Wizard Guide* is indeed an appeal to child readers of Harry Potter (note the original Amazon.com review titles):

"Harry Potter comes to life," October 23, 2001 / Reviewer: A reader from San Francisco, CA—When I first picked up this book, I thought it too good to be true. But after reading it, I am astounded by all the information that's in it. It is the closest thing to Harry Potter that I have read.[120]

"Good Starter Book for Kids," October 11, 2001 / Reviewer: pywacket from Ontario, Canada—The *Harry Potter* references were obvious in the title and in many of the chapter headings such as Divination and Defense Against the Dark Arts. . . . I found this book to be a fairly accurate book about witchcraft and magic. . . . Written in a very kid-accessible style, I was impressed with the solid beginner knowledge of the kind found in most adult books on witchcraft and paganism. I would highly recommend this book for any young adult looking to explore the real world of magick and witchcraft.[121]

A similar book, *The Real Witches' Handbook* (originally titled *The Young Witches' Handbook*) by Kate West—Pagan Federation vice president—takes advantage of Harry Potter popularity as well. This book specifically targets teenagers. The following advertisement for West's volume appeared at witchcraft.org—Web site of the neopagan group, The Children of Artemis:

Harry Potter, *Sabrina the Teenage Witch*, *Buffy the Vampire Slayer*, *Charmed*. It seems we can't get enough of all things magical or "witchy" at the moment. The result of all this interest is that Wicca has become the fastest growing religion in the UK.[122]

Such evidence linking Harry Potter to a growing youth interest in occultism continues to steadily increase. The whole attraction of occultism is power, excitement and entertainment—all of which is available in Harry Potter. Yet J.K. Rowling has dismissed outright any suggestions that *some* children might be turning to occultism because of her books.[123]

Ironically, it is on the Web site of Rowling's own publisher (Scholastic) that there appears a message from fourteen-year-old Rachel G., reading: "I like Ron, Hermione, and Harry a lot. . . . I would love to be a witch or a wizard."[124] The following is a but a small sampling of many other statements that Rowling has either not seen, or chosen to ignore—statements made by children who, because of the Harry Potter series, wish they could learn magick and/or be a witch/wizard:

- "I wish I could do magic! If I could do magic I might be a parseltongue [i.e., one who talks to snakes] or a necromancer" (Nicole, 13 years old).[125]

- "I dream about being a witch so I could get revenge on a few people" (Rebecca, 12 years old).[126]

- "Do I ever wish I could perform magic like Harry! Ever since I've started reading the series, I've daydreamed about that. . . . I'd love to go to a place like Hogwarts" (Grace, 13 years old).[127]

- "I think arithmancy is quite interesting! . . . I also am fascinated by Potions, because I like doing experiments" (Zhang, 12 years old).[128]

- "I like what they learned there [at Hogwarts] and I want to be a witch" (Gioia Bishop, 10 years old).[129]

- "I thought the story really made you feel like you could be a witch or a wizard" (Lily, 11 years old).[130]

It would be unrealistic to think that all of these youths, or all other children who share their feelings, will definitely get involved with occultism. But it would be equally improbable, as many Wiccans and neopagans have noted, to assume that none of them will do so. In reference to Rowling's perspective on her books, Robert Knight (Director of the Culture and Family Institute) observes,

Ms. Rowling dispatches legitimate concerns about *influence*. In the same way, defenders of "slasher" movies full of sex and violence say, "I've never heard of a kid seeing a film and then going right out and raping and murdering." This ignores the obvious, which is that kids, particularly those on the edge, are deeply affected by what they see and hear. Besides, some kids *do* go right out and copy what they have seen, like the teens who went on a killing spree after seeing the film *Natural Born Killers*. To say that kids won't immediately become witches after reading or viewing Harry Potter does not mean that many children won't take an unhealthy interest in witchcraft and the occult. It just might not materialize instantly.[131]

Some adults actually seem committed to nudging children toward occultism. Consider The Leaky Cauldron, a highly popular Web site for Rowling's fans. This Internet site includes a direct link to Harry's *real* astrological birth chart.[132] It was plotted by professional astrologer and author Barbara Schermer (*Astrology Alive*, HarperCollins, 1989), who has her own Internet site called "Astrology Alive."[133]

In addition to Harry's horoscope, Schermer's Web site contains her astrological interpretation of it, a "Your Horoscope" link for child fans, a link to Scholastic (Rowling's publisher), links to other fan sites, and links to serious books on astrology at Amazon.com (e.g., *Mythic Astrology*, *The Inner Dimensions of the Birth Chart*, and *Astrology, Karma & Transformation*).[134] For children visiting Schermer's Web site, or Web sites linking to it, the distance needed to travel from Rowling's fantasy world into the world of the occult is very short.

Children seeking information about Harry Potter in mid-2002 from Internet's Yahoo News were pointed by a "Related Subjects" link to a particularly interesting Discovery Channel Web site. It advertised the TV special *Real Magick: The Science of Wizardry*. This Web page in turn provided links to "The Wizard's Lair," "The Sorcerer's Guide" and additional "Weblinks"—Web sites where children could learn about real magick and objects used by occultists. The last link's subtitle stated: "Fortune tellers, mythic beasts and true tales of witchcraft await."[135]

Another example of adults boldly using Harry Potter to introduce children to occultism is *Beacham's Sourcebooks for Teaching Young Adult Fiction: Exploring Harry Potter* by Elizabeth Schafer. This teacher's guide to Rowling's books not only includes chapters covering the history of real magick and occult practices, but suggests that students research these practices and persons via Beacham's Internet companion resources Web site.[136]

Under "Reading for Research," Beacham lists *Drawing Down the Moon: Witches, Druids, Goddess-Worshippers and Other Pagans in America Today* by Wiccan Margot Adler (a very influential neopagan), and *An Encyclopedia of Occultism*, which Schafer describes as a "reprint of a classic encyclopedia source listing information about alchemy, the Philosopher's Stone, and the real Nicholas Flamel."[137] Beacham also lists *The Encyclopedia of Celtic Wisdom*, which "[d]iscusses subjects noted in the Harry Potter novels such as prophecy, divination, quests, initiations, shapeshifting, and ancestral worship."[138]

Occult Web sites featured by Beacham include: astrology .about.com, celticcrow.com (The Witches League for Public Awareness), themystica.com ("On-line Encyclopedia of the Occult, Mysticism, Magic, Paranormal, and More"), witchvox.com (a Wiccan Web site) and druidry.org (neopagan Web site of the Druidism-promoting "Order of Bards, Ovates, and Druids").[139]

These issues might be less significant if Rowling's story occurred in a place other than our world. Harry Potter then would fall into the category of mythopoetic literature—i.e., a story that takes place in a world disassociated from the world in which we live (e.g., Tolkien's The Lord of the Rings and C.S. Lewis' The Chronicles of Narnia). But Rowling's fantasy takes place here and now, in England, only a few hours' train ride from major British cities.[140]

The fine-line separation between our reality and Rowling's fiction may not be clear enough for *some* children to distinguish between the two worlds. Because children are moved by powerful images and characters, they often insert themselves into a book's characters and envision themselves doing what they see or read. This experience can at times be so strong that they forget that what they are reading is unreal. Young children are especially susceptible to powerful imagery and the desire to be part of a tale in which they are immersed. In an interview with *Newsweek*, Rowling confirmed the inclination:

> I get letters from children addressed to Professor Dumbledore, and it's not a joke, begging to be let into Hogwarts, and some of them are really sad. Because they want it to be true so badly they've convinced themselves it's true.[141]

This desperate desire to go to Hogwarts and actually be a witch or wizard appears again and again in the Harry Potter fan mail sent by children.[142] Even for older children who can distinguish between Harry Potter and real life, there is still the very tangible possibility that some of them may become so enthralled with magic and wizardry that they seek out the neopaganism, witchcraft and magick that is available in the real world. Rowling has revealed that some children actually are trying to cast her spells: "I have met people who assure me, very seriously, that they are trying to do them."[143] Rowling casually adds: "I can assure them, just as seriously, that they don't work."[144]

Parents must ask themselves, Will the ineffectiveness of Rowling's spells in Harry Potter mean the end of a child's interest in magick, or only the beginning of a child's dabbling with occultism? A 2001 article in *The Times* (London) suggests an answer. The story discusses how teachers' groups in England "are worried that nobody is monitoring the effect this fascination with the occult is having on its teenage followers."[145] *The Times* also states: "In a recent survey of 2,600 children aged 11 to 16, more than half said that they were interested in the occult." For many young people, their interest "was aroused, innocently enough, through television programs such as *Buffy the Vampire Slayer*."[146]

In response to these most recent findings, Britain's Association of Teachers and Lecturers wants schools to introduce classes advising young people of the risks of delving into the occult on the Internet. Peter Smith, the general secretary, said: "This goes beyond reading a Harry Potter story. This represents an extremely worrying trend among young people. Parents and teachers should educate children and young people about the dangers of dabbling in the occult before they become too deeply involved."[147]

Meanwhile, seemingly unfazed by the possible dangers posed to children by occultism, publishers continue churning out books that pique youth interest in the occult. As if to capitalize on their success with Harry Potter, for instance, Bloomsbury (Rowling's British publisher) released *Witch Child* (2000) by Celia Rees. It is not a fantasy, however, but a historical fiction novel for teenagers.

Witch Child tells the tale of a seventeenth-century adolescent girl who actually possesses the supernatural powers she is accused of using. She is exiled to Salem, Massachusetts, where she experiences numerous hardships—at the hands of Christian Puritans.[148] The book's recently released sequel, titled *Sorceress*, has received rave reviews. According to England's *The Independent*, "Rees has become a major writer for teenage readers."[149]

ROWLING'S MORAL RELATIVISM

Countless articles have applauded the morality and ethics of Rowling's "good" characters in Harry Potter. Rowling herself says, "I think they're very moral books."[150] Dozens of book reviewers agree that Harry and his companions are brave, honorable, kind, loyal, unselfish, noble and trustworthy.[151] In the Roman Catholic journal *First Things*, Wheaton College literature professor Alan Jacobs saluted the books, noting, "Rowling's moral compass throughout the three volumes is sound—indeed, I would say, acute."[152] The Dean of Gloucester, the Very Reverend Nicholas Bury, concurred: "[I]n the Potter books goodness, honesty, and integrity overcome lies and deceit."[153]

It is true that Harry and his companions demonstrate some praiseworthy characteristics. They display loyalty, bravery, rejection of materialism and an aversion to patently evil deeds: murder, hatred, torture, etc. However, Rowling's "moral compass" is not as "acute" as Potter fans assert. In fact, the morals and ethics displayed throughout Harry Potter are at best unclear and inconsistent; at worst, they are utterly confusing.

In many instances, Rowling's good characters behave contrary to anything that might be considered "good." They, in fact, indulge in activities not too different from what "bad" characters might do. Harry, Hermione, Ron, Hagrid and other "good" characters *habitually* lie, steal, cheat, ignore laws, break rules and disrespect authority. This occurs because each character bases his or her actions not on any objective standard of morality, but on his or her own subjective feelings; the characters are the embodiment of moral relativism, a close companion of situational ethics.

Like occultism, the moral relativism permeating Harry Potter reflects what has become not only acceptable, but popular in our society. Right and wrong, good and bad, righteous and evil—pop culture has relegated all of these concepts to subjective interpretation. As the computer junkies in the 1995 film *Hackers* put it, "There is no right or wrong, only fun and boring."[154]

Webster defines relativism as "the doctrine that knowledge of truth is relative and dependent upon place, and individual, and experience."[155] This philosophy usually translates to an "If it feels right, do it" mode of living—regardless of any external restrictions or moral standards. The result is convenient, flexible ethics. Bill Watkins, in *The New Absolutes*, explains:

> As truth goes, morality goes. . . . [People] say they believe that what is right for me may be wrong for you, and that no individual, group, or governing body has the right to set the ethical standard for anyone else.[156]

Rowling's "good" characters perfectly demonstrate relativistic thinking. She says, "By and large they go with their conscience."[157] But Rowling does not address how their subjectivity leads them into "bad" behavior. The Harry Potter books, far from presenting a world of consistent morality, portray a realm of moral ambiguity. As Charles Taylor observed in his Salon.com article, Harry learns to "balance his sense of what's right and his sense of what's necessary."[158]

Unfortunately, Harry often defines as "necessary" things that are not necessary at all—they are simply things he wants to do. Whether it entails breaking rules, disobeying laws or lying is inconsequential. Throughout all four books thus far released, Harry typically calls his own shots, making decisions based on what he feels. In *Sorcerer's Stone*, for example, he begins breaking Hogwarts' rules almost immediately after arriving.[159]

Harry consistently resorts to lying, cheating, crime and rule-breaking—yet he remains a hero. Oddly, most of the time Harry's unethical deeds are excused by adult characters, leaving him to continue on his way with few admonitions to change. Rarely does he suffer any consequences for his behavior. Sometimes, in fact, he is rewarded. Even when he is "punished" it usually does not amount to very much of a lesson. He is particularly fond of lying as a primary way of negotiating his way through life.

On page 34 of Book III, Harry lies to a bus driver. On page 155, he lies to Lupin, who is supposed to be his friend. On page 246, he again lies to Lupin, this time doing it "quickly." Harry then lies to Snape on page 283-285. In Book IV, Harry lies to Hagrid (p. 256), a house-elf (p. 408), Hermione (p. 443), Professor Snape (p. 516), Professor Trelawney (p. 577) and Cornelius Fudge, the Minister of Magic (p. 581)—all without negative consequence.

A good explanation for why so much lying exists at Hogwarts appears in Dumbledore's words to the student body in Book IV. He tells them his belief "that the truth is *generally* preferable to lies [emphasis added]."[160] Generally? Not surprisingly, Harry often lies to Dumbledore, who is himself a liar.

On page 353 of Book III, for instance, we learn that when Dumbledore first became Headmaster, he lied to his staff, the student body, all the students' parents and the citizens of a nearby town so Lupin (a werewolf) could attend Hogwarts when he was a boy. How did Lupin repay the favor? He disobeyed the rules, wandering off school grounds as a wolf and nearly causing the deaths of innocent people. Lupin explains how easily he dismissed his guilt:

> I sometimes felt guilty about betraying Dumbledore's trust. . . . [H]e had no idea I was breaking the rules he had set down for my own safety and others' safety. . . . But I always managed to forget my guilty feelings every time we [James, Sirius, and Peter] sat down to plan our next month's adventure.[161]

Readers finally find out in *Prisoner of Azkaban* why Harry seems so bent toward rule-breaking and lying. His father, James Potter, also "didn't set much store by rules."[162] In reference to Sirius Black and James Potter, Professor McGonagall remembers: "Black and Potter. Ringleaders of their little gang. Both very bright, of course—exceptionally bright, in fact—but I don't think we've ever had such a pair of troublemakers."[163]

Lupin, who was a close friend of James', reveals that Harry's father and two other Hogwarts students (Sirius Black and Peter Pettigrew) secretly and illegally became animagi—i.e., wizards who can turn themselves into animals. They were supposed to register with the Minister of Magic, but remained unregistered, again contrary to wizard law.[164]

In Book III Harry inherits a "Marauders' Map" from teenage twins Fred and George Weasley. This magical map shows all of the corridors in Hogwarts and displays moving figures that trace the movements of teachers and students. The map—originally made by Harry's father, Sirius Black, Peter Pettigrew and Remus Lupin—was stolen by the Weasley brothers from a drawer marked "Confiscated and Highly Dangerous." To activate the map, George taps it, saying, "*I solemnly swear that I am up to no good.*"[165] As Fred gives it to Harry, he solemnly sighs about the map's makers: "Noble men, working tirelessly to help a new generation of lawbreakers."[166]

Fred and George, in fact, are tirelessly disobedient themselves. Although depicted as good kids, they routinely disobey their parents, violate school ordinances and lie, all the while expressing gleeful satisfaction over their antics (see *Prisoner of Azkaban*). In Book IV, for instance, it is revealed that for years the twins have been ignoring their mother's instructions by continuing to invent dangerous magical gag-gifts.[167]

The twins also ignore their father's request not to gamble on the Quidditch World Cup game. Ultimately, a defeated Mr. Weasley capitulates to his sons, pleading: "*Don't* tell your mother you've been gambling."[168] Fred cheerfully responds, "Don't worry Dad.... We've got big plans for this money. We don't want it confiscated."[169] Interestingly, Mr. Weasley seems to be the very source of his sons' tendency toward rule-breaking and lying.

Although a Minister of Magic employee, he regularly circumvents wizard laws. He works in the "Misuse of Muggle Artifacts Office." His job is to prevent wizards from bewitching "things that are Muggle-made" (appliances, books, clothes, etc.). It is a way of protecting Muggles (nonmagical mortals) from objects that might prove to be harmful because they are bewitched.

To capture wizards/witches who have broken this law, Mr. Weasley conducts various raids and confiscates their illegally bewitched property. But Mr. Weasley is "crazy about everything to do with Muggles" and has a shed full of Muggle objects. His son, Ron, explains to Harry: "He takes it apart, puts spells on it, and puts it back together again. If he raided *our* house he'd have to put himself under arrest."[170] Mr. Weasley even lies to his wife about the extent to which he has bewitched his Muggle car.[171]

On page 45 of Book IV he admits to having illegally connected the Dursley's fireplace to the wizard's network of fireplaces (a

HARRY POTTER: MAGICK AND MORALITY   169

magical conduit of travel). "Muggle fireplaces aren't supposed to be connected, strictly speaking," he confesses. "[B]ut I've got a useful contact at the Floo Regulation Panel and he fixed it for me."[172]

Weasley even breaks rules for others. When the son of a friend landed in trouble for illegally bewitching a Muggle object, he "smoothed the whole thing over," effectively freeing the boy from punishment.[173] Weasley, far from being a model father or wizard, is a liar, hypocrite and lawbreaker. And as a parent he shows an appalling lack of control over his children.

Hagrid (Hogwarts Keeper of the Keys and Grounds), another "good" character, is even less inspiring as a role-model. He does little, for example, to correct Harry's attitude with regard to seeking revenge against foes. In one scene, Harry finds *Curses and Counter-Curses (Bewitch Your Friends and Befuddle Your Enemies with the Latest Revenges)* by Vindictus Viridian. He says: "I was trying to find out how to curse Dudley."[174] Instead of explaining a better way and pointing Harry in a psychologically healthier direction, Hagrid replies: "I'm not sayin' that's not a good idea, but yer not ter use magic in the Muggle world except in very special circumstances."[175]

Hagrid also could be considered an alcoholic. He constantly turns to strong drink and gets drunk when either depressed *or* joyful.[176] (This aspect of Hagrid's character was deleted from the movie version of Harry Potter.) At one point in Book III, Hermione actually has to tell him that he has had enough booze.[177] Moreover, Hagrid's integrity leaves much to be desired:

- He consistently performs spells even though he is not supposed to do magic (he was expelled from Hogwarts during his third year, which means he never graduated to the level of full wizard).[178]
- He repeatedly ignores legal statutes applicable to the entire wizard world. For instance, he raises an "illegal" dragon

against the 1709 Warlock's Convention law prohibiting
dragon breeding in Britain.[179]

- He often asks Harry and his friends to not tell anyone about
  his criminal activities and disobedience.[180]

Obviously, Harry is not alone in displaying less than admirable
behavior. Most if not all of Rowling's "good" characters indulge in
unethical conduct that is either rewarded or ignored. And they
rarely show any remorse over their misdeeds. The following list
presents only a small sampling of the many ethical lapses in Harry
Potter that occur without any negative results. (NOTE: These instances occurred in the story when no such behavior was necessary in order to combat evil, save a life or avert disaster.)

Harry: disobeys teachers (Book I: 148-150), lies (Book II:
128, 209; Book III: 155, 246, 283-285), disobeys school
rules (Book I: 153-158, 209-214; Book II: 164-165), steals
(Book II: 186-188), breaks wizard laws (Book I: 237-241;
Book II: 69), cheats (Book IV: 324-329, 341).

Ron: disobeys school rules (Book I: 153-158, 209-212; Book
II: 164-165), lies (Book III: 289), breaks wizard laws (Book I:
237-241; Book II: 69), uses profanity/swears/off-color slang
(Book II: 259).

Hermione : disobeys school rules (Book II: 164-165), steals
(Book II: 186-188), cheats (Book IV: 338-339).

Hagrid: disobeys conditions of his employment (Book I: 59,
64), breaks wizard laws (Book I: 230-233, 237-241; Book IV:
438), makes no effort to discourage the children from breaking rules (Book I: 64, 237), becomes drunk (Book I: 203-204;
Book II: 212; Book III: 121, 405), cheats (Book IV: 324-329).

Mr. Weasley: breaks wizard laws (Book II: 31; Book IV: 45,
61), keeps secrets from his wife (Book II: 66), uses profan-
ity/swears/off-color slang (Book IV: 43).

Fred and George: disobey school rules (Book III: 192), disobey parents (Book II: 30; Book IV: 88-89, 117, 367), break
wizard laws (Book II: 30).

Leprechauns: use profanity/swear/off-color slang (Book IV:
111—i.e., give an opposing sports team "the finger").

Dumbledore: breaks Hogwarts rules (Book I: 152, 165); lies
(Book III: 353).[181]

Interestingly, the only individuals who seem to care about discipline and following rules/laws are evil characters like the
Dursleys, or mean-spirited characters like Rita Skeeter (a reporter), Snape and Hogwarts' caretaker, Argus Filch. As Rowling
writes, "Filch burst suddenly through a tapestry to Harry's right,
wheezing and looking wildly about for the rule-breaker."[182]

In actuality, then, Rowling's good characters are hardly "good."
But if this is so, then why do they still appear good in the story?
Why do so many people maintain that Harry Potter is a tale of
good versus evil? Why do the lies, the disobedience and the self-
serving nature of Harry and other "good" characters remain relatively unchallenged by parents, educators and religious leaders?

It is a kind of literary illusion due to Rowling's radical redefini-
tion of good and evil. She has skillfully obscured the *mildly* evil
deeds of her "good" characters behind the *horrendously* evil deeds
of her "bad" characters. In other words, Rowling has made
Voldemort and his followers so repulsive, that the immoral/un-
ethical deeds of Harry and other "good" characters (e.g., lying,
cheating, etc.) take on an appearance of benevolence, fun and virtue. The result is a tacit acceptance of *mildly* evil characters as
"good" characters.[183]

Rowling further downplays the dismal morality in her books by
elevating two virtues *above all others*: bravery and courage. As she
herself has stated, "If the characters are brave and courageous, that
is rewarded."[184] Rowling fails to recognize, however, that "evil"
characters are brave and courageous too. They save each other's

lives, heal each other's wounds, remain loyal in the face of persecution and sacrifice for each other.

Toward the end of Book IV, for instance, we see Voldemort *rewarding* Pettigrew for his faithfulness (Rowling, p. 649). From
the Dark Lord's perspective, he is being "good" to Pettigrew who
helped him rise again even though enemies opposed him.
Voldemort also bestows honor upon those who remained true to
him and speaks of how he will someday greatly reward them for
the suffering they endured as a result of their faithfulness. To
Voldemort they are brave.[185]

Of course, Voldemort's method of operation may drastically
differ from Harry's, but the two characters share a similar motivation: self-interest. Voldemort wants what he wants, as does
Harry. The only difference between them rests in the rules they
choose to break, the lies they choose to tell and the goals they
choose to pursue.

This is why the whole "Harry-Potter-is-a-battle-between-
good-and-evil" argument is, in truth, without merit. Although
used as an oft-quoted defense of Rowling's works, it has little to
do with the books because they do not, in fact, contain a true "battle between good and evil."[186] The war in Harry Potter is a conflict
between *horrific* evil (Voldemort and his followers) and a *milder*
evil that only appears "good" (e.g., Harry and his companions)
because it is so less offensive than the greater evil.

What messages might children pick up from the actions of Mr.
Weasley, his twin boys, Harry, Hagrid and others? Several are obvious: 1) disobedience is not very serious; 2) try getting around
punishment, either by lying or using "connections"; 3) obedience
should be forsaken in favor of one's desires; 4) sometimes it is acceptable to deceive or conceal information from a spouse.

The incessant rule-breaking, criminal conduct (per wizard
law), lying, deception and overall unethical behavior of
Rowling's "good" characters ultimately outlines a threefold
moral code: 1) rules/laws are made to be broken if they do not

serve your own self-interests or if you don't see any reason for their existence; 2) ethics and morality are situational and flexible, dependent upon the circumstances; and 3) the end justifies the means by which you pursue your goal.[187]

While it is true that unrighteous deeds play a part in most fairy tales and fantasy adventures, there is usually at least an implied understanding that the characters involved are either: a) "evil" characters; or b) "good" characters undergoing a deep internal struggle over their actions. In some cases, these "good" characters are behaving "badly" only because they are somehow being deceived/bewitched. A classic example from fantasy literature containing a more honorable/consistent morality would be The Lord of the Rings.

TOLKIEN VS. ROWLING

Joseph Pearce, author of *Tolkien: Man and Myth*, observed, "Tolkien has no time for the amoral relativism that is so prevalent in much of what passes as modern entertainment."[188] Indeed, Tolkien's morality is far removed from the subjectivism of Rowling's works. This aspect of his stories is most evident in the character Frodo from The Lord of the Rings.

Frodo, unlike Harry, defeats evil by fidelity to truth. He does not resort to lying or deception, nor does he look to the very same powers used by his foe, the evil Sauron. Harry, on the other hand, uses some of the very same tactics employed by Voldemort and his followers—even the exact same magical spells.

But Tolkien shows that the defeat of evil *cannot* be obtained by gaining access to evil's power and using it for good. The Lord of the Rings demonstrates that conquering evil depends on humility, courage, love, self-sacrifice—i.e., natural human virtues. In The Lord of the Rings "morality and integrity are at stake and dealt with as important and significant concerns."[189]

Tolkien illustrates right and wrong (good and evil) not only through the choices his characters make, but how those choices affect others. He raises issues involving the consequences of disobedience, the merits of self-sacrifice, the detrimental effects of sin (e.g., pride, greed, lust), and the need to fulfill one's responsibilities for the benefit of others, even at one's own risk.

Tolkien additionally presents magic as a seductive and dangerous force that does not rightly belong to humanity (or hobbits). In Rowling's world, however, wizards are human and their powers are tapped and increased via real occultism. This contrast is even more stark because Tolkien's magic bears little outward resemblance to actual occult practices in our world.

So while a fan of Rowling's work could *easily* emulate the occult rituals in Harry Potter, a reader of Tolkien's books would be hard-pressed to copy anything within them. Consequently, it is not inconsistent for parents to view Tolkien's work as acceptable, while at the same time rejecting Harry Potter (see endnote for further information).[190]

The extreme dissimilarity between Rowling and Tolkien was highlighted in a 2001 article by Brian M. Carney, editorial writer for the *Wall Street Journal*, Europe:

> Harry, of course, is Good, and the wizard Voldemort, who killed Harry's parents, is Evil. Why is Voldemort evil? Well, he wants to "take over," we learn, and he kills people. Harry is good because he's nice, and we can't help sympathizing with him, since Voldemort killed his parents and all. This is very straightforward stuff, and there's little to argue with in it. But there's also little to argue for. Tolkien delves deeper. . . . In short, Tolkien is doubtful of man's ability to resist the temptation of absolute power. That is one of the great themes of the book. . . . Saruman, a scholar and originally a good man, is corrupted by the ring. He starts out studying its history and eventually becomes obsessed with having it. In the end he is ruined. . . . Another "good guy," the prince Boromir, underestimates the ring's dark temptations and argues that it should be used against the forces of evil; not to do so, he be-

lieves, is to accept defeat. He is wisely overruled, however, by others who decide that the ring must be brought straight to the heart of evil's domain and destroyed. . . . Even Frodo, the hobbit ring-bearer in Tolkien's tale, is not immune to the temptation to use the ring, and when the moment comes for him to destroy it, he cannot bring himself to cast it away. This kind of moral complexity is simply absent from Ms. Rowling's books. . . . In Tolkien's world the temptation of evil is one that all, or nearly all, of his characters must confront. . . . His story, for all its narrative brio [energy], presents a serious rebuttal to the idea that good ends justify using evil means. . . . It is time to shake off our moral complacency. "Harry Potter" will not help. For all its charms, it comes close to moral fatuousness by reducing good and evil to naughty and nice. Tolkien did much more—showing the ethical challenges we all face, as individuals and as nations. Unquestionably a writer for his times, Tolkien is also the better one for ours.[191]

In conclusion, the Harry Potter series presents morality inconsistently at best. Good characters behave badly. Heroes follow situational ethics, moral relativism and an "end-justifies-the-means" philosophy. Rowling's magickal universe is a topsy-turvy world rife with occultism with no firm rules of right and wrong or any consistent principles to determine the truly good from the truly evil. As former professional astrologer Marcia Montenegro remarks, "There is no moral center in Harry Potter. Good and evil are depicted as being two sides of the same coin, which is the occult worldview."[192]

IN THE FINAL ANALYSIS

Given the information in this chapter, all parents should have a reasonable level of concern about Harry Potter due to its inclusion of: a) real-world occultism; and b) inconsistent moral messages. Parental guidance, therefore, must be given to children reading Harry

Potter in order for them to avoid potential trouble in connection to real magick and emulation of unethical behavior. In *A Landscape with Dragons*, novelist Michael O'Brien explains the heart of the matter when it comes to children reading Harry Potter:

> If a child's reading is habitually in the area of the supernatural, is there not a risk that he will develop an insatiable appetite for it, an appetite that grows ever stronger as it is fed? Will he be able to recognize the boundaries between spiritually sound imaginative works and the deceptive ones? Here is another key point for parents to consider: Are we committed to discussing these issues with our children? Are we willing to accompany them, year after year, as their tastes develop, advising caution here, sanctioning liberality there, each of us, young and old, learning as we go? . . . Are we willing to sacrifice precious time to pre-read some novels about which we may have doubts? Are we willing to invest effort to help our children choose the right kind of fantasy literature from library and bookstore?[193]

No one, of course, is better equipped than parents to judge what is and what is not appropriate for their children. Parents of vulnerable or at-risk children may have to intervene to turn their children's interests in healthier directions. Children in this category would include those who are already showing deep fascination with occultism, are especially susceptible to peer pressure, are hanging around with a "bad crowd" of kids, are *preoccupied* with imaginary worlds and who are often obsessed with favorite books or movies.[194]

Unfortunately, many parents are being led to believe that there are no problems with Harry Potter. This confused position has been encouraged by a flood of misinformation and disinformation by biased news journalists, uninformed Potter fans, literature scholars (afraid of appearing narrow-minded) and even some religious leaders. The pro-Potter propaganda has been nothing short of impressive. It will be discussed in Part Four.

Part
Four

DEBATES, DISPUTES AND DECISIONS

He that answereth a matter before he heareth it, it
is folly and shame unto him.

—Proverbs 18:13 (KJV)

RALLYING
BEHIND ROWLING

"What the Muggles Don't Get: Why Harry Potter Succeeds While the Morality Police Fail"

Brown Alumni Magazine[1]

"Muddled Muggles: Conservatives Missing the Magic in Harry Potter"

The American Prospect[2]

The ongoing controversy over the child-appropriateness of Harry Potter has been unpleasant, to say the least. Throughout various communities—religious, literary and educational—debate has raged not only about witchcraft and the occult, but also religious freedom, First Amendment rights and censorship. Opposing viewpoints on these issues have sparked nothing less than emotional arguing, mean-spirited insults, irresponsible speculations, ugly rumors, misrepresentations of fact, malicious news articles and a significant level of disinformation. Persons on all sides of the debate have been guilty of fruitless bickering, which has produced far more heat than light.

Potter fans, for instance, have released scores of sensationalized diatribes falsely equating any and all concerns about Harry Potter with religious extremism and narrow-minded bigotry. Individuals using this ploy enumerate the worst examples of misguided zealotry (e.g., book burning), then with one stroke paint all concerned parents with the same broad brush.[3] On the other hand, it must be acknowledged that there have been some persons who have gone too far in voicing anti-Potter criticisms. They have called Rowling a witch, asserted that her books teach Wicca, claimed that Harry Potter contains Satanism, and spread fabricated stories about the alleged effects of Harry Potter on children.[4]

In an effort to sort fact from fiction, this chapter presents the views of Harry Potter supporters using their own words. Chapter 9 will offer comments that directly address their claims. Because most of the objections to Harry Potter have come from Christians, several of the pro-Potter articles excerpted have been taken from the Christian community. A few articles, however, are written by non-Christians. Bracketed numbers refer to points discussed in Chapter 9.

FROM "WILD ABOUT HARRY?"
by Bob Hostetler (*Hamilton [Ohio] Journal-News*)

[#1] Rowling accomplished something impressive in creating Harry Potter and his world. . . . [S]he created a cohesive alternative universe, in which few of the rules of our "universe" apply. . . . [T]hough Rowling fashioned an alternative "reality" for Harry Potter and the Hogwarts School of Witchcraft and Wizardry, it just wouldn't do for her to fashion an alternative morality. [#2] Thus, the "good guys" at Hogwarts are people who—like Harry—exhibit the classical virtues of love, loyalty, honesty, fairness, and courage. . . . [T]he "bad guys" in the books—whom the reader longs to see defeated—are bullies and liars who display rudeness, greed, and cruelty. . . . We—even those among us who profess not to believe in objective standards of morality—still admire the kind person far more than the cruel, the honest more than the dishonest, the brave more than the cowardly, the self-controlled more than the promiscuous. [#3] If we did not, Harry Potter would not be so popular, and his struggles with Voldemort and other forms of evil would not be so compelling.[5]

FROM " 'HARRY POTTER' RICH WITH CHRISTIAN ALLUSIONS"
by Baylor University Media Staff (Baylor University Tip Sheets)

[According to] Dr. Scott Moore, a Baylor University philosophy professor . . . [#4] Rowling understands the diverse world of Christian symbols, relying for instance on images of the phoenix and the unicorn in the early books. . . . "Both were commonly used by the medieval Church as images of Christ." In addition, Moore says Harry and his friends are being schooled in classical and Christian virtues and learn consistently about the value of truth from the school's headmaster. "Albus Dumbledore's insistence that one call [the book's villain] Voldemort by name is a reflection of his courage and his commitment to calling things by their proper names—truth-telling," Moore says. With a name meaning "willing death" (which is how Lucifer is frequently described in medieval theology), [#5] Voldemort cannot kill Harry because of the power of self-sacrificial love ("agape"—his mother died loving him).[6]

FROM "HARRY POTTER VS. THE MUGGLES: MYTH, MAGIC & JOY"
by Mike Hertenstein (*Cornerstone*)

[#6] For those who deem Harry Potter unacceptable, the easiest course is to condemn fantasy literature in toto. . . . [S]uch a critic's problem is to make the case that Rowling should be condemned for her use of magic, marvels and pagan references in a way that does not also render illegitimate the use of same by their favorite Christian authors. Here's a common argument: magical powers in Lewis's Narnia series are depicted as submitted to the rule of Aslan (the God figure), and therefore acceptable, while in the Potter books magic is a trade that must be learned, ergo, "there is no source that defines morality, only instinct and personal preference." . . . This argument only proves that the person making it prefers allegory, with its straightforward correspondences (Aslan = God) to myth. The fact that J.K. Rowling does not have a God figure in her stories doesn't make her stories godless; it makes them non-allegorical. . . .

[#7] There is also a persistent failure among critics of Harry Potter to distinguish between aesthetic and moral criticism; they seem unaware that these can be two different things. Most of the Potter criticism exhibits a reckless equation of badly made with bad, an approach that, if applied to most recent Christian fiction, could bring down an entire industry. The attempt to prove moral culpability by alleged poor literary quality, is unliterary, unethical, and illogical: it reduces to the argument "Harry Potter books are evil, and not only that, but they're also badly written, which proves they're evil." . . .

[#8] A similar debate once raged over whether Christians could eat food that had been originally offered to pagan idols. They most certainly can, insisted the Apostle Paul, provided they can eat with a clear conscience and be mindful of those "weaker brothers" who cannot. But Paul never suggested that weaker brothers must set the limits for everyone. Indeed, Tolkien notes, people make idols of anything, including money, science, nations and ideas. . . .

[#9] Most kids aren't going to be aware of some dark origin or an evil connection between Harry Potter and life: not unless some misguided adult suggests such things. . . Even then, the information won't really compute for most kids, though a certain kind will probably rejoice in having secret knowledge and feel a sense of power in exposing the "truth" about Harry Potter to his or her friends. Most of those friends, however, already know the truth about Harry Potter: that he has revealed to them the magic of life, that his story has been a medium of mythopoeic joy. . . .

For not only do kids find fantasy and reality less confusing than many adults think, or actually confuse the two less than many adults, they're also smarter than some adults seem to believe. . . .

Worse, they'll conclude their parents are willing to use dishonest means for the sake of what they tell them are Christian ends. In any case, Christianity will become Muggle-anity in the child's mind, and "Christian ethics" will come to mean a contradiction in terms. Meanwhile, if adults drum into kids the idea that what they go to Harry Potter for is what they'll also find in the occult, we shouldn't be surprised if an interest is sparked in Wicca.[7]

FROM "WITCHES AND WIZARDS: THE HARRY POTTER PHENOMENON"
by Chuck Colson (Breakpoint Commentary)

[#10] The books are enormously inventive, and include the kind of humor that makes many parents want to borrow the books from their kids. But if you're the parent of a Harry Potter fan, you may be concerned about the elements of witchcraft in these books. [#11] It may relieve you to know that the magic in these books is purely mechanical, as opposed to occultic. [#12] That is, Harry and his friends cast spells, read crystal balls, and turn themselves into animals—but they don't make contact with a supernatural world. [#13] Other parents are concerned with the dark themes and violence in the books. After all, Harry's parents are murdered in book one, and throughout the books, Harry is pursued by followers of a murderous wizard named Voldemort. . . . [But] the plots reinforce the theme that evil is real, and must be courageously opposed.[8]

COMMENTS ON/QUOTES FROM *WHAT'S A CHRISTIAN TO DO WITH HARRY POTTER?*
by Connie Neal (Waterbrook Press, 2001)

[#14] Most interesting is Neal's justification for the unethical behavior of Harry and his companions. She excuses their misconduct by advancing a philosophy of "doing 'the-wrong-thing-for-the-right-reason' " (Neal, p. 167). In other words, doing a "bad" deed for a "good" reason is not "outside the Judeo-Christian ethic" (Neal, p. 167). She further claims that both King David and Jesus Christ acted in such a way, contrary to Judeo-Christian ethics, and that their actions were approved by God. To support her assertion, she offers Mark 2:23-28, which according to Neal, recounts how Jesus and His disciples picked grain on the Sabbath— contrary to biblical law.

The Pharisees, of course, complained. Neal observes: "Notice that Jesus doesn't argue that it is not unlawful. It is" (Neal, p. 167). She then refers to Jesus' words about David going into the temple and feeding himself and his men (who were starving) with the consecrated bread, which according to the law, was to be eaten only by priests (Neal, p. 169). She concludes that if Jesus and David broke moral laws for higher moral reasons, then so, too, should "good" characters in Harry Potter be allowed to break rules and "sin" in order to fulfill higher moral goals (e.g., saving a life, defeating evil, etc.).

Neal also mentions several characters from Harry Potter. [#15] In reference to Nicholas Flamel, she says he "was a church-going man who had a dream one night [about a book].... Shortly thereafter a man sold him the book.... He deciphered the mysterious writings ... claimed to have succeeded in the 'Great Work' (making gold) ... became rich and made donations to churches" (pp. 41-42). Neal adds: "Flamel ... wanted to better understand how to live in harmony with the will of God the Father" (p. 42).

[#16] Others mentioned include Ron Weasley, who "belongs to a large but poor wizarding family that is loving and devoted to good" (Neal, p. 34) and Hermione, whom Neal says "consistently acts as the conscience of the group" (pp. 34-35). Neal further maintains, "Harry Potter appeals to kids' desire to be the best they can be" (p. 73) and when the characters on the side of good have moral lapses, "they are corrected in the course of the story" (Neal, p. 45).

[#17] Finally, Neal makes several observations concerning literature. She seeks to soften the occultism of Harry Potter by drawing parallels between it and other works such as *A Christmas Carol* by Charles Dickens:

> [I]t opens with Ebenezer Scrooge having a conversation with his dead partner. But Deuteronomy 18:10-11 clearly states, "Let no one be found among you who ... consults the dead." These are the same verses most often quoted to warn against Harry Potter. Isaiah 8:19 says, "Why consult the dead on behalf of the living?" ... [O]ne might rightly question a character who not only converses with the spirit of a dead man, but also welcomes three spirits in one night (Neal, p. 59).

Neal concludes by asking: "What does *A Christmas Carol* actually say about talking to spirits of the dead? What does it say about astral projection or leaving one's body to traverse space and time?" (Neal, p. 59). Her questions, of course, imply that it makes no sense to accept as appropriate *A Christmas Carol*, while rejecting Harry Potter.

FROM "HARRY POTTER'S MAGIC"
by Alan Jacobs (*First Things*)

[**#18**] Rowling has expressed her love for the Narnia books—one of the reasons there will be, God willing, seven Harry Potter books is that there are seven volumes of Narnia stories—but as a literary artist she bears a far greater resemblance to Tolkien. . . . [**#19**] It is true that Harry is often at odds with some of his teachers, but these particular teachers are not exactly admirable figures: they themselves are often at odds with the wise, benevolent, and powerful Headmaster, Albus Dumbledore, whom they sometimes attempt to undermine or outflank. But to Dumbledore, significantly, Harry is unswervingly faithful and obedient. . . .

[**#20**] But the matter of witchcraft remains, and it is not a matter to be trifled with. . . . So the issue is an important one, and worthy of serious reflection. . . . The place to begin is . . . the eight volumes Lynn Thorndike published between 1929 and

1941 under the collective title A History of Magic and Experimental Science. . . . In the thinking of most modern people, there should be two histories here: after all, are not magic and experimental science opposites? Is not magic governed by superstition, ignorance, and wishful thinking, while experimental science is rigorous, self-critical, and methodological?

While it may be true that the two paths have diverged to the point that they no longer have any point of contact, for much of their existence—and this is Lynn Thorndike's chief point—they constituted a single path with a single history. For both magic and experimental science are means of controlling and directing our natural environment (and people insofar as they are part of that environment). . . . [S]everal centuries of dedicated scientific experiment would have to pass before it was clear to anyone that the "scientific" physician could do more to cure illness than the old woman of the village with her herbs and potions and muttered charms.

In the Renaissance, alchemists were divided between those who sought to solve problems—the achievement of the philosopher's stone, for example (or should I say the sorcerer's stone?)—primarily through the use of what we would call mixtures of chemicals and those who relied more heavily on incantations, the drawing of mystical patterns and the invocation of spirits.

At least, it seems to us that the alchemists can be so divided. But that's because we know that one approach developed into chemistry, while the other became pure magic. The division may not have been nearly so evident at the time, when (to adapt Weber's famous phrase) the world had not yet become disenchanted. . . . This history provides a key to understanding the role of magic in Joanne Rowling's books, for she begins by positing a counterfactual history, a history in which magic was not a false and incompetent discipline, but rather a means of controlling the physical world at least as potent as experimental science. . . .

[#21] Hogwarts School of Witchcraft and Wizardry is in the business of teaching people how to harness and employ certain powers—that they are powers unrecognized by science is really beside the point—but cannot insure that people will use those powers wisely, responsibly, and for the common good. It is a choice . . . between magia and goetia: "high magic" (like the wisdom possessed by the magi in Christian legend) and "dark magic."[9]

FROM "HANDS OFF HARRY POTTER!"
by Chris Gregory (Salon.com)

[#22] Have critics of J.K. Rowling's books even read them? . . . [#23] If modern paganism could teach me to do half the stuff in these books, I'd be its most fervent convert. The students learn fun stuff like shrinking potions (which would certainly have enlivened my chemistry class), how to make a pineapple dance across your desk (which beats algebra, hands down) and how to fly on a broomstick (which leaves regular gym in the dust). Unfortunately, modern witchcraft bears as much resemblance to Hogwarts' curriculum as my eighth-grade chemistry class did to Professor Snape's potions class. . . .

It's worth noting also that the magic depicted by Rowlings [sic] does seem to have some moral sense attached to it. The few spells used to harm others usually backlash on the user in a riotously humorous or dreadful way. Thus, the evil Voldemort loses most of his powers after using magic to kill Harry's parents. And when Ron attempts to curse the school bully, Draco Malfoy, his wand backfires, and poor Ron spends the next few hours throwing up slugs. (Scenes like this explain why 10-year-olds love the books.)[10]

FROM "BURNING BOOKS, IDEAS IS THE REAL SORCERY"
by Michael Miller (*South Florida Business Journal*)

[#24] The Rev. George Bender, you're a putz. . . . You're also a book burner. I wish you could hear the contempt in my voice. . . . I don't question your love for God, Rev. Bender. You must have faith in a higher power if you think your earthly actions are going to go unpunished in the afterlife. . . .

[#25] The books show good kids making tough but honorable choices, with strong female equals and clear consequences for those who lie, cheat or hurt others. Harry gets through most of his battles on wit and teamwork, not sorcery. The most powerful magic in Harry Potter's world is love. The central adult figure in the books is Albus Dumbledore, a wizard in the Gandalf/Ben Kenobi tradition. I assume you know who those characters are, Rev. Bender, as surely you've burned a few copies of "Lord of the Rings" and "Star Wars" in your time.[11]

FROM "VIRTUE ON A BROOMSTICK," "SAINT FRODO AND THE POTTER DEMON" AND "POSITIVE ABOUT POTTER"
by Michael Maudlin and Ted Olsen (*Christianity Today*)

"Virtue on a Broomstick": Along comes a popular children's series about witchcraft and journalists scurry to their Rolodexes, looking under "F" for "frothy fundamentalists" to get a good quote. [#26] Thus when a relatively small number of Christian parents ask that their kids' schools not read Harry Potter, we read about it in all the major newspapers. . . . [But] I would guess that the vast majority of evangelicals in this country who have encountered Harry Potter are as smitten with him as the culture at large. . . .

[#27] The consensus is that *Goblet of Fire* is not only twice as long as any of the others but also better. The orphaned English wizard is now 14 and ready for more responsibility. It comes when he is illegally entered in the Triwizard Tournament (he is technically too young to participate). Harry knows that someone entered him in order to do him harm, but everyone thinks he rigged the ballot for his own glory. . . .

And how does Harry cope? Yes, he gets discouraged and angry, but overall he displays courage, loyalty, compassion, joy, humility, even love. During the tournament, Harry must choose between winning and ensuring that others remain free from danger; he chooses the latter while hardly batting an eye. And all the while he sounds like a typical 14-year-old. That is Rowling's triumph: creating a "cool" good kid. . . .

I think good and evil are clear and absolute in the books, just not fully explained—yet. It may be your "personal opinion" that it is right to serve Lord Voldemort, but every reader knows which side you have chosen. And I would shout a little more loudly the wonderful virtues that are modeled in the books, which is why Charles Colson and Fuller Seminary president Richard Mouw have reviewed the books positively.[12]

"Saint Frodo and the Potter Demon": Rowling's fantasy books have touched a raw nerve among some evangelicals. [T]he vitriol is not limited to the fringe element: [#28] take the venerable Ted Baehr, publisher of *Movieguide* and head of the Christian Film & Television Commission, a diplomatic mission to make connections between Hollywood and the Christian community. Normally cautious in his criticisms of the film industry and careful about making overgeneralizations that he may have to take back when meeting with studio heads, Baehr has openly campaigned against the Harry Potter movie. . . .

This primitive shunning of Harry Potter is made all the more strange when contrasted with the Christian response to The Lord of the Rings. . . . [#29] Both are fantasies by British authors who not only populate their stories with magical creatures but with magic as well. In fact, in both series magic is seen as a neutral instrument that can be used for either good or evil. And both authors allow their heroes to make full use of magic in their cause. So why are not both condemned equally? If one indulged in this paranoid game of spotting evil, then I think a case could be made that Tolkien stinks more of hell than Rowling. . . .

First, Middle-earth is surprisingly secular. We do not see any churches or temples, only monuments to past kings and historical figures. In fact, no wizard, elf, dwarf, human, or hobbit prays or mentions a deity (at least I don't remember such a reference in the five times I have read the series, but I am sure someone will tell me if I am wrong). At least Harry Potter celebrates Christmas. Suffice it to say that religious piety is not modeled in Tolkien.

Second, if you want to condemn a work for what it has inspired, then turn up the heat for Tolkien. While neither Tolkien or Rowling has ever encouraged people to mistake their magical worlds for the real one (in fact, both have made quite the opposite point), many fans have voluntarily entered Middle-earth. It would be hard not to link the occult-friendly role-playing game Dungeons and Dragons to the influence and popularity of Lord of the Rings, which has provided the imaginative landscape for much modern fantasy. One Web site even sells Lord of the Rings Tarot Cards. Have some people used Tolkien as an entry point to the occult? The answer must be yes.

[#30] And yet, where is the brouhaha over Lord of the Rings? I have not heard it. All I have heard are desperate, wrong-headed attempts at explaining why Tolkien's (and Lewis's Narnia series') use of magic is fine while Rowling's is bad. Even Harry's critics feel compelled to defend Tolkien. In fact, Tyndale House, the publisher of the Left Behind series and the New Living Translation of the Bible, has gone so far as to publish *Finding God in The Lord of the Rings*.

Written by a vice president at Focus on the Family (another organization that few would claim suffered from liberal leanings), Kurt Bruner and writer Jim Ware attempt to show the "strong Christian faith that inspired and informed [Tolkien's] imagination." No scent of hell in that. Bruner and Ware point out . . . "[T]he transcendent truths of Christianity bubble up throughout this story, baptizing our imaginations with realities better experienced than studied."

[#31] Bruner and Ware are right about Tolkien, but their observations apply equally to Rowling's Harry Potter books. Neither series makes much sense apart from a Christian ethic—whether or not this was the author's intent, especially in Rowling's case. Both works convey a palpable sense of Providence; both lift up agape love as the highest virtue; both flesh out what it means to have noble character; both see evil as coming from the heart and not "out there."[13]

"Positive About Potter": [A]s far as I can tell, [#32] while no major Christian leader has come out to condemn J.K. Rowling's series, many have given it the thumbs-up. If our readers know of any major Christian leader who has actually told Christians not to read the books, I'd be happy to know about it; but in my research, even those Christians known for criticizing all that is popular culture have been pretty positive about Potter.

One of the most quoted supporters of the Potter books is *Christianity Today* columnist Charles Colson. . . . Perhaps the most insightful discussion of the Potter books comes from Wheaton College professor Alan Jacobs. . . .

[#33] I'll give the final word to Harry Potter author J.K. Rowling, in a quote from a CNN interview: "I have met thousands of children now, and not even one time has a child come up to me and said, 'Ms. Rowling, I'm so glad I've read these books because now I want to be a witch.' They see it for what it is. It is a fantasy world and they understand that completely. I don't believe in magic, either."[14]

JUST THE FACTS: BYPASSING THE PROPAGANDA

9

> Rowling's voice speaks to children, rather than at them.
> They thus encounter the chicken-blood-and-brandy diet of
> baby dragons, vomit-flavored candy, and (mildly) off-color
> jokes, along with occasional drunkenness and violence.
>
> —*The Chronicle Review*[1]

This chapter corrects many of the factual errors commonly made by Harry Potter supporters. These errors are not subject to, nor do they concern, either personal preferences of literature or personal interpretations of indistinct aspects of Harry Potter—i.e., nothing that might be considered subjective. The corrections include errors relating to:

- Misleading depictions of what is contained in the Harry Potter books;
- Inaccurate descriptions of occult practices, techniques and/or historical persons;
- Faulty assessments of literature produced by C.S. Lewis, J.R.R. Tolkien and other popular writers;
- Out of context and/or misapplied biblical passages.

Hopefully, this chapter's points of discussion will help adults better judge the appropriateness of Harry Potter for children in their care. Whichever position a reader ultimately takes on the Harry Potter issue, making an informed decision based on verifi-

193

able facts and truth is essential. As Winston Churchill said, "The truth is incontrovertible. Panic may resent it. Ignorance may deride it. Malice may distort it. But there it is."[2]

THE HOSTETLER REPORT

Argument #1: Harry Potter's world is an alternate universe; a realm separate from our own; a parallel universe; a sub-creation.

This is the most oft-repeated piece of misinformation regarding Harry Potter. Christian literature professor Alan Jacobs, for example, like Hostetler, has declared, "One of the great pleasures for the reader of her books is the wealth of details, from large to small, that mark the Magic world as different from ours."[3] Rowling's story, however, is presented as taking place in the here and now, in England, only a few hours' train ride from major British cities.

Rowling has explained this during many interviews, saying: "The magical world of Hogwarts is like the real world only distorted. We're not going off to a different planet. It's a fantastic world which has to exist shoulder to shoulder with the real world."[4] On another occasion, Rowling said Muggles can even see Hogwarts: "When they look towards it, as a safety precaution, they see a ruin with a sign saying it's unsafe . . . they mustn't enter. They can't see it as it really is."[5]

Argument #2: Harry Potter is a classic good vs. evil story with clearly defined good characters.

Another common misconception concerns the morality of Harry Potter. Many fans say that it offers a classic good vs. evil tale and will readily describe the conduct of its evil characters. But they rarely give a complete summary of the behavior of her "good" characters. What goes unmentioned is how Rowling's "good guys" not only exhibit "classical virtues," but also cheat (Book IV: pp. 329, 334, 338-339, 341, 351, 465, 484-485, 490-491), lie (Book IV: pp. 408. 456, 516, 577), break laws/rules (see chapter 7), and are rude (Book I: pp. 92, 97).

The incorrigible Weasley twins are a perfect case in point. These boys excel at disobeying their parents, ignoring school authorities and breaking wizard law (see Books II-IV). They even engage in cruelty to animals. On pages 130-131 of Book II they blast off a Filibuster Firework (a bottle-rocket/firecracker/sparkler explosive) in the mouth of a salamander that emits loud sparks and bangs as it whizzes around the room, until finally landing in the fireplace where it explodes.[6] (Some Potter fans may argue that, in the fantasy, the salamander is a "fire-dwelling" being that is not injured by the firework; this is just begging the question, since the "humor" of the scene is based on the abuse of the salamander.)

The morality Rowling actually presents is moral relativism and situational ethics (see chapter 7). Many parents might find this information crucial to deciding whether to allow their children to read Harry Potter.

Argument #3: Harry Potter would not be so popular if he were not such a good character.

First, one must ask, who is defining "good"? Rowling defines "good" as any character opposed to Voldemort—regardless of "bad" behavior and immoral conduct. This is hardly an adequate definition of "good" and greatly blurs the distinctions between good and evil. Second, it is a fallacy to say that society only esteems "good" characters. Our culture is rife with highly popular books, showbiz personalities and TV/movie characters that reject and ridicule those values widely viewed as "good" (e.g., Goosebumps, "Beavis and Butthead," rap artist Eminem, MTV's "Jackass" program, and Freddie Kruger from the Nightmare on Elm Street series). Obviously, not all things popular model "good" virtues and exemplary behavior. In fact, a number of children have expressed that one of the reasons they enjoy Harry so much is that he is bad and mischievous—i.e., not good.[7]

Moore Propaganda

Argument #4: Harry Potter contains Christian teachings and symbolism (e.g., the phoenix, the unicorn).

This argument by Baylor University's Dr. Scott Moore falls into the realm of selective interpretation and speculation. The phoenix and unicorn were indeed used by medieval Christians, but they were originally pagan. There is no reason to assume that Rowling intended the symbols to be taken in any way remotely connected to Christianity, especially when in the broader context of her novels there are no allusions to Christianity—except passing remarks that effectively degrade the faith via references to that unfortunate period in history when witches were persecuted and burned (Book II, p. 150; Book III, pp. 1-2).

Equally false is the assertion that Harry and his friends are being schooled in "Christian virtues." The morality at Hogwarts mirrors secular humanism more than Christianity. For the lessons to be "Christian," they would have to be rooted in the person and work of Jesus Christ—hardly the case at Hogwarts! One example of Moore's faulty view can be seen in his suggestion that Dumbledore's willingness to call Voldemort by name is a Christian lesson in "truth-telling." But no such commandment to "call things by their proper name" exists in Christianity.

This particular teaching, however, is decidedly part of the magickal belief system, which holds that "one should call all things by their real name, for fear of a name increases fear of the thing named."[8] In the article "Magick: High and Low," neopagan Merlyn explains: "Magickal power is also traditionally believed to reside in peoples' secret or magickal names and other 'words of power.' For this reason these names and magickal incantations need to be kept secret to keep opponents from using them to place curses."[9]

Argument #5: Harry Potter contains examples of *agape* love, a foundational practice of Christians.

Moore contends that Voldemort cannot kill Harry because of the power of his mother's "self-sacrificial love." He then defines her love, borrowing the Greek term *agape*. But Moore incorrectly uses *agape*, especially as it applies to the Christian idea of self-sacrificial love. *Agape* is not just an emotional feeling for persons whom we love and who love us—even if it leads to sacrifice. That kind of a love reflects *phileo* (a reciprocal love).

Phileo is seen in the sacrifice of Harry's mother for her son and in Harry's life-risking deed during the Triwizard's Tournament when he attempts to save a friend from captivity. Such deeds are admirable, to be sure. But they do not qualify as *agape*. Why? Because many people would make a sacrifice—perhaps even of their lives—for a close friend or loved one. This is a natural, albeit difficult, response that both "good" and "evil" people demonstrate.

Agape, however, is a vastly different kind of love. It is the extraordinary capacity to sacrifice for enemies, or at the very least, people with whom we have little or no relationship. The apostle Paul explains the difference: "Very rarely will anyone die for a righteous man, though for a good man someone might possibly dare to die. But God demonstrates his own love [*agape*] for us in this: While we were still sinners, Christ died for us" (Romans 5:7-8).

The defrocked priest played by Gene Hackman in *The Poseidon Adventure* (1972) displayed such love when he sacrificed his life for fellow passengers whom he barely knew. Would Harry have made such an extraordinary sacrifice for Malfoy, Professor Snape or a stranger? That is doubtful.

Not once in all four books so far released has Harry displayed any concern for characters other than those that show concern for him. Moore completely sidesteps the words of Christ, which to paraphrase, teach, "If you only love those who love you, what special credit is that to you? Even evil people love those who love them. And if you only do good to those who do good to you, so what? Evil people do the same thing" (Luke 6:32-33, author paraphrase).

The true Christian definition of *agape*, then, biblically speaking, is sacrificial love that does not take necessarily into account the value to oneself of the other person being loved. It reaches out, in fact, to those who may have little or no particular value to oneself—even an enemy. This is not what we find in Harry Potter. Consequently, Moore is misrepresenting the contents of Rowling's series and/or redefining key terms to suit his purposes.

Hertenstein on Harry

Argument #6: Readers cannot legitimately object to Harry Potter because many popular Christian authors have used mythology, magic and pagan references just like Rowling has used them.

Hertenstein makes many erroneous statements in his article concerning literature, especially with regard to objections about the occult, pagan and mythological references in Harry Potter. He first suggests that Rowling and C.S. Lewis use mythology similarly, when in reality they do not. Moreover, the problem with Harry Potter is not that Rowling uses mythology and pagan references, but rather, *how* she uses them. She employs them in a broader environment that glamorizes occultism as part and parcel of a whole fantasy package—a single, unified "fun kit" that blends occultism, myth, legend and magick. Rowling makes extensive use of mythology in tight juxtaposition with real occultism, which creates a canvas for her story that is thoroughly occult-based.

C.S. Lewis, on the other hand, used mythology sparingly and only as a signpost of Christianity—i.e., "gleams of divine truth." Mythology and legend were not used by Lewis as a platter on which to serve up real occultism. Yet this is precisely what Rowling does; she makes no attempt to use myth as a vehicle for "gleams of divine truth." One might say she misuses myth and legend by too closely aligning it with occultism. The end result is more confusion over reality vs. fantasy and an unnecessary alignment of occultism with mythology.

Harry Potter critics have repeatedly demonstrated that it is indeed possible to be logically consistent in rejecting Rowling, while accepting Lewis and Tolkien. It is a false assumption to say, "[I]f we throw out Rowling's work for using mythological references or magic we must throw out Lewis and Tolkien as well." Interestingly, Hertenstein's comment exactly mirrors the argument given by Rowling herself against criticisms of her books.[10]

Hertenstein also states that it is inconsistent for Christians to accept the magic in Narnia just because it is submitted to the rule of Aslan (i.e., God), while rejecting the magic in Harry Potter because it has no God figure. This argument is one of the weakest of all objections to Rowling's novels, yet Hertenstein depicts it as a primary objection—perhaps because it is so easy to refute. Its destruction makes his position seem stronger, while at the same time making the view of Harry Potter critics seem weaker.

Very few people concerned about Harry Potter argue about its child-appropriateness based on whether it has a "God figure." A far more pressing concern is that the characters engage in real-world occult practices such as divination, which is defined as "[w]illful exploration of the future or the discovery of hidden things by various practices. Most common are astrology, dowsing, dreams, cards, crystal-gazing, numerology, palmistry, omens."[11]

Regarding the works of Lewis/Tolkien and Rowling, there still exist many other issues that clearly separate the writers. What about the difference between the way so-called "good" characters behave in Harry Potter and the way good characters behave in Lewis/Tolkien? What about the difference between how bad choices are pictured in Harry Potter and how bad choices are pictured in Lewis/Tolkien? What about the difference between the humor in Lewis/Tolkien and the profanity and crude/off-color jokes in the Potter series?

There is even a striking difference between the way evil is defeated in Harry Potter and the way it is defeated in Lewis and

Tolkien. Lewis' good characters (e.g., Peter, Lucy, Susan) do not overcome witchcraft by learning more witchcraft. They respond to evil by becoming servants of another good character, Aslan, who vanquishes the White Witch. Tolkien's characters likewise use strength of character to defeat evil—they do not use the Ring (Sauron's power).

Rowling's "good" characters, in contrast, overcome "evil" by using the same dualistic magical power employed by Voldemort and his Death Eaters. In fact, every good and evil magical character is trained by the same kinds of institutions. Harry's own school instructed Voldemort. Good and evil characters go so far as to use the exact same spells.

Furthermore, it must be recognized that Rowling's works, unlike those of C.S. Lewis, are completely dependent on magick. It is central to Rowling's story, whereas Lewis uses magic sparingly and in a highly stylized manner that does not connect with the real world. Moreover, the magickal arts used by Harry and his friends are locatable in the occult section of any bookstore or on the Internet. As one journalist observed: "Lewisian magic seems a bit pale and remote compared with Rowling's; it is far easier to imagine a Harry Potter fan thinking: 'Wow, that sounds like fun! If only I could find a way to . . .' "[12]

Lewis' works also offer morality lessons different from those found in Rowling's books. Consider the disobedience of Edmund Pevensie in The Chronicles of Narnia. He is a little boy whose errant ways subject him to the wicked White Witch. To rescue Edmund, Aslan offers himself as a sacrifice on the ancient Stone Table. Although he is killed, Aslan rises again through a "deeper" magic unknown to the witch. This sacrificial love—true *agape*—convicts Edmund of his evil, and he repents. The once mischievous Edmund is transformed by Aslan's love into Narnia's "King Edmund the Just."

Argument #7: Harry Potter critics are only saying the books are evil because they believe the fantasy series is

poorly written, which is an absurd reason to condemn a book.

This is a "strawman argument"—i.e., an attack on a caricature or false description of something that is opposed, which leads to an apparent victory after the false description has been easily refuted. It is rare to find Christians condemning Harry Potter because they feel it is poorly written. In fact, many Christians have said that the books are written quite well. It was renowned secular critic Harold Bloom who called Harry Potter "slop."[13] Other secular reviewers have expressed similarly negative opinions, which were quoted earlier in this book. Even if a small number of Christians are calling the books evil just because they are poorly written, their illegitimate objection does not negate the many legitimate objections to the series (e.g., its profanity, inconsistent morality, ethical relativism, gratuitous violence, crass humor and real occultism).

Argument #8: Whether or not Harry Potter is child-appropriate is an issue of Christian freedoms.

After tackling literary issues, Hertenstein turns his attention to biblical verses that are pivotal in the religious debate over Harry Potter—Romans 14-15 and First Corinthians 8-10. These passages relate to Christian "freedoms." Such freedoms in Christ are activities not specifically condemned in the Bible (e.g., manner of dress, wearing jewelry, moderate consumption of distilled beverages, going to church on a day other than Sunday). Christians are "free" to enjoy such activities, even though not all Christians may agree on the issue. The thrust of this argument is that enjoying Harry Potter is a freedom about which no one need worry.

But the current Harry Potter controversy is not about freedoms in Christ. The issue is threefold:

1. Do the books contain positive presentations of real-world occultism?
2. Do the books glamorize unethical behavior?

3. Do the books contain enough real occultism and/or unethical conduct to adversely affect some children?

All three of these questions, I believe, have only one valid answer: yes. The applicable Scripture, then, would be: " 'Everything is permissible for me'—but not everything is beneficial" (1 Corinthians 6:12).

Argument #9: Even though some kids may start dabbling in occultism because of Harry Potter, the number will be small, so there is no need to worry. Besides, most kids aren't even going to catch on to the real occultism in the books.

When it comes to the effects of Harry Potter on youth, Hertenstein makes two rather startling comments for an evangelical (not excerpted in chapter 8): 1) "In the case of the Harry Potter stories, there will no doubt be bad readers who stay on the surface of the plot, projecting themselves into the action merely to experience the vicarious thrill of hexing the teacher"; and 2) "Harry Potter may or may not be evil or may or may not turn kids into occultists."[14]

It appears Hertenstein is stating that there will be a degree of literary "collateral damage" to some children (i.e., "bad readers")—but the most important thing is for "good readers" to have an opportunity to "plunge below the surface to experience that awakened sense of longing."[15] The logical end of such thinking is that some children "may or may not" fall through the cracks into occultism. This, to Hertenstein, seems to be an acceptable consequence.

While it certainly may be true that children deserve the right to enjoy fun and exciting literature, it is also true that sometimes safeguards need to be erected by parents and adults. Such safeguards are to prevent a small, but no less precious, percentage of children from heading toward a religious belief system that they may be too young to handle. Hertenstein seems to be saying that any harm coming to children actually is their own fault for being "bad readers."

Hertenstein then concludes his article with three groundless assumptions:

1. Kids are not going to be aware of the connections between Harry Potter and real occultism (even though several books making the connections have already been published).
2. Child confusion over the positive presentation of symbols once associated with evil will not be as harmful to them as associating mythopoeic literature with evil.
3. Kids will not fall into occultism due to Harry Potter because they are smarter than adults think they are and have less difficulty distinguishing fact from fiction than grown-ups (even though child development experts disagree).

On what basis are these assertions made? These are merely unverifiable declarations of Hertenstein's personal opinions—not facts. Consider the following:

- No supporting studies or observations from child development experts or child psychologists are given.
- No in-depth studies are cited that deal with the way children learn from fantasy and fictional characters.
- No children were interviewed and quoted about these issues.
- No follow-up studies/polls on children who started reading the books several years ago when they were first published has been conducted.

Furthermore, Hertenstein directly contradicts documentation that shows kids are already gravitating toward occultism in Britain and the U.S. because of Harry Potter (see chapter 7). Oddly, Hertenstein suggests that any children who get involved in occultism will probably end up there thanks to adults who "drum into kids the idea that what they go to Harry Potter for is what they'll also find in the occult." On what basis is such a claim made?

Neopagans/Wiccans have attributed Harry Potter-related youth interest in the occult and Wicca to the books—not any interaction with adults by children.

Finally, Hertenstein all but completely dismisses the possibility that anyone would want to be involved in the occult after discovering that spellcasting does not work. But whether or not spells work has not dissuaded hundreds of thousands of Wiccans, many of whom have recently taken up the Craft due to the current popularity of witchcraft and occultism. They seem to be bothered very little by the fact that spells do not work (see chapter 6). Will children respond any differently than adults have to such popularity?

COLSON'S COMMENTARY

Argument #10: Harry Potter contains wonderful humor appropriate and fun for both adults and children.

This is a particularly interesting argument since a fair degree of the humor found in Harry Potter is not only juvenile, but mildly off-color, crass and gratuitously violent. Such forms of humor are not normally thought of as Christian. One set of supposedly funny scenes involves Rowling's macabre depiction of lessons relating to the use of mandrake. People used to believe this root, which looks vaguely like a small human, had magical properties.

A Handbook on Witches explains that the historical beliefs surrounding the oddly shaped plant made it a virtual symbol of witchcraft during the Middle Ages:

> [I]ts root may be considered—with a little imagination—to look like a dead, shriveled baby. It is gnarled, and forked into two little "legs." Mandrakes were therefore regarded as the progeny of the Devil, said to grow in places where he had spilt his seed on the ground (while romping with witches?). *They were said to shriek in protest when they were drawn out of the earth* [emphasis added]. Nevertheless many

people, witches included, must have braved this ordeal, since mandragora appears in a large number of spells.[16]

Not only does Rowling stress the significance of the mandrake root for the potion needed in Book II, but her storyline details a rather gruesome procedure that involves pulling live Mandrake-babies from the ground and growing them to maturity before "cutting them up and stewing them."[17] To add more color to the story, Rowling has the children wearing earmuffs to protect them from the Mandrake-babies' screams that ring out whenever they are repotted. This distasteful imagery is periodically referred to as a sort of running joke.[18]

Off-color humor, drunkenness and cursing are added amusements for Rowling's fans. In Book IV, for instance, a suggestive sentence structure allows readers to fill in the blank: "Ron told Malfoy to do something that Harry knew he would never have dared say in front of Mrs. Weasley" (Rowling, p. 121). Later Harry says, "Yeah, give Ron a good kick up the—" (Rowling, p. 290). Hagrid, of course, plays the part of the comic drunk in Books I-IV.[19]

More child-inappropriate humor appears on page 111 of Book IV in the form of a vulgar hand gesture Rowling couches in humor. It occurs during the Quidditch World Cup, after a foul by Bulgaria, the mascots for Ireland—an unruly throng of leprechauns—float into the air to form "a giant hand, which was making a very rude sign indeed."[20] Such humor is in no way compatible with what many parents want their children reading.

A great deal of humor also is rather low-brow. In Book I, for instance, there are references to "troll boogers" (Rowling p. 177). Book II continues in like manner, describing one potion as "the khaki color of booger" (Rowling, p. 216). Another scene has Ron accidentally cursing himself, which causes him to belch up hundreds of slugs—so many, in fact, that they fill up a basin and spray all over the ground.[21] Additionally, Book II includes a game of Head Hockey, in which a dozen headless horsemen play a polo match with a ghost's head.[22]

Book III merrily trundles down this same path of humor, which is reminiscent of contemporary horror/comedy films. On page 50, Rowling describes a wizard game called Gobstones in which "stones squirt a nasty-smelling liquid into the other players' face when they lose a point."[23] Book IV supplies stupendously gross scenes involving bubotubers, which are black, squirming plants that fourth-year students must squeeze in order to harvest the vegetation's "pus" into bottles. This foul substance is used as "[a]n excellent remedy for more stubborn forms of acne."[24]

Book IV, *Harry Potter and the Goblet of Fire*, pushes the bounds of gutter humor even further. During one divination class in which students are studying the planets, a girl named Lavender discovers an unexpected planet. Professor Trelawney explains, "It is Uranus, my dear." Ron Weasley jokes, "Can I have a look at Uranus too, Lavender?"[25] In another scene, an elderly wizard complains about having to trade his loose-fitting robe in for pants, saying: "I'm not putting them on. . . . I like a healthy breeze 'round my privates, thanks."[26]

Rowling obviously understands what children like to read and has delivered it to them. But are these images appropriate for all kids? Parents must ask themselves: Is this the kind of humor that should be encouraged? Are there other books that might present more wholesome avenues of entertainment? Apparently Colson believes such examples of humor are not only appropriate for children, but highly entertaining for adults.

Argument #11: The magic in Harry Potter is not real, just mechanical—i.e., pretend magic, similar to hi-tech devices used in science fiction.

The most obvious problem with the analogy in this argument is that the technology in most sci-fi stories cannot be duplicated, nor do they have anything to do with occultism. In Harry Potter, however, characters go beyond unrealistic "mechanical" magic by delving into real magick/witchcraft, including divination. It is important to note here that Harry Potter fans consistently say Rowling uses her characters to make fun of divination. But such a claim is not entirely true. Trelawney (Hogwarts' divination teacher) is indeed painted as an off-beat witch whose forté is a very "imprecise" branch of magic.[27] At the same time, though, Trelawney accurately predicts the future during a classic episode of spirit channeling. And Hermione excels at arithmancy (a form of divination).

Argument #12: The good characters in Harry Potter do not make contact with the supernatural world.

Harry and his friends are constantly communicating with the spirit realm via ghosts, magical creatures and enchanted objects (books, mirrors, etc.). Ghosts include Professor Binns (a Hogwarts teacher), Peeves (a poltergeist), Moaning Myrtle (a murdered Hogwarts student) and Nearly Headless Nick (Gryffindor's resident apparition). Each student dorm, in fact, has its own house-ghost.

In Book III, Headmaster Dumbledore uses these and countless other ghosts to send messages to the students.[28] In occultism, ghosts are defined as the "disembodied spirit or image of a deceased person, appearing to be living. . . . Ghosts are believed to haunt specific localities, either dwellings associated with their earthly life or locales with a tragic history."[29]

Additionally, a ghoul lives with the Weasleys, who are content let it dwell with them as a long-term guest. A ghoul, according to occult legend, is

> [a]n evil spirit supposed to rob graves and feed upon human corpses. . . . Amongst Hindus there are similar beliefs of the vetala, a demon that haunts cemeteries and animates dead bodies, or the rakshasas, a whole order of evil demons that disturb sacrifices, harass devout people, or devour human beings.[30]

Perhaps the clearest contradiction of Colson's assertion about "contact with a supernatural world" can be seen in an episode with Madame Trelawney (Book IV). Trelawney becomes momentarily possessed by someone (or something), which speaks through her mouth, using a loud, harsh voice described as "quite unlike her own."[31] The scene occurs when Harry and Trelawney are engaged in a form of divination called scrying. Suddenly, Trelawney went "rigid in her armchair; her eyes were unfocused and her mouth sagging."[32]

From her gaping jaws, the voice (which Rowling never identifies) declares, "IT WILL HAPPEN TONIGHT." The voice continues to make its prophecy, while Trelawney remains transfixed, completely unaware of what is going on:

> THE DARK LORD LIES ALONE AND FRIENDLESS, ABANDONED BY HIS FOLLOWERS. HIS SERVANT HAS BEEN CHAINED THESE TWELVE YEARS. TONIGHT, BEFORE MIDNIGHT . . . THE SERVANT WILL BREAK FREE AND SET OUT TO REJOIN HIS MASTER. THE DARK LORD WILL RISE AGAIN WITH HIS SERVANT'S AID, GREATER AND MORE TERRIBLE THAN EVER HE WAS. TONIGHT . . . BEFORE MIDNIGHT . . . THE SERVANT . . . WILL SET OUT . . . TO REJOIN . . . HIS MASTER.[33]

Trelawney's head then falls forward onto her chest, and she makes "a grunting sort of noise" as if she is exhausted. This incident is nothing less than mediumship. The history of spiritualism is filled with mediums, who have always held prominence in occultism as persons "qualified in some special manner to form a link between the dead and the living."[34] According to the *Encyclopedia of Occultism and Parapsychology*, "[t]he essential qualification of a medium is an abnormal sensitiveness, which enables him or her to be readily 'controlled' by disembodied spirits."[35]

Argument #13: There's not that much violence in Harry Potter, just enough to show that evil is real.

Colson excuses the "dark themes and violence" in Harry Potter by parroting Rowling's explanation that her books only show that "evil is real." He refers to the murder of Harry's parents and the pursuit of Harry by Voldemort. But these aspects of the story are not what many parents are concerned over. Concerns are being raised about the gratuitous and unnecessarily graphic violence in the books.

Consider Book IV, which begins on pages 2-3 with Voldemort murdering his father and grandparents. Next comes a discussion about the murder of a witch named Bertha Jorkins, who was "tortured" before being killed.[36] Then, Voldemort kills a gardener named Frank Bryce.[37] At the Quidditch World Cup, evil wizards torment a family of Muggles by contorting their bodies "into grotesque shapes" and levitating them into the sky.[38]

On page 465 of Book IV readers encounter the ghost of Moaning Myrtle (c.f., *Chamber of Secrets*), who laments the day she was murdered in a Hogwarts bathroom: "Nobody missed me even when I was alive. Took them hours and hours to find my body . . . Olive Hornby came into the bathroom . . . . And she saw my body . . . ooooh, she didn't forget it until her dying day, I made sure of that."[39] Book IV also mentions:

- Muggle killings "done for fun" by Voldemort's followers;
- the killing of two evil wizards;
- the killing of another Death Eater;
- the "torture" of countless Muggles;
- a good wizard and his witch wife being tortured to the point of insanity;
- Cedric's murder in front of Harry;
- Pettigrew severing off his own hand to put in a boiling cauldron;

- Harry having blood drained into a vial after being slashed in the arm by Pettigrew;
- Voldemort's revelation that his survival depends on drinking a mixture of snake venom and unicorn blood;
- a child killing his father, turning the body into a bone, and burying it.[40]

Rowling herself has repeatedly stated that this is only the tip of a very sinister iceberg of evil that will gradually be revealed in successive books. "I can tell you that the books are getting darker," Rowling has warned. "Harry's going to have quite a bit to deal with as he gets older."[41] And sure enough, each volume has been markedly harsher than the last. Steve Bonta, in *The New American*, observes: "[E]ach new book seems a bit darker and more morbidly tragic than the one preceding."[42] In agreement, Rowling has said: "[D]eath and bereavement and what death means, I would say, is one of the central themes in all seven books."[43]

Goblet of Fire is already being compared to Stephen King's horror novels by some reviewers.[44] Even several nonreligious critiques of Book IV and Rowling's other books have included warnings about their violence and gore:

- "[P]arents expecting a respite from the violence in popular culture will be surprised by the amount of violence that Rowling introduces into her tales. I cannot think of any classic children's story that has as much of it. . . . At one point, she even has Harry and his friends pointing their wands and kicking in a door. Legs get broken, the children get thrown against walls, blood drips, bones crunch."[45]
- "Parents should be aware that there are some really dark and spooky scenes in this novel; more so than the first three. Some of the scenes involving this character [Voldemort] could really have the kids checking under the bed for monsters."[46]

- "[T]his is a different, darker story from the first page of J.K. Rowling's new novel. It just might be time to rethink that whole "Harry Potter is a children's book" theory. Letting an 8- to 9-year-old read this right before bedtime might not be the best way to ensure untroubled sleep."[47]

- "Images of death and violence, however, do haunt the story, and it is here that the rising idea that the Potter books are some sort of universal literature [for adults and kids] needs to be questioned. My five-year-old assistant critic had a troubled Saturday night after hearing the first one hundred pages."[48]

How much darker can Rowling's books get? In one of her more recent interviews with the BBC (December 2001), Rowling pledged to take on even more delicate subjects in her next book. "There are deaths, more deaths coming," she said, adding that one character's end will be "horrible to write." She also commented that she plans to deal with some of life's more challenging topics. "They are 15 now, hormones working over-time," she told the BBC.[49]

CONNIE'S CAMPAIGN

Argument #14: Harry and his friends should not be condemned for breaking rules or laws because even Jesus and his followers broke various laws, as the Pharisees rightly pointed out. Besides, Rowling's good characters only break rules/laws when they are forced to do so in response to a danger.

First, the Pharisees did not accuse *Jesus* of breaking the Sabbath, but His *disciples*, as the text cited by Neal (Luke 6:1-5) reveals.

Second, Christ called himself "Lord of the Sabbath," meaning that He, as Creator of the Sabbath, had authority over it and could, if He so desired, suspend it if necessary (unlike Harry

Potter, who did not, in the context of Rowling's story, create any of the rules he breaks).

Third, the "laws" broken by the disciples were not originally part of the Sabbath Law. Religiously legalistic Pharisees added a no-grain-picking restriction to God's original command about keeping the Sabbath holy. So, technically, not even the disciples were breaking God's Sabbath Law. They actually were disobeying unrighteous restrictions that had been added to the perfect moral law of God.

Fourth, in the case of King David, he did not break any moral laws (unlike those broken in Harry Potter—e.g., lying, stealing, cheating). David merely disregarded ceremony, over which life preservation needs will always take precedence. Ceremony, not morality, gave way to a higher purpose.

Fifth, concerning the Potter books, it is only on rare occasion that "good" characters in the series break a law/rule in order to fulfill a higher moral imperative (e.g., defend a life or save someone from injury). Neal, however, makes it seem as if their unethical behavior often results from having to make such a choice. On most occasions, Harry and his companions display unethical behavior simply as a matter of choice (see chapter 7).

Argument #15: Nicholas Flamel, the alchemist mentioned in Rowling's first book, actually was a "churchgoing man" who sought to serve God the Father.

Neal's sanitized version of Flamel's life might easily mislead readers into thinking that he was a Christian. Such an assumption, however, would be a mistake, since being a "churchgoing man" (a common practice in the fourteenth century) would have had little bearing on whether Flamel lived as a devoted follower of Christ. Flamel, in fact, was not a Christian. According to the occult Rosicrucian Order (A.M.O.R.C.), he was an occultist, a Rosicrucianist.[50] Neal also left out a number of other important details concerning Flamel:

- First, Flamel did not just "have a dream" about a book (see Neal's comments in chapter 8). It was shown to him in a dream by an "angel of light," which would fall under the warnings in the Bible that "Satan himself masquerades as an angel of light" (2 Corinthians 11:14), and condemns even "an angel from heaven" who preaches a false gospel (Galatians 1:8).

- Second, the book, known as *The Book of Abraham the Jew*, was supposedly written by the Hebrew patriarch, Abraham, but there is no historical evidence suggesting that this text was anything but a spurious manuscript of occult origin. (Interestingly, the book contained "great curses and threats against anyone who set eyes on it unless he was either a priest or a scribe"—yet there were no Jewish priests or scribes in Abraham's day!)

- Third, Flamel deciphered the writings only after acquiring secret knowledge from a follower of the Cabala, an old occult source of magick beliefs.

- Fourth, Flamel's attempts to convert base metal into gold was not the "Great Work" alchemists pursued. What alchemists sought was the soul's inner transformation by which they would come to a full realization of their godhood (i.e., divinity). Transmutation of metals was simply a mirror of the alchemist's "transmutation of the human into the divine."[51]

- Fifth, alchemists did not believe in a "God the Father" in any way that Christians believe in a personal God. Alchemists were more pantheistic in their views—i.e., they believed God exists in all things.

In other words, any depiction of Nicholas Flamel as a pious churchgoer who held beliefs similar to today's Christians is wildly inaccurate. Nevertheless, this picture of Flamel has been repeated again and again by well-meaning Christians seeking to link Harry Potter with Christianity, rather than the occult.

Argument #16: No one should criticize Harry Potter when the story includes a family like the Weasleys (who

are "devoted to good") and Hermione (who serves as a moral conscience).

The "devoted to good" Weasley family includes a father who habitually lies to his wife (Book II, p. 31; Book IV, p. 89), breaks wizard laws (Book II, pp. 31, 66; Book IV, pp. 45, 61), approves of his children breaking wizard laws (Book II, p. 39) and is a hypocrite—he arrests other wizards/witches for breaking the laws he himself violates (Book II, p. 66). Ron's two brothers—Fred and George—are notorious for lying (Book II, p. 32) cruelty to animals (Book II, pp. 131-132), blatantly disobeying their parents (Book II, p. 32; Book IV, pp. 88-89, 117, 367), misbehaving at school (Book III, p. 192) and encouraging others to misbehave just for the fun of it (Book III, p. 193). Only Percy Weasley, Ron's older brother, adheres to rules and laws. But he is painted by as a dreadful stick-in-the-mud who is "a great believer in rigidly following rules" (Book IV, p. 90).

Regarding Hermione, she only serves as a moral conscience during early segments of *Sorcerer's Stone*. Hermione quickly joins other "good" characters in less than admirable behavior by breaking wizard laws (Book I, p. 237), breaking school rules (Book I, p. 237; Book II, p. 159), stealing (Book II, 186), punching another student (Book III, p. 326) and cheating (Book IV, pp. 338-339).

As previously mentioned, Harry Potter does not appeal to children exclusively because Harry and his companions are "good." Furthermore, the good characters are rarely corrected in the course of the story for their "moral lapses." Neal's claims simply do not reflect what is contained in the Harry Potter books.

Argument #17: If someone is going to condemn Harry Potter based on biblical verses like Deuteronomy 18 and Isaiah 8, then to be consistent, Scrooge in *A Christmas Carol* by Charles Dickens would have to be condemned as well. This classic even contains astral travel!

This argument is flawed for two reasons. First, the Deuteronomy and Isaiah passages are not applicable to Scrooge because they refer to people who seek out spirits of the dead for the purpose of obtaining otherwise unknowable information (i.e., necromancy). Scrooge did no such thing. He had no choice in the matter. He begged the ghost of Marley to leave and had no desire to meet the so-called "ghosts" of Christmas that visited him, but he was made to go with them. In Harry Potter, spirits are regularly spoken to, welcomed as friends and used to convey messages.

Second, the three "Christmas spirits" in *A Christmas Carol* are not even spirits of the dead! They are symbolic-animate representations of various Christmas periods of time that come into existence yearly. Each one enjoys a limited time of "life." Christmas past, for instance, can only interact with Scrooge until Christmas arrives. Then, Christmas present takes over, but only as long as it is indeed Christmas present. Obviously, these are not "ghosts" in the true sense of the word. So the parallel Neal implies in her first question does not exist.

Third, Neal's comments seriously misrepresent not only the storyline of *A Christmas Carol*, but also astral projection, which is the occult practice wherein a person's spirit allegedly leaves his body. Scrooge, however, never left his body in *A Christmas Carol*. He traveled in his physical body to another dimension (Christmas past/future) as well as to locations in the real world (Christmas present). Labeling such activity "astral projection" is incorrect. Even if Scrooge had left his body, it still would not be astral projection because this a specific modern practice popularized by the New Age Movement and always includes the presence of a spiritual "silver cord" that keeps the soul attached to the body. Neal has blended two widely divergent subjects that cannot legitimately be merged.

FIRST THINGS FIRST

Argument #18: No one should be condemning Rowling when her writings are so much like Lewis and Tolkien, even to the point of her decision to write seven volumes because seven novels are in The Chronicles of Narnia.

This argument is absolutely false. Rowling's stated reason for writing seven volumes is linked to her belief that the number seven has magical/mystical powers. Regarding Tolkien's works, Rowling herself has indeed compared them to her novels, but contrary to Jacobs' assertion, she has said that the "similarities are fairly superficial."[52]

Argument #19: Harry is justified in being disobedient because he only disobeys characters that are themselves evil or against good.

Noteworthy is this unique justification, which argues that Harry's poor ethical conduct is acceptable because the recipients of his misbehavior are teachers at odds with Dumbledore. In other words, to Jacobs, disobeying and lying to people may be acceptable as long as those who are being disobeyed and lied to are not admirable people. This is a blatant contradiction of Christian morality. Moreover, he asserts: "[T]o Dumbledore, significantly, Harry is unswervingly faithful and obedient." But this too is untrue.

Harry consistently breaks rules at Hogwarts (of which Dumbledore is headmaster) and conceals information from Dumbledore (Book II, p. 209). And despite Jacobs' claims, there is little evidence that Harry ever "wonders and worries" about the self-justifications he uses to excuse his less than virtuous deeds. For example, Harry chooses without reservation to travel to the city of Hogsmeade when he does not have permission to do so (see Book III). During this particular adventure he uses a highly "dangerous" magical map that no student is supposed to even possess.

Argument #20: The magic in Harry Potter is more like science than anything else, especially with regard to alchemy.

Jacobs also makes some very odd comments about magick and witchcraft in his supportive statements about Harry Potter. He basically equates magick with science, differentiating them only by the fact that at one point in history they parted company. Science, as Jacobs points out, won the race to find ways of understanding and harnessing natural forces. But to Jacobs it seems that the differences are barely noteworthy and hardly a cause for concern—even for Christians. He even takes time to discuss alchemy, probably because it is such a prominent feature of Rowling's first book.

According to Jacobs, "alchemists were divided between those who sought to solve problems . . . primarily through the use of what we would call mixtures of chemicals and those who relied more heavily on incantations, the drawing of mystical patterns, and the invocation of spirits." This appears to be an attempt to distance so-called nonreligious/non-occult, "problem-solving" alchemists (e.g., Flamel in *Sorcerer's Stone*) from occult alchemists.

Such a delineation, however, although it may soften the occult aspects of Harry Potter, cannot be so easily drawn—especially with Flamel on the side of non-occult alchemists. Most medieval alchemists, including Flamel, held views contrary to Christian doctrine.[53] In order to veil their occult beliefs and teachings, they often attended church, termed their activities a "gift of God" and used mystical drawings with Christian symbolism. They did this in order to not draw negative attention from the church, which in the fourteenth century, could have sentenced them to prison or death.[54]

The quest for the philosopher's stone (or should I say sorcerer's stone?) was wholly intertwined with occult beliefs and the pursuit of spiritual truths incompatible with Christianity. There was no clear distinction between various alchemists, although alchemy had various branches. As *The Encyclopedia of Witches & Witchcraft* explains, "The esoteric purpose of alchemy was mystical and concerned the spiritual regeneration of man."[55] Flamel is commonly associated with the occult side of alchemy rather than its more scientific side—the very opposite of what Jacobs intimates in his article.

Argument #21: Harry Potter is just a story about children learning simple lessons about how to use powers for good—how to not choose black magic.

Jacobs declares that Hogwarts is "in the business of teaching people how to harness and employ certain powers—that they are powers unrecognized by science is really beside the point—but cannot insure that people will use those powers wisely, responsibly, and for the common good." This comment seems intended to alleviate any fears that Harry Potter might contain certain aspects of true magick and real witchcraft.

Ironically, Jacobs' statement mirrors the very definition of magick and modern witchcraft! The popular Man, Myth and Magic series reads, "Magicians are concerned with forces of Na-ture, even if they are peculiar, generally unrecognized, or even, to a sceptic's eye, non-existent forces. . . . Magic is concerned above all else with the acquisition and exercise of power."[56] Likewise, the famous Aleister Crowley, who popularized "magick," wrote,

> The laws of magick are closely related to those of other physical sciences. A century or so ago men were ignorant of a dozen important properties of matter: thermal conductiv-ity, electrical resistance. . . . Magick deals principally with certain physical forces still unrecognized by the vulgar [i.e., non-occult persons]; but those forces are just as real, just as material—if indeed you can call them so, for all things are ultimately spiritual.[57]

Jacobs' reference to Harry Potter characters needing to use their powers wisely also reflects occult teachings. The "Teen Wicca" Web site article "What is Wicca?," for instance, proclaims, "We do not believe in the concept of ultimate good or ultimate evil. Instead we believe that all is power and it therefore depends on how the power is used. It is up to us to use this power wisely."[58] Branwen, the Wiccan founder of Branwen's Cauldron of Light, agrees: "Power is a sacred gift and must be used wisely and with humility."[59] Far from distancing Harry Potter from real magick or witchcraft, Jacobs actually supplies more evidence that the books contain accurate representations of occult teachings.

The most erroneous passage in Jacobs' article concerns his assertion that the choice faced by Harry and his companions may be reduced to a choice "between *magia* and *goetia*: 'high magic' (like the wisdom possessed by the magi in Christian legend) and 'dark magic.' "

First, most occultists (e.g., Wiccans) do not even draw a qualitative distinction between dark and light magick. Magick simply is. It exists as a neutral, amoral power.[60] The Wiccan belief system does not even include any objective definition of good or evil. Hence, there can be no rigid definition of either white or black magick. As the celebrated and highly influential witch Doreen Valiente taught: "[T]he distinction between black and white magic has no validity."[61]

Second, when the relatively modern division between black and white magick is mentioned by occultists, it usually is in reference to rituals that depend "upon sharp contrasts between good and evil spirits" or "the use of repulsive means, such as blood sacrifice."[62] But such things have nothing to do with the parental concern about Harry Potter, which is whether or not Rowling's fantasy contains any real magick (black or white) that might influence children toward the occult.

Third, Jacobs' statement that Rowling's characters face a choice between *magia* and *goetia* misrepresents and misapplies these terms. *Magia* can indeed be traced to the Magi, the learned men of the Assyro-Babylonian kingdom; the word describes their many practices and is a term that today still applies to most forms of magick. Contrary to what Jacobs claims, the magickal arts of the Magi went far beyond mere "wisdom" or science-like activity. They used occult ritual as a means of religious expression and spirituality. Their brand of "high magic" has been defined by the *Encyclopedia of Wicca & Witchcraft* as follows:

> High magick refers to ceremonial magick in which ritual tools, magickal correspondences, and structured rites are employed. High magick is a more formal, traditional form of magick.[63]

This definition applies to all forms of "high magick." It might best be viewed as any formal brand of occult or magick-based religion. In other words, "high magick" is not even an issue in Harry Potter because the novels contain no references to any official religion.[64] The article "Types of Magick" explains:

> High Magick includes full Wiccan workings, ceremonies of both covens and solitaries. It involving [sic] a highly ritualised invocation of Divine power. Also called "Theurgy" in some grimoires, High Magick is always part of [a] greater philosophy (or theosophy) and belief system, including rituals of Qabbala or the Hermetic Orders. Examples of Wiccan High Magick are the Great Rite or Calling Down the Moon, or invocations of the God or Goddess.[65]

So rather than distancing Harry Potter from Wicca or the occult, Jacobs has unintentionally and erroneously declared that Wicca, as a religion (i.e., "High Magic"), is present in the stories! Harry and his friends obviously have nothing to do with any religious system. Consequently, Jacobs has incorrectly defined High Magick and inaccurately presented the contents of the Harry Potter books as well.

What do Harry and his friends practice? They engage in something termed "low magick," which is defined by occultists as "the realm of folk spells, herbs, potions, candle magick, and things of this nature."[66] Low magick (e.g., divination, runes and spellcasting) can be practiced by anyone and is what most Wiccans use as part of their High Magick belief system.

Oddly, Jacobs makes no mention whatsoever of low magick in his article. To do so, of course, would have severely undermined his premise that Harry Potter contains no occultism about which parents need be concerned. Consequently, readers of "Harry Potter's Magic" have adopted several misconceptions about "high magic" and the contents of Rowling's fantasy. Moreover, low magick and high magick have "nothing to do with good and bad," according to the Internet's neopagan Web site Sophia Net.[67] This is confirmed in many works on magick written by Wiccans, neopagans and other occultists. Low magick, occultists claim, can be used positively or negatively, as is the case in Harry Potter.[68]

Finally, Jacobs' readers might easily be led to believe that the Magi's use of *magia* is tantamount to a Christian endorsement of these practices. Such an assumption, however, would be quite false. *Magia*, in all forms, is condemned by the Bible. Although the Magi who visited the infant Jesus were certainly of the *magia* class of priests, there is no historical evidence suggesting that they continued their occult practices after leaving Bethlehem. Nor do we really know the extent of their activities with the occult just prior to making their trip to Israel.[69]

Regarding *goetia*, Jacobs rightly reports that it is primarily confined to "black magic." What he neglects to mention is that the magickal arts used by black magicians who practice *goetia* are the same ones employed by those practicing "low magic." This is the case in our real world as well as in Harry Potter. So contrary to what Jacobs says about Rowling's books (i.e., they contain little or no occultism and they present a choice between white and black magic), Harry Potter presents "low magic" used by both her good and evil characters. "High magic" (i.e., magick within the context of a formalized religion) is not even an issue.

SALON TALK

Argument #22: Most Harry Potter critics have not even read the books.

In actuality, Rowling's most articulate critics—novelist Michael O'Brien, renowned literary critic Harold Bloom, Concordia University English professor Gene Veith, and former professional astrologer Marcia Montenegro, to name but a few—have read all of her volumes. Their arguments are cogent, well-reasoned and balanced. But Chris Gregory and other fans continue portraying critics as ignorant.

Argument #23: It's ridiculous to object to Harry Potter simply because its cheerful depiction of magic causes pineapples to dance and brooms to fly.

It is not the "cheerful depiction" of fairy tale magic in Harry Potter that concerns parents, but rather the accurate and positive depiction of real-world occultism, including various beliefs, lore and history associated with magick. It might cause some children—Christian and non-Christian—to experiment with and dabble in a religious belief system they cannot emotionally or psychologically handle (see Appendix A).

Like many Harry Potter fans, Gregory resorts to sarcasm, stating that he himself would convert to paganism if it indeed included flying broomsticks, shrinking potions and spells to make pineapples dance. Such flip commentary, however, does little to address the real concern of parents. None of the fairy tale examples of magic he gives have anything to do with the many magickal principles and teachings present in the books. It is true that modern Witchcraft (capital "W") bears no resemblance to Hogwarts, but modern witchcraft (small "w") is another story.

Gregory casts aside serious reflection on the issues to engage in frivolity and mockery. He also misrepresents the novels by saying that the few spells used to harm others in Harry Potter "usually backlash on the user in a riotously humorous or dreadful way." The fact is that on many occasions magic is used by good characters in a less than "good" way.[70]

BURNING MAD

Argument #24: Harry Potter critics are just a bunch of idiotic, book-burning fools.

Michael Miller's diatribe perfectly illustrates the kind of anti-religious, anti-Christian rhetoric that pervades the Harry Potter controversy. Such mean-spirited language does not help anyone enter the realm of rational discourse. Yet similar attacks have appeared in a wide variety of newspaper and magazine stories. Rather than representing both sides fairly or, at the very least, consistently quoting well-reasoned Christian responses, journalists have taken great pains to paint Harry Potter critics as ignorant Bible-thumpers whose objections are inconsistent, illogical and groundless.

Numerous articles have even resorted to mocking Christians as "narrow-minded moralists."[71] Other stories have derided as "paranoid" anyone raising objections against the novels.[72] A *London Review of Books* article went so far as to label parental objections as stupid, specifically referring to "born-again" Christians.[73] One particularly harsh *Jewish World Review* article titled "Casual Censors and Deadly Know-Nothings" called Rowling's critics "Barbarians" whose attacks amounted to "ignorance parading as piety."[74]

To be fair, concern over book burning is legitimate. It can lead to all manner of unnecessary censorship if book-burners attempt to impose by force their values on others. However, book-burning, like other forms of free expression, is an American freedom. As much as someone may disagree with such a form of public self-expression, it is no worse than, perhaps not even as bad as, flag-burning. True tolerance, which so many Harry Potter fans claim to espouse, should include toleration of unpopular and contrary opinions.

And the common practice of linking book-burning with censorship is yet another mistake. Book-burning is simply self-expression. Censorship is when you burn *other people's* books. But by invoking the hated specters of censorship and book-burning, many Potter fans have attacked with great rancor anyone voicing anti-Potter sentiments. In a 1999 *New York Times* op-ed column, for instance,

well-known author Judy Blume attacked those concerned about
Harry Potter, saying,

> [T]he Harry Potter series has recently come under fire. . . .
> The only surprise is that it took so long—as long as it took
> for the zealots who claim they're protecting children from
> evil (and evil can be found lurking everywhere these days)
> to discover that children actually like these books. If chil-
> dren are excited about a book, it must be suspect.[75]

The accusation in this brief tirade is absurd. It intimates that
concerned parents actually do not want their children reading! It
is a groundless assertion, but succeeds in venting a great deal of
hostility. Blume then decries censorship, as if it does not exist legitimately, when in fact, it is prevalent everywhere—not only in
public schools, but also in places frequented by the general public
(e.g., libraries). Society enforces numerous laws to protect children from harmful literature (note the plastic-wrapped, paper-
covered pornography in convenience stores covered by signs that
read, "18 YEARS OLD—NO READING IN STORE").

Parents forbidding their children to read certain material is not
even censorship. It is good parenting. People also should remember that censorship, which is all around us, is not the same as
book-banning. It is simply the way any society (or a segment of it)
deems certain material (e.g., racist literature, pornographic publications, anti-Semitic/hate propaganda) inappropriate for a specific location and/or readership. These materials are censored with
little or no adverse news coverage or public outcry. English professor Gene Edward Veith makes an astute observation:

> [J]ust because the government is not allowed to exercise
> censorship does not mean that private citizens cannot say
> no to objectionable material. Yet, parents who object to
> their children reading certain books are accused of censor-
> ship. Retail stores that refuse to sell objectionable CDs are
> charged with censoring them. Conversely, that the govern-

ment is not allowed to prevent certain kinds of material from being published is taken to mean that libraries, schools, and bookstores have an obligation to put it on their shelves. . . . [P]rivate citizens are free to do things that the government is not allowed to do.[76]

Censorship is simply treating with caution certain materials that may be harmful to a specific segment of the population, such as children. Moreover, it is not even an issue for many parents concerned about Harry Potter. Only a handful of individuals are advocating any kind of censorship regarding the books. An even smaller minority advocate such extreme measures as book burning. The majority of persons concerned about Harry Potter are far more reasonable. They simply want to offer words of caution about the possible negative effects of the books on some children.

Nevertheless, Potter fans and the media have reveled in condemning various individuals who have sought to not only ban, but also burn, Harry Potter books. Anti-Potter extremism makes for tantalizing news stories, but it is hardly representative of the vast majority of concerned parents. By continuing to propagate misinformation, Potter fans are doing a disservice to themselves. Casually dismissing all concerns about Harry Potter as the ranting and raving of extremists has caused legitimate concerns to be overlooked.

Argument #25: Surely Harry Potter is good for kids since it shows children making honorable choices and has strong female role models.

One need only take a cursory look at all four volumes to see that Harry persistently wins his battles, accomplishes his tasks and achieves his goals primarily through reliance on magic. Wit and teamwork do come into play, but not as decisively and at such exclusion to magic as Miller makes it seem. Regarding female role models, even secular reviewers have observed that Harry Potter lacks strong female characters. It is a decidedly male-dominated story, perhaps even sexist, as several secular commentators have argued.[77]

CHRISTIANITY TODAY?

One of the most surprising pockets of support for Harry Potter has been *Christianity Today* (*CT*), a publication widely recognized as solidly evangelical. This periodical, as of mid-2002, had run several pro-Potter articles and reviews in its main publication and sister publication *Christian Parenting Today*.[78] The editorial staff has not only given support to Rowling's works, but has gone so far as to criticize fellow Christians voicing contrary opinions, labeling such persons and their concerns as "primitive" and "paranoid," and in some cases motivated by a desire to "capitalize" on the Potter phenomenon.

This is a radical departure from biblical standards, which encourage love and kindness, while still allowing freedom of thought and disagreement regarding issues not essential to the faith. It has always been within Christian parameters to publicly correct errors and offer alternative viewpoints, but *CT* seems to have gone beyond such parameters by taking on a tone of condescension and condemnation reminiscent of secular media stories.

Argument #26: Only a small number of extremist Christians are objecting to Harry Potter.

Michael Maudlin begins his first article with an apparent need to discredit what he sees as the secular media's unfair caricaturing of Christians as "uptight," "ridiculous" and/or "bigoted." Unfortunately, Maudlin goes out of his way to distance himself and *CT* from such depictions by holding out a "Harry-Potter-Is-Fine" position as proof of their open-minded, nonextremist identity. He downplays concerns about Harry Potter by stating that critics of the books from a religious perspective are "a relatively small number."

No statistics, however, are given that might substantiate this claim. No surveys or polls are cited. Nor are any major newspaper stories quoted wherein social commentators make a similar observation. Maudlin adds a second unsubstantiated claim, saying, "the vast majority of evangelicals" adore Harry Potter and have no problems whatsoever with the novels. Again, no documentation is given to indicate a "vast majority" of Christians hold the view Maudlin claims they hold.

Argument #27: Rowling's books are clearly great literature because they just keep getting better and more compatible with Christianity.

Both assertions in this argument are false, as is demonstrated by numerous secular reviews of Rowling's most recent book, *Goblet of Fire*:

> *USA Today*: " 'Goblet of Fire' Burns Out— . . . . This installment has the telltale loping pace and paper-chewing verbosity that best-selling authors develop when they try to write a book a year. There is a reason this baby is more than 700 pages, and it's not the plot. There were dreaded signs of this syndrome in the third installment, *Harry Potter and the Prisoner of Azkaban*, but the disease is full-blown in *Harry Potter and the Goblet of Fire*."[79]

> *New York Times*: " 'Goblet' is as long as 'Chamber' and 'Prisoner' combined. Is it more textured than the first three? More thought-provoking? Sorry, no."[80]

> *CNN*: " 'Harry Potter and the Goblet of Fire' . . . is not great literature. . . . [Rowling's] prose has more in common with your typical beach-blanket fare than, say, 'Pride and Prejudice.' . . . The farther she gets into her planned seven-book series, the more difficult it will be for her to put some oomph into the beginning of each book; already, she's getting bogged down in the minutiae of introducing her characters to new readers."[81]

Arizona Daily Star: "*Goblet of Fire* boldly burns darker than had been expected. . . . Readers who want a superbly crafted one-off will likely be disappointed [in Book IV]; if you're among these, head for Rowling's third book, *Harry Potter and the Prisoner of Azkaban*."[82]

Schoolsnet and *The Guardian*: "[Harry Potter] has suffered an early and unexpected defeat at the hands of this year's Whitbread book award judges. *Harry Potter and the Goblet of Fire* . . . has failed to reach the shortlist stage of the children's book award because 'it was not as good as the last Harry Potter.'[83] . . . [A]uthor Michael Morpurgo, said: 'I think we just felt it was not as good as the last Harry Potter. We had other books which were very, very good.' "[84]

Arcfan.com (sci-fi fan Web site): "[T]he question remains is it [Book IV] any good? Yes and No. My initial instinct is that if Rowling was a more skilled author she could have compressed the book by about a third and removed some of the more cloying sentiment and commentary. . . . [A]s we have seen from the other books she's not afraid to deal with the adult topics of fear, hate, death and the nature of evil, she builds on these. The language of the characters, especially of Harry and Ron, is growing more adult and the faintest suggestion of bad language is creeping in. I would not, for example, be surprised to see the F word in the last book."[85]

Secular reviews also have noted that Book IV is significantly darker in tone and may be inappropriate for younger readers.

Christian Science Monitor: "[*Goblet of Fire* is] just too scary for kids under 12. (I know, I know, what does some stupid adult know, especially one who would use a phrase like 'perfect literary sense.') It's also true that there's no way kids are going to put the books down for a year or two, so at the least, I'd recommend parents read the last 100 pages with anyone under 5 feet."[86]

Time Magazine: "[S]ome of those parents may want to keep the book [IV] away from their younger ones. The rumors that Goblet of Fire is darker and more violent than the first three turn out to be true."[87]

Young Adult Books Central: "[M]any young readers (younger than ten) will read this book. Some of the scenes may frighten them and the best defense is a good offense. . . . If you are a parent or teacher of a young reader, be sure to discuss the darker scenes with them."[88]

Concerning the main plot of Book IV, Maudlin lauds the way Harry makes it through the Triwizard Tournament, saying that he overall he displays "courage, loyalty, compassion, joy, humility, even love." What is not mentioned, however, is that Harry only makes it through the competition by consistently cheating! He not only cheats himself, but either allows or causes others to cheat with him (Book IV, pp. 322-325, 328-329, 334, 341, 344, 351, 357, 365, 464-465, 490-491). He then lies about cheating (Book IV, pp. 357, 516). Others who cheat to help Harry include Hagrid, Hermione, Ron, Cedric, Dobey, Ludo Bagman and Moody.

Oddly, Maudlin adheres to the notion that the good and evil in Harry Potter is "clear and absolute." But he does not explain how such a position lines up with how Rowling has her good characters indulging in classically "bad" behavior. Nor does he explain how lying, stealing, rule-breaking, criminal activity (according to wizard law) and profanity are behaviors consistent with "wonderful virtues."

Argument #28: Christians objecting to Harry Potter are displaying nothing but a terribly primitive way of looking at literature.

In Maudlin's second article, which is marked by an increased level of hostility and loaded language directed against Harry Potter critics, he first repeats the erroneous idea that Rowling's fantasy does not contain real occultism. He then proceeds to downplay the views of widely respected leaders within the religious community, most notably Ted Baehr, whose reputation as a balanced, thoughtful, Christian critic is well-known throughout Hollywood and the entertainment industry. Maudlin admits Baehr is "venerable" and "diplomatic." Yet suddenly, when it comes to Harry Potter, Maudlin paints Baehr as becoming inexplicably "primitive" in his shunning of the novels. Why?

Apparently, just the sheer fact that Baehr holds a different opinion than *CT* is enough to earn him such heavy-handed criticisms. No other reasons are cited. It is in preparation for discussing The Lord of the Rings (henceforth referred to as LOTR) that Maudlin takes this rather "low blow" against Baehr and others. The word "primitive" usually is defined as crude, rudimentary or underdeveloped. Yet this is hardly a fair characterization of Baehr and others he condemns, among whom are respected Christian authors, seminary professors and journalists.

Argument #29: Rowling's use of magic is hardly any different than what is found in Tolkien's The Lord of the Rings.

Regarding Tolkien's fantasy, Maudlin displays a decidedly sophomoric understanding of it. His claim that LOTR and Harry Potter both utilize magic as a "neutral instrument" is inaccurate and sidesteps several other differences between the magic used in these two tales (see Table 9.1). The most striking difference involves the fact that magic in Tolkien actually corrupts any characters that come in contact with it if they are not magical by nature (e.g., humans and hobbits). Sauron's Ring begins corrupting Frodo's goodness. The magic rings of the nine kings turned them into Dark Riders.

Even good magical characters (e.g., Galadriel and Gandalf) must be wary of accepting the Ring because it is so closely associ-

ated with the Dark Lord. Obviously, magic in Middle-earth is far
different from magic in Harry Potter's world. Moreover,
Tolkien's characters do not hone their skills via real-world occult
practices that can be emulated by young readers. And none of the
good characters in Tolkien resort to using the exact same spells
and magic used by evil characters to defeat evil. The same cannot
be said for Rowling's good characters, who are even trained at the
same schools as evil characters.

Tolkien's Magic	Rowling's Magick
Takes place in an alternate reality; another realm entirely separate from our world.	Takes place in our reality; not in another realm separate from our own world.
Based on imaginary concepts of magic; only loosely connected to real-world mythology and legend.	Based primarily on real occult practices (e.g., spellcasting, herbology, alchemy, astrology, crystal-gazing, divination).
Does not make use of realistic historical figures from the occult.	Makes use of realistic historical figures from the occult.
Good characters do not use the same magic that is used by evil characters.	Good characters do use the same magic that is used by evil characters.
Magic is not completely neutral, but can indeed have evil properties.	Magic is entirely neutral and cannot have evil properties.
Magic activities cannot be readily copied by children.	Magic activities can be readily copied by children.

Table 9.1

Contrary to Maudlin's article, both Tolkien and Rowling do
not "allow their heroes to make full use of magic." Only Rowling
allows her characters to use magic at the drop of a hat to fix situations. In The Lord of the Rings, however, Gandalf uses magic
sparingly and on rare occasion, usually opting instead to rely on,

and encourage the use of, one's own resourcefulness, physical strength and/or intellect. As for Frodo, he is warned again and again to avoid using the Ring at all costs. His companions in the Fellowship of the Ring—Gimly, Boromir, Merry and Pippin—do not use magic at all!

Maudlin continues his attack, claiming that Harry Potter critics are playing a "paranoid game of spotting evil." He opines that if Tolkien is subjected to similar scrutiny, he "stinks more of hell than Rowling." Again, such harsh rhetoric is not only unnecessary, but is an extreme departure from biblical mandates against malice, slander, abrasive words and abusive speech (Colossians 3:8, 4:6; Titus 2:8).

To support his charge against Tolkien, Maudlin points out that Middle-earth is secular. But he is wrong. Although LOTR makes no mention of churches, temples or prayer, *The Silmarillion* makes it clear that Middle-earth is indeed religious, but has lost its religion as consequence of the Dark Lord's presence. Tolkien confirmed this aspect of Middle-earth in 1954.[89] It also must be recognized that Maudlin is using yet another strawman argument, since very few persons have criticized Harry Potter (or LOTR, for that matter) for the lack of God or religion overtly represented in them.

Christmas is then mentioned in the article as if it somehow proves Harry Potter is compatible with Christianity. But occultists, atheists, agnostics and assorted other non-Christians celebrate commercialized "Christmas" every year. It is no longer necessarily a religious holiday with many people, but instead, it is a time to enjoy pretty lights, hot cider, partying with friends and exchanging gifts. It has nothing to do with celebrating the birth of Jesus Christ.

Maudlin's argument that Tolkien and Rowling are similar because both might lead children to occultism is only partially correct. It is true that readers of Tolkien have indeed utilized aspects of it to initiate themselves into occult-like forms of entertainment. However, this reality only hurts Maudlin's overall argument since Rowling's work is even more closely aligned with real occult practices than is Tolkien's.

In other words, if children have gotten involved with occultism due to the extremely vague and indirect links to the occult that might be found in Tolkien, then how much easier will it be for children to get involved with the occult when Harry Potter contains explicit and deep references to real-world occult practices, beliefs, lore and historical persons?

Argument #30: Christians do not even have any good reasons for objecting to Harry Potter. All they have are desperate, illogical rantings.

Maudlin's third denunciation of Harry Potter critics accuses them of only voicing "desperate, wrong-headed attempts at explaining why Tolkien's (and Lewis's Narnia series') use of magic is fine while Rowling's is bad." Yet he gives no examples of such attempts, nor shows why they are desperate or wrong-headed. Instead, Maudlin refers to *Finding God in The Lord of the Rings*, a book which makes no comparisons between Rowling and Tolkien—in fact, it does not mention Rowling even once throughout its 120 pages!

Argument #31: The truths of Christianity are just as evident in Rowling's works as they are in Tolkien's fantasy novels.

Maudlin's assertion that "the transcendent truths of Christianity bubble up throughout" both Rowling's books and Tolkien's LOTR is a blatant contradiction of his earlier statement that "Middle Earth is surprisingly secular." Is LOTR secular or Christian? Moreover, nowhere in Harry Potter is there any mention of Christianity, aside from a few degrading remarks about the faith in reference to that unfortunate period in history when witches were persecuted and burned (Book II, p. 150; Book III, pp. 1-2).

Oddly, Maudlin actually goes so far as to say that Rowling's books must be interpreted in light of "Christian ethics" even more so than Tolkien's works! This is a difficult claim to support since LOTR, unlike Harry Potter, contains no profanity, no off-color humor, no sexual innuendo and no juvenile/vulgar imagery (e.g., boogers, snot, pus, vomit candy, etc.). Even more surprising is Maudlin's claim that both tales "convey a palpable sense of Providence"—i.e, a God figure. This is a direct contradiction of the statements of other Harry Potter supporters like Mike Hertenstein, who says there is neither a God figure, nor any allusions to one, in Harry Potter. So is there a sense of Providence (i.e., God) in Harry Potter or not?

Argument #32: Not a single major Christian leader has even criticized Harry Potter, let alone told followers to not read the books.

This argument is simply untrue. First, since Olsen never defines "major leader," his argument is a meaningless statement. Second, outspoken critics of Harry Potter, in fact, do include several Christian leaders, such as Douglas Groothuis (associate professor of philosophy at Denver Seminary and best-selling author of books on the New Age movement), Gene Edward Veith (professor of English at Concordia University, Wisconsin, whose book *Postmodern Times* received a *Christianity Today* Book Award as one of the top 25 religious books of 1994) and Hank Hanegraaff (best-selling author, Gold Medallion Book Award winner and president of the Christian Research Institute, America's largest counter-cult ministry).

A most unusual remark by Olsen is: "If our readers know of any major Christian leader who has actually told Christians *not to read the books*, I'd be happy to know about it [emphasis added]." Olsen adds that his research has revealed none. But what many readers may not consider is that an absence of such leaders is likely due to the fact that no competent, biblically sound Christian leader ever *would* authoritatively tell Christians "not to read the books." Such a command would not only contradict Christian teachings on free will, but also run contrary to biblical passages dealing with freedom in Christ. In other words, Olsen is asking for something that no one will *ever* find! Consequently, the lack of Christian leaders telling people "not to read the books" is meaningless.

Argument #33: There's no reason to object to Harry Potter since many Christian leaders have spoken in favor of the books. Besides, J.K. Rowling herself has stated that she has not run into a single child who wanted to become a witch because of Harry Potter.

Near his conclusion, Olsen simply appeals to the same limited sources that most Harry Potter supporters use against critics—i.e., Alan Jacobs and Chuck Colson. Their arguments, however, have long since been addressed by persons concerned about Harry Potter. Finally, Olsen allows J.K. Rowling the last word, quoting her famous lines about not meeting any children who have wanted to become witches because of Harry Potter. But these quotes too have been shown to be shallow and insubstantial dismissals of a very real problem. A number of children have indeed expressed such an interest and continue to do so.

QUESTIONS MOST FREQUENTLY ASKED

> [Harry Potter] critics have been too easily dismissed as ig-
> noramuses and "censors." . . . The argument being used to
> defend Harry Potter is essentially the same as one that was
> used to defend Little Black Sambo in the 1960s. . . . Ques-
> tions about a book's suitability can only be answered
> through open discussion.
>
> *Education Weekly*[1]

The Harry Potter controversy has generated a wide variety of questions in the minds of parents, educators, librarians, religious leaders and other adults with children in their care. Issues raised have related not just to Harry Potter, but also to fantasy literature in general, the occult, the current popularity of The Lord of the Rings, censorship, Christianity, religious extremism, separation of church and state, the First Amendment and the power of the media. Unfortunately, there exists neither a storehouse of information, nor an answer book dedicated to Harry Potter and the many debates it has spawned.

This chapter attempts to answer at least some of the questions that have commonly been asked since 1997, the year J.K. Rowling's first book—*Harry Potter and the Philosopher's Stone*—was published in Britain. This chapter contains actual questions collected from e-mails, Internet message boards, fan club Web sites, educational institution articles, and personal conversations with parents, bookstore owners, librarians, social workers, teachers, pastors and youth counselors. They are grouped into the following categories: Harry Potter, The Lord of the Rings, Censorship and Schools, Occultism, and Christianity and Scripture.

HARRY POTTER

How is Harry Potter more "satanic" than C.S. Lewis' Narnia series, Tolkien's The Lord of the Rings, Hans C. Andersen's *Hansel and Gretel*, Disney's *Sleeping Beauty* movie or any number of other stories?

The most articulate critics of Harry Potter are not saying the novels are "satanic." Satanism is vastly different from Wicca. Moreover, Wicca *per se* is not even in the books. However, magick and occultism can be found in Rowling's volumes, as previously shown. It is the presence of this real-world occultism that separates Harry Potter from many other fantasy works.

Isn't Hogwarts School of Witchcraft and Wizardry a perfect fantasy model to show how children need the guidance of wise and competent adults in order to get through life?

Actually, the adults in Harry Potter—i.e., the good characters, including Dumbledore—serve minor purposes and are fairly incompetent as well as oblivious to the goings-on at Hogwarts. Even favorable reviews have noted as much, saying such things as, "Though Rowling's child heroes are imperfect . . . they are usually smarter and braver than adults. Some of the nicest teachers at Hogwarts, though friendly and knowledgeable, often don't have a clue to what's going on around them. Others are weak and incompetent, or complete phonies."[2] Another reviewer writes,

> [M]ost of the adults in these books are deeply flawed. At Hogwarts the teachers drink like fish; the gentle giant,

> Hagrid, positively staggers through the first three books. . . .
> Professor Trelawney is a New Age flake. Professor Snape, the
> potions master, is a slime. Cornelius Fudge, the minister of
> magic, is a dithering [fool]. These people constantly boss the
> kids around. But most of the adults are knuckleheads. The
> kids disobey them and, as a result, save the day. In *Prisoner of
> Azkaban*, for example, everyone tells Harry not to leave the
> school grounds. Naturally, he immediately scampers out
> through a forbidden passage. By the end of the book we learn
> that Harry's father, one of Hogwarts's great mischief makers,
> would have been highly disappointed if his son had never
> found any of the secret passages out of the castle."[3]

Obviously, the adults in Harry Potter leave much to be desired
when it comes to showing children the benefits of mature guidance. Part of the story's attraction is how adults, especially parents, are not central to the action. They are taken out of the way
and this appeals to a child's desire to be away from adult control,
which is a natural desire.

**Harry Potter has sparked interest in reading among chil-
dren. Isn't that a positive sign? Shouldn't the books be applauded for pulling kids away from Nintendo and finally
getting them to read?**

Renowned literature expert Mem Fox—formerly associate
professor at Flinders University and a highly regarded literacy
consultant in Australia, the United States and many other
countries—has stated that reading is not inherently "good."[4]
Many educators agree with Fox. Nevertheless, the general public and media have persisted in fostering the opposite mind-set.

ABC News reporter John Stossel, for instance, on a *20/20* segment, said, "It's odd that adults are upset about a book that more
than any other has inspired kids to read." And NBC's Katie
Couric, in an hour-long special that aired on November 11, 2001,

stated that the Harry Potter books had "reintroduced [kids] to the lost art of reading."[5]

Comments like these suggest that it does not matter what children are reading as long as they are reading. But just because a child may be reading does not mean that what is being read is beneficial. Some material is not emotionally, psychologically or spiritually healthy. To think otherwise leaves a door open for children to read anything regardless of content, including violent, pornographic or racist literature.

Few persons would distribute *Playboy* to children for its humor and interesting news articles, even though quite a few adolescent boys might appreciate the gesture and be happy to "read" the magazine. The same could be said for white supremacist literature. Novelist Michael O'Brien comments,

> The basis of this question is an erroneous notion that the habit of reading is intrinsically good and valuable regardless of the reading material. While it is true that the Potter books are hooking a generation on reading, I must say that this is a superficial defense of the series. Will the 100 million young fans of Harry now turn to Tolkien and Dickens and Twain? Or will they go searching for more of the thrills Rowling has whetted their appetite for? There is a lot of corrupt literature out there, well-written material that may indeed stimulate a literary habit, as it speeds the degeneration of moral consciousness. A discerning literacy—the true literacy—is of very great importance in a child's formation. But literacy alone can never be enough. Is an appetite for reading fiction a higher value than a child's moral formation? Is any book better than no book? Would we give our children a bowl of stew in which there was a dose of poison, simply because there were also good ingredients mixed into the recipe? Of course we wouldn't.[6]

The real problem today, then, is not necessarily that kids are not reading, but rather, the substance of what they are reading.

Don't most occult experts agree that the world of wizards and spells created by Rowling is not the same as the occult-type practices?

No. There exists no documentation to support the contention that a majority of "experts" on occultism believe the wizards and spells in Rowling's novels are wholly different than actual occultism. The media has repeatedly quoted only a few so-called authorities, who, in reality, are not occult experts. The four Christian sources regularly cited as supporters of Harry Potter are: 1) Charles Colson, who is primarily a social commentator and evangelist to prisoners; 2) Alan Jacobs of Wheaton College, a literature professor; 3) Connie Neal, an author specializing in the area of family and marriage; and 4) *Christianity Today*, which is a social-cultural magazine that specializes in covering events relating to the Christian community. None of these sources are "occult experts." Numerous knowledgeable "experts" on occultism have voiced concerns about the books and continue to do so.[7]

Why is there so much concern about Harry Potter when it is obvious that a lot of kids reading the books are not suffering any psychological/spiritual problems or being drawn into occultism?

First, "a lot" of kids do not represent all kids. Just because most children may remain unaffected by Harry Potter is no reason to completely dismiss concerns that some children might indeed be drawn into witchcraft, magick, or the occult. Second, it would take many years and several surveys to measure with any exactitude a correlation between Harry Potter and youth occultism. Nevertheless, there are signs that some children are gravitating toward occultism due to the books (see chapter 7).

Who could object to Harry Potter when, unlike so many other movies and books, it does not contain any sexual innuendos, swear words, delinquent behavior or anything that's not good clean fun?

Harry Potter does contain some swearing by good characters. In Book IV, for instance, there appears the following: Mr. Weasley ("Damn"); Bill Weasley ("damn"), Ludo Bagman ("Damn them"), Snape ("I don't give a damn"), Cedric ("What the hell").[8] There also is off-color humor, for example, when the leprechauns in *Goblet of Fire* give the finger to the opposing Quidditch team. Sexual innuendos are present when Ron and Harry almost lose control over the sexy Veelas dancing erotically at a Quidditch match. These Veelas dance in such a sexually suggestive manner that they caused "wild, half-formed thoughts" to race through Harry's "dazed mind."[9]

Isn't it a bit paranoid to think that, just because some of the good characters in Harry Potter do a few bad things, children will be affected adversely?

Fantasy, no matter how imaginative it may be, teaches some form of morality—usually one that reflects the author's views. Literature, in this way, can either reinforce or alter the moral universe in a child's mind. The problem is that many children reading Harry Potter are so young (as young as six) that they still have little or no discernment about the worldview being presented to them through the books. Hence, the images and indirect lessons of the text could significantly sway their behavior in years to come.

Why? First, because children engage in seeking lessons about life from stories even more intensely than adults. Second, they do so via an indirect method: rather than pondering which traits of a character they most want to adopt, they simply decide which character in total they most want to be like. Consequently, rather than emulating just the "good" aspects of a particular character, a child will emulate that character's entire persona—good and bad traits, mannerisms, thoughts, attitudes, and behavior.

A clear delineation between good and evil, therefore, must be present for children to nurture within themselves a moral center of being. This, however, does not occur in the Harry Potter series. Rowling's fantasy presents a morally confusing world where good characters, such as Harry, Ron, Hermione, Lupin and others, consistently resort to such unethical behavior as lying, cheating, stealing and deception to further their own goals (that are supposedly "good").

Isn't Rowling just showing the human side of Harry, Ron, Hermione and others when they break rules, misbehave or do something immoral?

No. Rowling is not simply using these actions as a way of showing the humanity of her characters. She goes beyond using it as a literary device by not correcting the bad conduct and even presenting such activity as "fun" and exciting. This does not help children see a better way to live. It only reinforces how children naturally want to act. The problem is not that Rowling's good characters are imperfect. We have that in all good stories. The problem is that their imperfections are glamorized.

Rowling exalts as acceptable various forms of disobedience, misbehavior and law-breaking (by children and adults). Moreover, her so-called "good characters" rarely suffer negative consequences as a result of their bad deeds. Consequently, the overall message of Rowling's books might be paraphrased as, "Doing bad things can be really fun, especially for kids, when they can get away with it. Besides, adults do it too, and they're just fine and it's fun for them."

Aren't critics of Harry Potter overreacting just a bit, since the books, after all, are pure fiction?

No critic of Harry Potter is foolish enough to believe that it is actually true. Obviously, the bulk of it—i.e., the main characters, plot, fairy tale magic (e.g., riding brooms)—is fictional. However, into this fictional story Rowling has inserted real occult practices, history, beliefs, lore and personalities. Many children probably will not be harmed by the books. But younger children, who may not be mature enough to handle the material, may respond differently. This is the concern being voiced by critics.

THE LORD OF THE RINGS

What was Tolkien's motivation for writing The Lord of the Rings?

Tolkien said he created Middle-earth in hopes of providing England with an ancient "myth" to call its own. He loved mythology and it saddened him that England had no extensive mythology. He believed that his mythology of Middle-earth might help reveal deeper truths about life, human nature and evil. The wizardry, elves and hobbits were tools in that truth-revealing myth.

Isn't there a lot of violence and death in The Lord of the Rings, just like in Harry Potter?

Violence and death are not intrinsically bad for children to read about if such episodes in fantasy are not gratuitous in nature. Wars and battles, death and loss, are often inextricably linked to any tale that deals with human tragedy and suffering. The key to good literature is its placement in the story, its relevance to the plot and whether or not it delves too deeply into morbid details—i.e., gore for the sake of gore.

How can anyone say The Lord of the Rings is different from Harry Potter when they both deal with magic and wizards?

As previously explained (see chapter 7), the magic and wizardry found in Harry Potter and The Lord of the Rings are vastly different. Rowling's fantasy includes magick, while Tolkien's tale employs imaginative, highly stylized fairy tale magic (i.e., enchantment). Also, the wizards in Tolkien's works are in actuality physical manifestations of angelic-like beings known as Maiar, whereas the wizards/witches in Harry Potter are children and adults with whom readers can closely identify.

How can any Christian support a movie like The Lord of the Rings when it includes images of demons and evil?

The only way to show evil is to show evil. Evil can be not only ugly, but in many ways beautiful, which is a concept also illustrated in The Lord of the Rings. Showing evil is not itself evil, especially when the evil is clearly painted as such and is contrasted with the value of goodness. Tolkien's work expertly does just that. In the end it exalts many admirable qualities of the human spirit that are the strengths a person can draw upon when faced with evil. The images of evil and demonic entities in The Lord of the Rings trilogy and movies should not be rejected outright as non-Christian or unacceptable. However, with regard to the movie, parents must certainly take into consideration any images that may be too frightening for children younger than, let's say, ten years of age.

CENSORSHIP AND SCHOOLS

Isn't it a bit narrow-minded to say that just because Harry Potter books contain occultism they should not be read or discussed in public schools?

Unlike the bulk of fantasy stories read by students in public schools, Rowling's works tread well within the realm of religion because the world of Harry Potter includes so many actual forms of religious expression (i.e., occult practices). These practices are then discussed in a positive light and used as the basis for classroom activities. This violates public school policies. According to the Anti-Defamation League's "ABC's of Religion in the Curriculum," religion in public schools "must be discussed in a neutral, objective, balanced and factual manner. The curriculum's approach may not be devotional or doctrinal, nor have the effect of promoting or inhibiting religion."[10]

But some of the classroom projects and discussions now taking place in public schools because of Harry Potter do not adhere to this condition. Several of the projects are patently anti-Christian in their bias. Some of the most egregious examples are in Dr. Elizabeth Schafer's *Beacham's Sourcebooks for Teaching Young Adult Fiction: Exploring Harry Potter*. This educator's guide not only includes chapters on the history of real magick and occult practices such as alchemy, but attempts to get students to research these practices and the personalities associated with them. Consider these assignments found on Beacham's online companion resource Web site:

- "Investigate and write a paper about alchemy. When and why did humans begin to practice alchemy? What did different metals such as gold symbolize to alchemists?"

- "Look up the names mentioned on the wizard cards [in *Sorcerer's Stone*] . . . and list whether they are real or fictional. If they are historical figures, write a paragraph about each magician, witch or wizard."

- "Learn about the role of witchcraft [i.e., real witchcraft] in different cultures. Either make a costume for yourself . . . or use construction paper to design the attire of witches in a specific geographic location."

- "[W]rite a poem, short play, literary non-fiction, or other form of expression about magic or witchcraft."[11]

One can only wonder how many public schools in America would permit Schafer's projects if they were to be Christianized as follows:

- "Investigate and write a paper about Christian prayer. When and why did people begin to pray to Jesus?"

- "Look up the names mentioned on Foxe's Book of Martyrs. . . . Write a paragraph about each apostle, Christian or church leader."

- "Learn about the role of Christianity in different cultures. Either make a costume for yourself . . . or use construction paper to design the attire of Christians in a specific geographic location."

- "[W]rite a poem, short play, literary non-fiction, or other form of expression about Jesus Christ or Christianity."

Such activities probably would elicit strong protests from organizations such as American Atheists and the American Civil Liberties Union. But because occultism/paganism has become the fashionable religion of our era, Rowling's Harry Potter series and the educational lessons based on it continue to go largely unchallenged.

Other projects from this resource encourage children to research anti-Christian books that include misleading and inaccurate information about Christianity, such as *The Power of Myth* by Joseph Campbell, who referred to Judeo-Christian worship as "monkey-holiness."[12] Schafer's book clearly reflects a number of ideas compatible with Campbell's adaptation of Carl Jung's theories on "collective unconscious" and "archetypes."[13]

Schafer, like Campbell, suggests that Genesis is a "primitive" myth which, when viewed by researchers, conflicts "with the logic of reason and history."[14] She also suggests that the entire Bible—its "demons and sorcerers, unexplained wonders, and brutal tortures and murders"—are merely "archetypal experiences." In other words, Scripture is little more than a group of mythological stories that reflect or symbolize various truths (e.g., good, evil, suffering) embedded in society's collective unconscious. Schafer even implies that belief in an "invisible" God is similar to children who "often see things that aren't real."[15]

Additionally, Schafer poses extremely biased (i.e., pro-occult and anti-Christian) discussion questions pertaining to occultism in general, the controversies surrounding occultism, its relation to Harry Potter and other debates concerning religion. Some of these questions, comments and projects actually seem to be an attempt to influence public school policy and children's opinions in favor of occultism. Still others are plainly anti-Christian, such as

the ones that compare today's conservative Christians to perpe-
trators of the murderous witch hunts that took place in the fif-
teenth to seventeenth centuries. Consider the following examples
of both types of material:

- "Write a paper about how efforts to ban the Harry Potter novels because of their themes of evil, sorcery, or witchcraft, and
  to forbid children from wearing witch and devil costumes, resemble historic witch hunts."
- "Has your school or community ruled that children cannot
  wear witch or devil costumes at Halloween? . . . Write a letter
  to the editor of your school or local newspaper expressing
  your opinion about this."[16]

Schafer boldly offers questions and projects that clearly delve
into an area that should be off-limits in public schools: religiously based concepts of morality and ethics. Some of these
questions bring the Bible and methods of biblical interpretations into classroom discussions, even though there is no guar-
antee that any teacher leading the discussions will be qualified
to deal with these issues with accuracy and objectivity:

- "Some parents have complained about Harry Potter novels on
  religious grounds. Explain how you think the novels do or do
  not parallel evil, violence, and miracles in the Bible."
- "Compare a Harry Potter character to a biblical character."
- "Can lies ever be created to achieve good goals or are they told
  for solely malicious intentions?"[17]

It must be admitted that simply reading the Harry Potter
novels in a classroom setting might encourage a student to pursue activities like astrology, numerology and spellcasting,
which are religious practices performed by pagans/witches and
other occultists. Would the school systems allow a well-written
book to be read in classrooms and used for school projects if it
featured a Christian orphan, who defeats an evil foe through

Christian prayer and various miracles that occur by the hand of an intervening Son of God named Jesus Christ? Of course not.

Isn't restricting access to books children want to read a violation of their First Amendment rights?

No. To believe that restricting children's access to certain books is some kind of constitutional violation is not only illogical, but legally inaccurate. First, children already are restricted from reading and purchasing materials that state and local governments have ruled as obscene, adult and/or inappropriate for children. Second, children also are prevented from engaging in activities many adults are allowed by virtue of age and maturity: voting, smoking, drinking, driving, etc.

Isn't it possible that keeping children from reading Harry Potter in schools is just going to help produce an illiterate society?

It does not logically follow that widespread illiteracy among our nation's youth will be the end result of not allowing children to read one book amid the thousands of volumes unanimously viewed as appropriate for children. The reading problem in our society is far more complex than whether or not children like to read what is available. Plenty of excellent literature is available.

OCCULTISM

Aren't Christians really saying that the only good books are books written by other Christians whose works uphold Christian teachings and have a God mentioned in them?

No. A book's merits cannot be judged exclusively on one's personal beliefs, motivation for writing or whether the work mentions God. Good intentions sometimes produce anti-Christian results and intentions not necessarily "Christian" can sometimes produce Christian-like results (Genesis 50:20). For example, Stephen King's book *Desperation* actually has a great deal of Christian teaching in it and is quite favorable toward Christianity. It also shows the beauty of one's personal relationship to God and the power of Christian prayer over evil.

How can a fairy tale or a fantasy—images that are not real—convey any harmful messages?

Some images convey good messages, while other images convey harmful messages. For example, in Aesop's fable "The Hare and the Tortoise," the image of that slow and steady turtle conveys a good message centering around the value of patient and consistent work. Obviously, the race between the turtle and the rabbit never took place. Nevertheless, the moral to the story is learned.

Other images, however, convey different messages. This is especially known to advertisers. Consider the Camel cigarettes' cartoon figure of Joe Cool, the camel. So many adults objected to the particular message being conveyed by Joe smoking a cigarette that the image was banned from magazine ads and billboards.

Aren't children able to tell the difference between fantasy and reality well enough to know that books like Harry Potter are not true?

Whether or not children know that Harry Potter is not a true story is completely irrelevant to the issues at hand. Children being entertained by fantasy or reality, on TV or in a book, tend to copy what they enjoy (see chapter 7). Additionally, very young children do have a difficult time separating fact from fiction. As Rowling herself stated in a *Newsweek* article,

> I get letters from children addressed to Professor Dumble-
> dore, and it's not a joke, begging to be let into Hogwarts, and
> some of them are really sad. Because they want it to be true so
> badly they've convinced themselves it's true.[18]

Bernice Cullinan, former president of the International Reading Association, has observed that children have no problem with fantasy as long as they can tell what is real and what is make-believe. This ability is well-formed by the second grade. "But those six years old and younger will certainly have more trouble making such a distinction."[19] Best-selling author Michael O'Brien makes several observations on this issue in relation to Harry Potter:

> It is important to note that children read fiction with a different consciousness than adults. This is something that has been overlooked by those Christian leaders who have written pro-Potter commentaries. They forget that children are in a state of formation, that their understanding of reality is being forged at every turn.[20]

The important point O'Brien is making is that books like the Harry Potter series definitely convey certain messages that children may not be equipped to properly dissect. Regardless of their maturity level, a child will not see, read, enjoy or reflect on a piece of literature the way an adult would do so. This is a critical fact that many people seem to be forgetting when it comes to determining the potential influence of Harry Potter.

Shouldn't children just be allowed to make their own decisions about what they want to read?

Not completely. With regard to certain kinds of literature, sometimes it is just not possible for children to decide for themselves what is best. Being a parent means guiding, leading, teaching, and sometimes—at least until a child is closer to adulthood—making decisions about what is best for a child, even concerning reading material. Children are notorious for choosing bad things for themselves. Recently, for example, it was found that teen smoking and drug use have not decreased significantly, even though TV ads and commercials about the dangers of cigarettes/drugs have been airing for several years.

CHRISTIANITY AND SCRIPTURE

Where does it say in the Bible that witchcraft is wrong?

Deuteronomy 18:10-12 is the classic Old Testament passage wherein many occult practices are condemned. They include divination, astrology, witchcraft, charms, spells, wizardry and necromancy (communication with spirits of the dead). Other Old Testament passages contain similar condemnations (2 Kings 17:17; Leviticus 19:26; Joshua 13:22; 2 Chronicles 33:6; Isaiah 44:25, 47:13-15; Jeremiah 27:9, 29:8; Ezekiel 13:9, 23; 22:28; Zechariah 10:2).

"Magick" also is prohibited by both the Old and New Testaments, often through the use of different words. One such term, *kashap*, can be found in Exodus 7:11 as well as in Deuteronomy 18:10, Daniel 2:2 and Malachi 3:5. It means to practice magick or sorcery, to use witchcraft or to enchant. It is the feminine form of *kashap* that appears in Exodus 22:18, the well-known verse in which God tells Israel that the penalty for being a witch is execution. Obviously, practicing magick/sorcery/witchcraft must be an extremely profane activity to the Judeo-Christian God (cf. 2 Chronicles 33:6).

Keshep, which is the corresponding noun form of the verb *kashap*, is another general term used for magick. It means magick or magical arts, sorcery or sorceries, soothsayer, spell or witchcraft. It is sternly condemned in several biblical passages (i.e., 2 Kings 9:22; Isaiah 47:9, 12; Micah 5:12). Consider the intense displeasure of *"keshep"* that is especially apparent throughout the condemnation of Ninevah in Nahum 3:4-7:

> Because of the multitude of the whoredoms of the well-favoured harlot, the mistress of witchcrafts [*keshep*], that selleth nations through her whoredoms, and families through her witchcrafts [*keshep*]. Behold I am against thee. . . . I will show the nations thy nakedness, and the kingdoms thy shame. And I will cast abominable

filth upon thee, and make thee vile, and will set thee as a gazingstock [i.e., a spectacle]. . . . And it shall come to pass, that all they that look upon thee shall flee from thee, and say, Nineveh is laid waste. (KJV)

There is an equally strong emphasis against magick in the New Testament. Acts 8:9-24 speaks of Simon the sorcerer/magician who astonished the people of Samaria through his magickal arts. Although he pretended to be a convert to Christianity, the biblical account of Simon the sorcerer ends with him offering the apostles money for the secret of their power and Peter rebuking him for still living bound in his sins (8:23). There also is Acts 19:19, which describes how Ephesian converts to Christianity gathered together and burned all of their books relating to magick.

Another relevant passage is Galatians 5:20, which puts magick/witchcraft alongside hatred, strife, and murder. Similarly, there are Revelation 9:20-21 and 18:23, both of which describe magick/sorcery as harmful behavior. Clearly, the art of magick—i.e., seeking to bring about change in accordance with one's own will through various ceremonies, rites, rituals, spells, witchcraft or charms—is resoundingly condemned by the Bible.

Isn't it true that the word for "witch" in the Bible is "poisoner" of the body or mind, which would mean that the Bible is not condemning real witchcraft as people know it today?

In order to dismiss Christian concerns about witchcraft, Wiccans and other occultists (as well as the media) have often repeated an extremely popular piece of misinformation. It involves the word "witch." According to their argument, the word translated as "witch" in Exodus 22:18 ("Thou shalt not suffer a witch to live," KJV) actually should be translated "poisoner" (either of the body or mind). Wiccans agree that it is understandable why the Israelites would not want poisoners among them, but since witches are not poisoners, then the Bible really does not condemn witches.

Well-known witch Doreen Valiente, for instance, regarding
Exodus 22:18, stated in her book *An ABC of Witchcraft* that the
text does not "refer to witchcraft at all." She added: "The word
translated as 'witch' is the Hebrew *chasaph*, which means a poisoner. In the Latin version of the Bible called the Septuagint,
this word is given as *veneficus*, which also means a poisoner."[21]

Such an assertion, however, is a prime example of how people
can make utterly false statements, yet have them widely repeated
and believed. First, Valiente actually misspelled the Hebrew word
translated as "witch." It is *kashap* or *kashaph*, not *chasaph*.

Second, *kashap* does not mean "poisoner." According to *The
New International Dictionary of the Bible*, the word means "to
practice sorcery."[22] This is confirmed by countless language
dictionaries and encyclopedias including, but not limited to,
*The New Brown-Driver-Briggs-Gesenius Hebrew and English
Lexicon* and *The International Standard Bible Encyclopedia*.[23]

Third, contrary to Valiente, the Latin version of the Bible is not
the Septuagint. The Septuagint is the Greek translation of only the
Old Testament. And the Greek word used in it for "witch" in Exodus 18:22 is *pharmakos*, not *veneficus* (i.e., a Latin word).

Fourth, the Latin version of the Bible known as the Latin
Vulgate (transl. by Jerome, c. 383-405 A.D.) does not use the
word *veneficus*, either, but the word *maleficus*, which means a
practitioner of magick/sorcery.

A witch, then, biblically speaking, is anyone who practices occultism in any one of a variety of forms that include: divination,
magick, astrology, sorcery, and spiritism. Modern-day Wiccans,
as well as most neopagans, practice such arts. Therefore, their belief system and rituals would indeed be condemned by the Bible.

The rumor that states a "witch" (as condemned in the Bible) is
nothing but a "poisoner" may have come from a misunderstand-
ing of the origins of the modern word "pharmacy." It derives from
the Greek word *pharmakon*, which has a meaning linked not only
to the idea of a drug or poison, but also to the concepts of magic

or charm. These root meanings stem from the fact that "witches" have traditionally been associated with herbs and potions (which if used improperly might have been poisonous).

But such an association does not mean that the word "witch," as defined in the Bible (either Hebrew or Greek versions), exclusively means a "poisoner." It seems that at some point a supporter of witchcraft erroneously assumed that since the Greek word *pharmakon* is linked to poison, then the Greek word *pharmakos* (as found in the Septuagint) must mean a "witch" is a poisoner. This simplistic view of word usages and language, however, completely misses the accurate meaning of the word "witch" and the various contexts in which it is used.

If a few books about wizards and broomsticks are going to prompt a kid to get into occultism, doesn't that indicate that several other variables are at work in the equation somewhere?

Many former occultists have readily admitted that they first became involved with occultism via curiosity that started after reading a book, watching a movie or seeing a TV program on occultism. That is all it took for them to begin their journey into the occult world.

A 1997 Purdue University study has explained a possible reason for such an experience. It found that "exposure to paranormal phenomena on television affected belief in such things as unidentified flying objects, ghosts, devils and extrasensory perception."[24] Particularly susceptible to these media influences are those persons who have no prior personal experiences with the paranormal (e.g., children).

In other words, a child does not necessarily have to possess a vulnerability or propensity toward occultism. Curiosity about occultism can be inspired in any child at virtually any time in during their developmental years. This is one reason why parents must be aware of their children's activities and how they might respond to occult-glamorizing entertainment.

Is it even possible for a child to convert to Witchcraft?

In April 1974, the Council of American Witches adopted a set of principles of Wiccan Belief. One principle read: "We acknowledge a depth of power far greater than that apparent to the average person. Because it is far greater than ordinary, it is sometimes called supernatural. But we see it as lying within that which is naturally potential to all."[25] Another principle declared: "This same creative power lies in all people."[26]

Everyone, then, according to witches, has the potential to be a witch—even children. All they need to do is embrace the principles of Wicca and tap into their magical powers within. This is why witches today are actively seeking to convert children (contrary to their claims) via witchcraft books that target teens and children. Noteworthy is the fact that some of these same books are now capitalizing on the popularity of Harry Potter and its brand of witchcraft as a sort of lure for children (see chapter 7).

Interestingly, any child can convert to Witchcraft without his or her parents even knowing it. Wicca is a religion that can easily be practiced in secret with little paraphernalia or outward show of conversion. It can be a fairly solitary religion, or a belief system that is practiced with others. This is one reason why so many teenagers, especially girls, are now turning to Wicca. A significant number may already be practitioners without their parents' consent or knowledge.

Why are Christians still upset over Harry Potter when so many Christian leaders have said the books are just fine?

Novelist Michael O'Brien answered this question very well in a recent interview, saying:

> I'm surprised by the promotion of the Potter series in certain Christian circles, even among some Catholic academics. Perhaps this is due to their naïveté about the power of fantasy. Possibly it's an over-reliance on individual reason, as if to say, "I am so intelligent, and my child is so intelligent, that we can

enjoy the irrational and the corrupt without being affected by it, and therefore it's not really corrupt."

This non sequitur is based on the mistaken belief that the imagination can be safely contained within an airtight compartment of the mind. I'm guessing here, but I suspect there is also a certain fear at work in their adamant and not always objective reaction to criticism of the Potter series. Is their overreaction caused by a fear of anti-intellectualism? A fear of "fundamentalism"? Perhaps even a fear of loss of credibility among other academics? I'm not certain.

At the very least it indicates a lack of understanding about the integral relationship between faith and culture, between imagination and the world of action. Consistently, the pro-Potter advocates extract details from the books that point to some kind of "morality" in the series, actually more a set of "values"—to use the modern term—than genuine morality. Their approach is, I think, rather revealing. Any serious scholar should know that empirical "evidence" for any theory can be found by dipping selectively into a large body of source material, and that this can be highly misleading.

When a scholar operates from an *a priori* need to find supportive data for his gut attraction, truth gets lost in the process. And this is the crux of the problem for all of us: Regardless of whether we are impelled by a gut attraction or a gut repulsion to the world of Harry Potter, we must ask ourselves if we are thinking according to principles, or are we articulating impressively as we let ourselves be driven by feelings.[27]

How can any Christian object to the violence and death in Harry Potter when the Bible is filled with all kinds of violence, adultery, evil and descriptions of horrible wars?

Drawing an analogy between Harry Potter and the Bible is terribly flawed in many ways. Moreover, such an analogy is

symptomatic of the kind of anti-Christian rhetoric filling newspaper stories and other media reports.

First, the Bible is not intended to be read as entertainment by
children, nor is it meant to be a tool for stimulating their imagination. In other words, the violence is not presented "for fun" or
amusement.

Second, the literature category of Harry Potter is fantasy/fic-
tion, whereas the Bible is historical narrative. The Bible tells the
story of the ancient nation of Israel (Old Testament) and the life
of Jesus of Nazareth (New Testament). It is absurd to compare
the Harry Potter series and the Bible. It would be like comparing
the Harry Potter movie to a PBS or History Channel documen-
tary on the Nazi Holocaust.

Third, the Bible does not seem to contain any references to violence that are in any way gratuitous. Harry Potter, on the other
hand, excels at presenting episodes designed to startle the senses
by virtue of their gore. For example, Rowling has her characters
pulling up Mandrake babies that scream and cry until they are cut
up for stew (Book II, pp. 92-94). And then there are Fred and
George Weasley who set off a "Filibuster firework" in the mouth
of a salamander (Book II, 130-131). Kids really don't need to get
used to the idea that this kind of stuff is funny.

Aren't Christians the last people who should be complain-ing about anything since they are the ones who are actually hurting society with their narrow-minded bigotry?

This question raises a common attack unfairly made against all
Christians of all varieties. There may indeed be some individuals
who call themselves Christians and exhibit a lack of sophistication
about certain issues. However, labeling all Christians as narrow-
minded bigots seems more of an attack against the Christian religion than against any arguments against Harry Potter. Persons
who would ask this question commonly ignore some very beneficial aspects of the Christian faith:

- Christian shelters for the homeless;
- Christian foster parents who open their homes to abused children;
- Christian-built orphanages in third-world countries;
- Christian hospitals;
- Christian-owned and operated food centers for the poor throughout our inner cities;
- Christian organizations like Samaritan's Purse that send relief aid and supplies to war-torn and disaster-stricken regions in the world;
- Christian crisis pregnancy centers such as CareNet.

Interestingly, no one seems to be asking a number of other questions that would be politically incorrect: e.g., How many hospitals or homeless shelters have Wiccans built in the world? How often do covens go to the inner city to feed the poor? How much money have Wiccans given as a group to help the hungry and poverty-stricken across the globe? How many orphanages have Wiccans built?

Charles Perrault (above) was the first to publish a book of fairy tales (1697) that included some of today's most well-known stories: e.g., "Little Red Riding Hood" and "Sleeping Beauty." Below are pictured brothers Jacob Grimm (1785-1863) and Wilhelm Grimm (1786-1859), who collected fairy tales told by country folk. Their publication in 1812-15 included "Snow White" and "Hansel and Gretel."

An 1804 engraving from *Tabart's Popular Stories* shows the adult nature of some versions of classic fairy tales: "Taking a sharp knife he ripped open his own belly."

An indication of how far back fairy tales date in history can be found in these two printed versions of the famous story of Tom Thumb. The title page from the earliest existing English text of *The History of Tom Thumbe* (left) is from 1621. Another title page from *Tom Thumbe, His Life and Death* (right) is from 1630. It shows Tom riding King Arthur's horse. This latter version was published in metrical verse.

These covers from four of R.L. Stine's Fear Street books for teens and pre-teens show a disturbing consistency of plot: the brutal victimization of young women. As of 2002, Stine's volumes had sold more than 100 million copies.

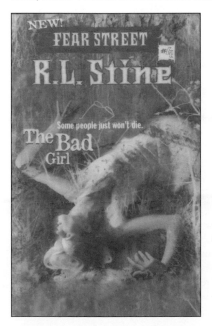

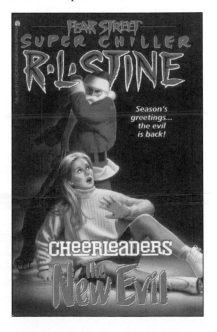

The covers from two of R.L. Stines' Goosebumps books (produced by Scholastic, the publisher of the Harry Potter series) show the frightening nature of these volumes, even though they are marketed to children as young as seven and eight years old. Interestingly, to frighten young minds, Stine often resorts to taking familiar or safe objects/characters—e.g., parents, friends, toys (left), or household pets (right)—and then turns them either into monsters or murderous stalkers.

This cover is from a compilation of ten R.L. Stine horror stories. It is advertised for children ages nine to twelve. Its contents include "Make Me a Witch," "The Dead Body," "Afraid of Clowns," "Nightmare Inn" and "The Most Evil Sorcerer," which is introduced as being about "a world of sorcerers and evil magic." Photos and illustrations on the inside include: a woman carrying a bloody and dismembered foot, a decomposing body and sadistic sharp-toothed clowns abducting a small boy.

J.R.R. Tolkien (left) in his study only a few months before his death in 1973. He ben-
efitted greatly during his childhood by having Roman Catholic priest, Francis
Morgan (right), as a father figure. Morgan became the legal guardian of both J.R.R.
and his brother, Hilary, when their mother died in 1904. Tolkien was twelve years old
at that time. (J.R.R. Tolkien, courtesy of Douglas Gilbert; Father Francis Morgan,
courtesy of the Fathers of the Birmingham Oratory.)

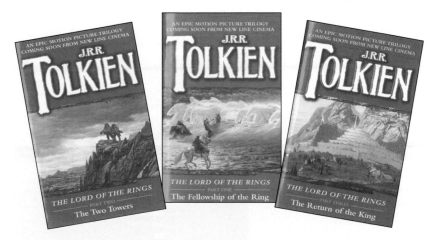

Cover designs and illustrations on more recent editions of Tolkien's The Lord of the
Rings trilogy—perhaps the greatest fantasy series ever written.

Two screen shots from the Web site featuring the T*Witches series of books by Scholastic, publisher of the Harry Potter series. The T*Witches books, advertised for children ages nine to twelve, follow the adventures of twin teenage witches. This Scholastic Web site includes pages containing spells children can use and discussions about "magick," which is spelled with a "k" (both images). The Web site even gives magick "tips," one such tip being how to use animal "energy" to boost the efficacy of spells. This is a classic occult teaching that fans of T*Witch and Harry Potter may learn through Scholastic Publishing. Notice the title of the Web page is "Kids Fun Online."

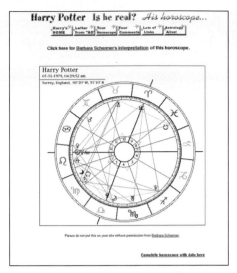

Harry Potter's horoscope, according to professional astrologer Barbara Schermer, who makes this chart available to child fans of Rowling's books. Links to Schermer's astrologyalive.com Web site are on many different Harry Potter fan Web sites regularly visited by children. Schermer also offers kids their own horoscope readings and recommends occult literature to them through links on her Web site. This is only one of the numerous ways children are being introduced to real occultism and encouraged to partake in it through the Harry Potter books.

This step-by-step guide to practicing Wicca by well-known witch Sirona Knight specifically targets teenagers and pre-teens. To attract young buyers, one advertisement on a Wiccan/Neopagan Web site reads, "A complete guide to doing the magic in Harry Potter using modern Wiccan Techniques." The volume's back cover states, "For anyone who has ever wanted to be a Witch or a Wizard and to make real magic." Knight herself writes in its introduction, "[W]ith the unparalleled popularity of the Harry Potter books by J.K. Rowling, a whole new generation—young and old—are adventuring into the magical world of witches and wizards. . . . Transforming what seems like fiction into nonfiction can look like a difficult task, but it isn't."

This animated graphic awaits children visiting the Discovery Channel's Web site in 2002 (http://dsc.discovery.com/convergence/realmagick/realmagick.html). The Web site highlights the various topics covered in the channel's TV special *Real Magick: The Science of Wizardry*. Notice that the title word magick is spelled with a "k," thereby placing the subjects discussed in the program well within the realm of real occultism. This Web site is linked with a Harry Potter fan Web site for children at Yahoo.com.

Image captured from: http://dsc.discovery.com/convergence/realmagick/interactive/interactive.html

Children can access the "Wizard's Lair" Web page (pictured above) and "The Sorcerer's Guide" Web page from the Discovery Channel's *Real Magick: The Science of Wizardry* Web site. Visitors to both Web pages can learn answers to a series of questions about magick and/or click on any object pictured and learn more about that object's use in the real world of magick, Wicca and occultism. Various statements given by the game/exercise include: (1) "The wizards may have believed the rods were moved by spirits" (the divination rods); (2) "Through your drum-induced trance you can enter an alternate reality" (the drum); (3) "I will focus your energy" (the wand); (4) "Mandrake root allowed wizards to 'fly.' It would be prepared as an ointment and put on the skin to seep into the bloodstream" (roots placed on book).

WHAT'S SO BAD
ABOUT OCCULTISM?

The title of this section remains a common question. One's perspective determines the answer. Christians, of course, view occultism as problematic because it clearly is prohibited by the Bible (Exodus 7:11, 22:18; Leviticus 19:26; Deuteronomy 18:10-12; Joshua 13:22; 1 Samuel 15:23; 2 Kings 17:17; 2 Chronicles 33:6; Isaiah 44:25; 47:13-15; Jeremiah 27:9; 29:8; Ezekiel 13:9, 23; 22:28; Zechariah 10:2; Acts 16:16-18; and many other places).

This fact, however, understandably means very little to persons who do not happen to be Christian or who do not believe in the reliability of Scripture (e.g., skeptics, atheists, agnostics, occultists, people of other faiths). Regardless of whether or not a person is Christian has no bearing on the fact that there exists a variety of *nonreligious* reasons to avoid occultism, especially when it comes to youth involvement.

First, occult practices are notorious for not working. Consequently, they may be little more than a waste of time, energy and money. Divination, psychic readings (including telephone hotlines), ESP and occult prophecies are extremely unreliable methods of obtaining accurate information about the world, ourselves, others and the future.

Consider famed psychic Gordon-Michael Scallion, who claims to average nearly eighty-nine percent accuracy with his predictions.[1] But out of sixty-six predictions made for 1995, only a few came to pass, and all of those were so vague and so in line with existing trends that it would have been difficult for them not to come true (e.g., UFO sightings will increase, herb sales will soar, media programming on metaphysics and the world of the spirit will expand).[2]

The renowned psychic Edgar Cayce (a.k.a. the Sleeping Prophet) has an equally dismal record. His failed predictions include: the complete geographical annihilation of Japan, America and the Arctic sometime between 1958-1998; the destruction within "one generation" of 1941 of New York City, Los Angeles and San Francisco; the appearance of the mythical continent of Atlantis by 1968-1969; and worldwide devastation via a "pole shift" in the year 2001.[3]

Astrologers have not fared any better at predicting the future. Consider the results from the following studies that have been done on this form of divination:

- A 1979 advertisement in *Ici Paris* offered a free horoscope reading, and those who responded were asked to judge how accurate they and their friends found it to be. Of the first 150 replies, ninety-four percent said it was accurate, along with ninety percent of their friends and family. It was later revealed that the respondents all received the same horoscope reading—that of a notorious mass murderer.

- In 1982, the Australian Skeptics organization compared the horoscopes from thirteen different newspapers for the same week and found that they gave a wide variety of *differing* predictions for the *same* astrological sign. After rating the predictions for such topics as health, luck, relationships and finance, the researchers concluded that "most signs had a fairly even spread so, for instance, you could find one paper telling you it would be a lucky week and another saying the opposite."

- In 1989, in response to a $100,000 TV challenge to any psychic or astrologer who could prove the truth of his claims, an astrologer cast the charts of twelve people after being given their birth information. Then he interviewed the twelve and attempted to match them to their horoscopes. He did not get a single one right.

- In 1994, six astrologers and psychics were challenged by the Melbourne *Sunday Age* to predict the winner of the Melbourne Cup. Not one of them came close.[4]

Second, many occult practices involve entering an altered state of consciousness (ASC) wherein one's normal everyday awareness (or consciousness) is replaced by an alternate (or altered) awareness. An ASC is induced when anything interrupts or brings to a halt "the normal patterns of conceptual thought without extinguishing or diminishing consciousness itself."[5] A hypnotic trance, for example, is an ASC. This is problematic because, during an ASC, persons cannot separate fact from fiction. They function under a confused sense of reality.

Third, teen and young adult occult involvement *sometimes* is accompanied by violent and/or criminal behavior.[6] In fact, occult involvement has been identified as one of the early warning signs of potential violence in a child. This, according to many nationally recognized authorities on the subject, including Dr. Reid Kimbrough, psychologist and executive director of The Justice Group. His credentials are impressive:

- 20-year veteran police officer;
- Master of arts degree in psychology/professional psychology;
- Doctorate in behavioral science, with emphasis in psychology;
- Consultant to the U.S. Department of Justice;
- Behavioral scientist,
- Police psychologist; and
- Member of the adjunct faculty of the Tennessee Law Enforcement Training Academy.[7]

Since 1997, Kimbrough has been conducting seminars nationwide for law enforcement personnel and educators con-

cerned about youth and school violence. His "Children at High
Risk for Violent Behavior" course includes material that explains occultism's link to youth violence. Warning signs may include: 1) a student listening to music which has death or suicide
in its lyrics; 2) possessing paraphernalia such as skulls, black
candles or a satanic bible; 3) preoccupation with a Ouija board
or tarot cards, drawing satanic symbols on themselves or property; and 4) wearing black clothing.[8]

These assertions, far from being reactionary or sensationalistic,
are a balanced assessment of how youths respond to various types
of stimuli that they receive at a critical time in their emotional and
psychological development. Others see the correlation as well.
For example, a link between juvenile violence and occultism has
been detailed in *Chasing Shadows: Confronting Juvenile Violence
in America* by Gordon A. Crews, Ph.D. (associate professor and
head of the criminal justice department, Jacksonville State University) and Reid H. Montgomery, Jr. (associate professor, College of Criminal Justice, University of South Carolina).[9]

Norvin Richard, professor of philosophy at the University of
Alabama, agrees. He believes youths who gravitate toward occultism could be looking for a value system that opposes the values of
previous generations. "I think one could say those who dabble in
the occult have lost faith in ordinary senses of good and evil," he
stated. "They've lost faith in the principles and the sources of
those principles that are more conventional and they're looking
for direction elsewhere."[10]

TODAY'S
"CHRISTIAN" WITCHES

S ince the early 1990s a movement spearheaded by Wiccans and assorted neopagans has been quietly gaining momentum within the Christian community. Zealous purveyors of goddess worship have been ever so steadily infiltrating mainstream Protestant denominations as well as the Roman Catholic Church. Their numbers, interestingly, have not been limited to lay members of congregations. Some witches and neopagans are now senior pastors of large denominational flocks. It is an event unprecedented in the history of Christendom. This section of *Fantasy and Your Family* takes a brief look at some of the most visible representatives of the new movement and their efforts to literally paganize Christianity in the twenty-first century.

CATHOLIC WITCHES

In *Catholics and the New Age* Father Mitch Pacwa reveals some surprising information regarding the infiltration of witchcraft and occultism into American Catholicism:

- A well-known Catholic women's college not only offers workshops in Wicca and the goddess within, but prints astrology columns in its school newspaper.
- A Chicago parish hosts a professional astrologer to lecture on the stars and inform parishioners where they can go for further astrological consultations.

- A Franciscan convent offers "enlightenment" classes that include Wicca (witchcraft), I Ching (Chinese fortune-telling) and Oriental meditation. The nuns staff "The Christine Center for Meditation," teaching yoga, astrology and tarot card readings.[1]

During an interview with *Insight*, Pacwa—a professor at the University of Dallas—explained the contrariness of such activities with Catholicism, saying: "The Catholic Catechism forbids divination, sorcery and magic as a mortal sin against the first commandment—and that includes Wicca."[2] The Catechism of the Catholic Church makes it clear that the occult is not morally neutral. All aspects of it, including neopaganism and Wicca, are to be strictly avoided.[3]

Despite the anti-occult tenets of Catholicism, an increasing number of Catholic educators, priests, nuns, scholars and lay leaders are endorsing occult practices, neopaganism and witchcraft. In fact, it was reported in May 2002 that Vivienne Crowley—an internationally-known Wiccan initiated into both the Alexandrian and Gardnerian traditions of witchcraft—had been offered a teaching position at a Jesuit college in North London.[4]

Two examples of prominent Catholic witches would be feminists Mary Hunt and Diann Neu—codirectors of W.A.T.E.R. (Women's Alliance for Theology, Ethics and Ritual). The penetration of Roman Catholicism by Wicca is so crucial to them that they have begun publishing a newsletter: *Waterwheel*. The front-page editorial of one recent issue reads,

> [Renowned witch] Starhawk gets it right in her new introduction to the twentieth anniversary edition of *The Spiral Dance*, the book that launched Goddess religion into the contemporary mainstream. How do I learn this . . . how do I pass this on?[5]

In the center of this same newsletter appeared a liturgy for All Saint's Day, honoring the gracious mother goddess, Wisdom (i.e.,

Sophia), written by Diann Neu. She states: "This liturgy is a resource for others to use on their own or in their denomination."
In 1999, Hunt explained that although W.A.T.E.R is not officially
affiliated with the Catholic church, she and other like-minded believers are definitely seeking "to influence it however and receive
funding from some Catholic bishops."[6]

PROTESTANT WITCHES

Like the Catholic church, several Protestant denominations
have faced an infiltration of occultism. Heretical concepts based
on occultism, neopaganism and Wicca, in fact, now circulate
freely throughout many Protestant congregations. These beliefs
usually relate in some way to radical feminist theology, the proponents of which are actively seeking to replace God the Father and
Jesus with images of "the goddess" worshiped by neopagans.[7]

For example, a 1990 event sponsored by the Perkins School of
Theology at Southern Methodist University took place at the
Highland Park United Methodist Church in Dallas. This
"Women's Week" conference featured Linda Finnell, a Wiccan,
who spoke on the subject of "Returning to the Goddess Through
Dianic Witchcraft."[8] During the event, which promoted tarot
cards, channeling energy and communication with spirit guides,
Finnell actually built an altar to the goddess Diana.[9]

The year 1994 saw the publication *Wellsprings: A Journal for
United Methodist Clergywomen* by the Division of Ordained Ministry, General Board of Higher Education and Ministry of the
United Methodist Church. It included two articles: "A Croning
Ritual" and "Reflections from a New Crone."[10] The first article
was written by Rev. Nancy Webb, minister of Christian education
at Foundry United Methodist Church (Washington, D.C.), attended by former President Clinton. The second was penned by
Rev. Mary Kraus of Dumbarton United Methodist Church in
Georgetown. Both stories highlighted the Wiccan "croning ritual," a rite of passage ceremony that marks a witch's fiftieth birth-

day. The celebration relates to the worship of the Wiccan goddess, whom witches see existing in three stages: maiden, representing sexual ripeness; mother, representing birth; and crone, representing old age.[11]

When Connie Alt, a former Methodist clergywoman, telephoned Foundry Methodist Church to voice concerns about the article, author Nancy Webb informed Alt that she found Northern European practices of Wicca very helpful. Webb then recommended Alt read *The Spiral Dance*, by Wiccan high priestess Starhawk.[12] As of May 2002, Webb was still serving at the church as "minister of Christian education" and Mary Kraus was still senior pastor of Dumbarton United Methodist Church.[13]

Another UMC pastor, Susan Cady (Emmanuel United Methodist Church, Philadelphia), has gone so far as to write two books advocating Wiccan beliefs: *Sophia: the Future of Feminist Spirituality* and *Wisdom Feast*. In the *SCP Journal* article titled "Goddess Worship," Tal Brooke and Russ Wise explain that Cady's first book says "Sophia is a female, goddesslike figure appearing clearly in the Scriptures of the Hebrew tradition."[14] In her second book, Cady declares "Sophia as a separate goddess, with Jesus as her prophet, hence replacing Jesus with the feminine deity Sophia."[15]

Witchcraft has been accepted not only in many United Methodist churches, but also in some Presbyterian Church (PCUSA) congregations. At the PCUSA-owned Ghost Ranch retreat center in New Mexico, for instance, a 1998 retreat invited women to

> celebrate the sacred feminine goddess in the land of enchantment with art, movement, ritual and song. Honor the goddess within each woman. . . . Create art with your symbolic Goddess language. . . . Dance at the temple of the Living Goddess. Connect us with a sacred circle with very special women for mutual transformation. Share the Magic![16]

And then there is self-professed "butch-lesbian" Mary Daly, the highly visible Boston College tenured professor, who has become widely known as one of the most radical feminist witches in America.[17] She is active in both Protestant *and* Catholic circles. Daly adamantly has declared on more than one occasion a rather controversial goal, saying: "I propose that Christianity itself should be castrated."[18] She has gained a sizable following from the ranks of many different churches, and is spearheading a campaign to turn Christianity into nothing less than a neopagan, goddess-worshiping religion.

The theological views held by these so-called Christian witches were perhaps best illustrated at the October 1999 "Jesus: A Feminist, Womanist Perspective" conference at Kanuga, a retreat center affiliated with the Episcopal church. The order of service proceeded around Psalm 121, which had been rewritten to Godde, the Lady and Mother. The song performed by conference coordinator Rosemary Crow was titled "You Can Be a Heretic Too."[19] Speakers included Carter Heyward (a professor at Episcopal Divinity School in Cambridge, Massachusetts) and Delores Williams (professor at Union Theological Seminary).

RE-IMAGINING GOD

Mary Daly, Nancy Webb, Mary Kraus and Susan Cady are only some of the many like-minded witches seeking to raise a church-changing force within the evangelical Christian community. Their influence is most visible at the regularly held "Re-Imagining" Women's Conferences held at various locations throughout America. These conferences, which celebrate neopagan feminism and goddess worship, present speakers that include lesbians, radical feminists, Wiccans and neopagans.

The events are designed to bring spiritual awakening to Wicca and related traditions. They are designed to "re-imagine" the Bible and Christian theology into a feminist/neopagan mold. Although not *officially* funded by Christian churches, many women in attendance are leaders from mainline denominations. The 2000 conference, for instance, was coordinated by Lutheran Joan Regal.

Another member of the coordinating committee was retired Methodist pastor Jeanne Powers.

The first such gathering in Minneapolis (1993) drew more than 2,000 participants from twenty-seven countries, forty-nine states and fifteen denominations. Dozens of high-ranking denominational officials attended. One of the main speakers was Korean radical feminist Chung Hyung Kyung, who "drew substantially from New Age and animistic religions, expressing God as an all-encompassing energy force in nature."[20] Kyung repeatedly led women in *prana* (psychic energy) exercises and often referred to the Gnostic Gospels (a set of occult texts rejected centuries ago by the church as being heretical).[21]

According to a detailed account of the event published by *Watchman Fellowship* (a counter-cult organization), there were "regular convocations during the conference to the goddess Sophia, the source of everyone's divinity, the creator god who dwells within all."[22] The conference concluded with a perversion of the Lord's Supper (i.e., communion). It was turned into a Wiccan ritual called "Milk and Honey," wherein participants chanted: "Our Maker Sophia, we are women in your image, with the hot blood of our wombs we give form to new life . . . with nectar between our thighs we invite a lover . . . with our warm body fluids we remind the world of its pleasure and sensations."[23]

The 1998 Conference drew nearly 1,000 attendees. Again, participants "shared milk and honey in a communion-like ritual affirming the sensuality of women." They spoke of savoring "the life-giving juices of our bodies and the planet" and prayed to Sophia, who was identified as the Goddess of Wisdom. This 1998 event began "in a darkened room with primal fires and beating drums to summon the 'First Woman.' " The Re-Imaginers then conjured up spirits of the dead under the guise of praying.[24]

ENDNOTES

INTRODUCTION: TO BE A CHILD AGAIN

1. David McCord, "Books Fall Open," in *One at a Time* (Boston: Little Brown, 1977), 343.
2. Richard Savill, "Occult Fears Prompt Store Owner to Ban Harry Potter Toys" [on-line], September 24, 2001. *Daily Telegraph.* July 16, 2002. Available from: <http://www.dailytelegraph.com/news/main.jhtml?xml=%2Fnews%2F2001%2 F09%2F24%2Fnpott24.xml>; Elizabeth A. Wittman, "Occult Trends in Children's Literature" [on-line], October 2000. *Homiletic & Pastoral Review.* July 16, 2002. Available from: <http://www.catholic.net/rcc/Periodicals/Homiletic/ 2000-10/wittman.html>; Sarah Tippitt, "Harry Potter Film: Invitation to Join Occult?" [on-line], November 17, 2001. *Reuters.* July 16, 2002. Available from: <http://in.news.yahoo.com/011117/14/18ycr.html>; "Potter Fans Turning to Witchcraft" [on-line], August 4, 2000. *This Is London.* July 16, 2002. Available from: <http://www.thisislondon.co.uk/dynamic/news/story.html?in_review_id= 306029&in_review_text_id=250010>.
3. J.P. Zmirak, "Tolkien, Hitler, and Nordic Heroism" [on-line], December 20, 2001. FrontPageMagazine.com. July 16, 2001. Available from: <http://www.frontpage magazine.com>; Michael O'Brien and Sandra Miesel, "Tolkien and Rowling: Common Ground?" [on-line], July 2001. *Catholic World Report.* July 16, 2002. Available from: <http://www.catholiceducation.org/articles/arts/al0105.html>; WNDU-TV, "Movies of Witchcraft and Wizards: Is This Good Entertainment?" [on-line], December 12, 2001. *WNDU-TV Faith Report.* July 16, 2002. Available from: <http://www.wndu.com/news/faithreport/faithreport_1727.php>.
4. WisdomWorks, Press Release, "New Study Looks at Effect of Harry Potter on Teens" [on-line], May 16, 2002. August 1, 2002. Available from: <http://gospel-net.com/cgi-bin/newspro/viewnews.php?newsid=1022876329,20310,>. The poll also found that only one percent of Potter readers/viewers said they were less interested in witchcraft as a result of the Potter stories; while most (86%) said that reading/viewing it had made no difference to their overall interest in witchcraft. The data contained in this report originated through a research project conducted by the Barna Research Group, Ltd. of Ventura, California. Mark Matlock of Wisdom-Works Ministries commissioned the research. In total, this study includes the perspectives of 612 teenagers. The research questionnaires were designed by the Barna Research Group based on information objectives supplied by representatives and consultants of WisdomWorks. The surveys were administered by telephone and were conducted by telephone between March 14 and March 25, 2002.
5. WisdomWorks, available from: <http://gospel-net.com/cgi-bin/newspro/view news.php?newsid=1022876329,20310,>.

CHAPTER ONE: THE WONDER OF FANTASY

1. *The Oxford Universal Dictionary*, quoted in Jack Zipes, *Spells of Enchantment: The Wondrous Fairy Tales of Western Culture* (New York: Viking Penguin, 1991), xiv.

2. Perri Klass, quoted in Association of American Publishers, "Literacy Facts and Factoids" [on-line], n.d. July 16, 2002. Available from: <http://www.publishers.org/abouta/camp/literacyfacts.htm>.

3. Northrup Frye, *The Educated Imagination* (Bloomington, IN: Indiana University Press, 1964; 1970 edition), 101.

4. Mem Fox, *Reading Magic: Why Reading Aloud to Our Children Will Change Their Lives Forever* (New York: Harcourt Inc., 2001), 136. Fox writes:

   > Fairy tales—like the best picture books and novels—provide children with rules for living. They uplift us all with their grand examples of love and sorrow, courage and fortitude, being brave against the odds, living by one's wits, and caring for the downtrodden. They're the best sermons in literature, thundering into children's memories and remaining there as signposts to a well-lived life. (Experts tell us that many young criminals who have never been exposed to the cause-and-effect elements that abound in stories—particularly fairy tales—literally cannot imagine the consequences of their crimes. To correct this, some rehabilitation programs actually include reading stories aloud to young offenders.)

5. Leon Garfield, "The Outlaw," *Horn Book Magazine*, March/April 1990, 169-70. *Horn Book Magazine* is available on-line at <http://www.hbook.com/mag.shtml>.

6. Hazel Rochman, *Against Borders: Promoting Books for a Multicultural World* (Chicago: Booklist Publications/American Library Association Books, 1993), 19.

7. Bernice E. Cullinan, *Literature and the Child* (New York: Harcourt Brace Jovanovich, 1989), 5.

8. Some individuals also would place myths and legends into the folklore category.

9. Zena Sutherland and May Hill Arbuthnot, *Children and Books* (New York: Harper Collins, 1991; eighth edition), 182.

10. Jane Yolen, *Touch Magic: Fantasy, Faerie & Folklore in the Literature of Childhood* (Little Rock, AR: August House Publishers, 1981; 2000 edition), 15-7.

11. Rebecca J. Lukens, *A Critical Handbook of Children's Literature* (Glenview, IL: Scott, Foresman, and Co., 1976; 1990 fourth edition), 23.

12. John Buchan, "The Novel and the Fairy Tale," in *The English Association Pamphlet No. 79*, July 1931. Reprinted in Virginia Haviland, ed., *Children and Literature* (New York: Lothrop, Lee & Shepard Co., 1973), 221.

13. James E. Higgins, *Beyond Words: Mystical Fancy in Children's Literature* (New York: Teachers College Press, 1970), 4.

14. Buchan, 221-2.

15. Lang's books greatly influenced J.R.R. Tolkien.

16. Adapted from Sutherland and Arbuthnot, 187-9.

17. Fables are similar to fairy tales in that they have morals, but are much shorter in length. Moreover, a fable's sole purpose is to put forth a moral lesson. In fact, unlike the ending of a fairy tale, the ending of a fable is punctuated by an explicitly stated moral, such as "Slow and steady wins the race" or "Don't cry wolf."

18. Other hallmarks of the fairy tale and folktale are equally as striking:
    - The plots are simple.
    - The first few sentences quickly establish characters and setting, while at the same time the precise location of the story's events remains deliberately vague.
    - The good characters are supremely good, and the bad characters are excessively bad.

- The characters are established along stereotypical socio-economic lines to assist in painting easily identifiable characters.
- The characters do not behave in ways inconsistent with their overall personality traits. There is no subtlety of character—i.e., the wicked, wise, foolish, violent, disloyal all perform throughout the story in predictable ways.
- The main story section succinctly establishes the main character's dilemma and pushes toward a resolution using straightforward, uncomplicated language.
- The ending cleanly resolves the problem, leaving no complications.
- The characters "live happily ever after" (Cullinan, 230).

19. Nicholas Tucker, *The Child and the Book: A Psychological and Literary Exploration* (Cambridge University Press, 1981), 95-6.
20. Richard Le Gallienne, "Concerning Fairy-Tales," in *Attitudes and Avowals* (New York: Jane Lane Co., 1910), 36-7.
21. Eudora Welty, "And They All Lived Happily Ever After," *New York Times* (Book Review), November 10, 1963.
22. Sheldon Cashdan, *The Witch Must Die: How Fairy Tales Shape Our Lives* (New York: Basic Books, 1999), 6.
23. A version of this fairy tale appears in Maria Tatar, ed., *The Classic Fairy Tales* (New York: W.W. Norton & Co., 1999), 109-16. A number of equally horrific tales can be found in early publications of fairy tales. In the Grimms' collection, for instance, there is "The Juniper Tree." It is about a woman who decapitates her stepson, chops his corpse into small pieces, and cooks him in a stew that her husband devours. Countless other tales in their unedited form are just as macabre and gruesome (see Maria Tatar, *The Hard Facts of the Grimms' Fairy Tales* [Princeton: Princeton University Press, 1987]).
24. Zipes, xi.
25. Zipes, 15.
26. Zipes, 15.
27. A legend, in this context, should not be confused with an "urban legend," which is an altogether different story form of more recent origin (although a few long-term urban legends go back hundreds of years). An "urban legend" is a supposedly true story that is simply too good to be true. They quickly infect a society and usually express some kind of anxiety specific to a particular place, time or group of people. Moreover, not only is it entirely false, but it is sometimes deliberately fabricated by one or more persons who usually are never identified. They often take the form of something that happened to a friend of a friend of a friend. Urban legends may be used to demonize certain individuals or groups, while at other times they might be employed as a means of either frightening or showing as gullible the very people to whom it is being told. One example of a contemporary urban legend would be the false claim that the president of Proctor and Gamble admitted to being a Satanist on a national TV talk show (usually any one of a dozen popular programs). Another example would be the rumor that claims the now-infamous atheist, Madalyn Murray O'Hair, has a Senate bill up for vote that will force the FCC to ban all religious programming. (Oddly, this urban legend continues to circulate even though O'Hair has been dead for several years.) For more information on urban legends, see Jan Harold Brunvand, *Too Good to Be True: The Colossal Book of Urban Legends* (New York: W.W. Norton & Company).

28. An excellent introduction to mythology is *Bulfinch's Mythology: The Age of Fable, the Age of Chivalry, Legends of Charlemagne* (New York: Harper Collins, 1991), edited by Princeton University classicist and mythologist Richard P. Martin. It contains all of the original text by Thomas Bulfinch (1796-1867), including his notes and introductions to *The Age of Fable, The Age of Chivalry, and Legends of Charlemagne*. Also included are commentaries by Martin, who introduces each myth and legend with comments comparing Bulfinch's interpretations with current scholarship and teaching.
29. Malcolm Edwards and Robert Holdstock, *Realms of Fantasy* (New York: Doubleday, 1983), 5.
30. Edwards and Holdstock, 5.
31. J.R.R. Tolkien, "On Fairie Stories," in Christopher Tolkien, ed., *J.R.R. Tolkien: The Monsters & the Critics and Other Essays* (New York: Houghton Mifflin Co., 1984), 109. This essay was originally a lecture given at the University of St. Andrews on March 8, 1939.
32. Edwards and Holdstock, 7.
33. Tolkien, "On Fairie Stories," 122, 132.
34. Edwards and Holdstock, 5.
35. Natalie Babbitt, "The Purpose of Fantasy," in Barbara Harrison and Gregory Maguire, *Innocence and Experience: Essays and Conversations on Children's Literature* (New York: Lothrop, Lee & Shepard Books, 1987), 180.
36. Ursula Le Guin, "From Elfland to Poughkeepsie," quoted in Edwards and Holdstock, 9.
37. Higgins, 5.
38. E.F. Bleiler, *A Checklist of Modern Fantastic Literature* (Shasta Publishers, 1948), 3. Quoted in C.N. Manlove, *Modern Fantasy: Five Studies* (London: Cambridge University Press, 1975), 1.
39. Elizabeth Cook, *The Ordinary and the Fabulous: An Introduction to Myths, Legends and Fairy Tales for Teachers and Storytellers* (New York: Cambridge University Press, 1969), 2.
40. Cook, 5.
41. Madeleine L'Engle, "Fantasy Is What Fantasy Does," in Janet Hickman and Bernice Cullinan, eds., *Children's Literature in the Classroom: Weaving Charlotte's Web* (Norwood, MA: Christopher Gordon Publishers, 1989), 129-30.

CHAPTER TWO: TRUSTING SOULS

1. Cullinan, 5.
2. Margaret S. Steffensen, Chitra Joag-Dev and Richard C. Anderson, "A Cross-Cultural Perspective on Reading Comprehension," *Reading Research Quarterly*, vol. 15, no. 1 (1979): 10-29. Cited in Cullinan, 45.
3. Cullinan, 50.
4. Cullinan, 8.
5. Cullinan, 12.
6. C.S. Lewis, "On Stories," in *Essays Presented to Charles Williams* (London: Oxford University Press, 1947), 100.
7. Wolfgang Iser, "The Reading Process: A Phenomenological Approach," in *The Implied Reader* (Baltimore: John Hopkins University Press, 1974), 274-94. Cited in Cullinan, 9.

8. Elizabeth Fitzgerald Howard, "Delight and Definition: The Nuts and Bolts of Evaluating Children's Literature," *Top of the News*, 43, no. 4 (summer 1987): 363.

9. Declaration of the Rights of the Child (1959), adopted by the United Nations.

10. Bernice E. Cullinan, Kathy T. Harwood and S. Lee Galda, "The Reader and the Story: Comprehension and Response," *Journal of Research and Development in Education* 16, no. 3 (spring 1983): 29-38; cf. Cullinan, 49.

11. Sutherland and Arbuthnot, 35.

12. André Favat, *Child and Tale: The Origins of Interest* (Urbana, IL: National Council of Teachers of English, 1977), 38, 50. Bernice E. Cullinan observes: "[Children] consider it just when the scoundrel cook in 'The Pink' is forced to eat live coals for having deceived the king or when the maid-in-waiting is put naked into a barrel stuck with nails and dragged along the streets for having posed as the true princess in 'The Goose Girl.' . . . [F]airy tales embody an accurate representation of the child's conception of morality" (Cullinan, 18).

13. James Miller, Jr., "Literature and the Moral Imagination," in James R. Squire, ed., *Response to Literature* (Urbana, IL: National Council of Teachers of English, 1968), 30.

14. Sutherland and Arbuthnot, 36.

15. James Britton, *Language and Learning* (Harmondsworth, England: Penguin Books, 1970), 11. Cited in Cullinan, 22.

16. A more mature outworking of this phenomenon is the playing of Dungeons and Dragons by adolescents and young adults (as well as some older adults).

17. Cullinan, 23.

18. See J. Piaget, *The Origins of Intelligence in Children* (New York: International Universities Press, 1952; transl. by M. Cook).

19. Frye, 55.

20. Cullinan, 19.

21. Yolen, 26.

22. Higgins, 50.

23. Higgins, 49.

24. Without realizing it, my young friend had echoed the teachings of the learned Apostle Paul, who in Romans stated, "[T]hat which may be known of God is manifest in them [i.e., all human beings]; for God hath shewed it unto them. For the invisible things of him from the creation of the world are clearly seen, being understood by the things that are made, even his eternal power and Godhead" (Romans 1:19-20, KJV). This child also unknowingly summed up one of the most sophisticated philosophical lines of reasoning used to validate God's existence: The Teleological Argument, also known as Intelligent Design. In its most basic form, Intelligent Design asserts that creation, and the elaborate "design" inherent within it, suggests there must have been a "designer"—i.e., God. One analogy was offered by William Paley (1743-1805), the archdeacon of Carlisle, who compared the rationale behind Intelligent Design to the natural observation one might make if they were to find a watch in an empty field. Anyone would rightly conclude that it had a watchmaker because of its obvious design. It did not simply appear by random chance. The Teleological Argument is a complex proposition that has been discussed and debated by some of the most brilliant minds since the days of Socrates and Plato (see Norman Geisler, *Baker Encyclopedia of Christian Apologetics* [Grand Rapids: Baker Books, 1999], 715).

25. Higgins, 51.

26. Higgins, 51-2.
27. Le Gallienne, 37.
28. Lloyd Alexander, "Wishful Thinking—or Hopeful Dreaming," in Robert H. Boyer and Kenneth J. Zahorski, eds., *Fantasists On Fantasy: A Collection of Critical Reflections by Eighteen Masters of the Art* (New York: Avon Books, 1984), 145.
29. Alexander, 145-6.
30. Alexander, 147.
31. Alexander, 148.
32. Terry Pratchett, "When the Children Read Fantasy" [on-line], July 28, 1999. *Concatenation* (1994). July 16, 2002. Available from: <http://www.concatenation.org/articles/pratchett.html>.
33. Alexander, 148.
34. G.K. Chesterton. Quoted in Pratchett, available from: <http://www.concatenation.org/articles/pratchett.html>.
35. Countless occultists use the spelling "magick" with reference to their practices. The *Encyclopedia of Wicca & Witchcraft* reads: "The letter 'K' has traditionally been added to the word magic to distinguish it from sleight-of-hand stage magic" (Raven Grimassi, *Encyclopedia of Wicca & Witchcraft* [St. Paul: Llewellyn Publications, 2000], 232).
36. J.R.R. Tolkien, *Tree and Leaf* (London: Allen & Unwin, 1964), 44.
37. Tolkien, 48; cf. Ann Swinfen, *In Defense of Fantasy* (London: Routledge & Kegan Paul, 1984), 6-7. Swinfen, a novelist and teaching professor at the University of Dundee (Scotland), draws a distinction as well, writing: "Fantasy may be said to aspire rather to the 'elvish craft' of enchantment. At its heart lies creative desire, like Dante's: 'In this world it [i.e., fantasy magic] is for men unsatisfiable, and so imperishable. Uncorrupted it does not seek delusion, nor bewitchment and domination; it seeks shared enrichment, partners in making and delight, not slaves' [Tolkien, 49]. . . . Fantasy [including the use of magic] draws much of its strength from certain 'primordial desires' for the enrichment of life: the desire to survey vast depths of space and time, the desire to behold marvelous creatures, the desire to share the speech of the animals, the desire to escape from ancient limitations of man's primary world condition."
38. C.S. Lewis, "Sometimes Fairy Stories May Say Best What's to Be Said," in Boyer and Zahorski, eds., 118.

CHAPTER THREE: THE FALL OF FANTASY

1. Jack Zipes, *Sticks and Stones* (New York: Routledge, 2001), 5-6.
2. Margaret R. Marshall, *An Introduction to the World of Children's Books* (London: Gower, 1982; 1988 edition), 13.
3. Zipes, *Sticks and Stones*, 7.
4. Jonathan Cott, *Piper's at the Gates of Dawn: The Wisdom of Children's Literature* (New York: Random House, 1981; 1983 edition), xx.
5. A number of statistics and articles on literacy in America is available on-line from Training Wheels for Literacy: Our Reading Problem at <http://www.implicity.com/reading/app1problem.htm#schoolstats>.
6. Teen Research Unlimited, "Today's Teens" [on-line], 1998 survey. July 16, 2002. Available from: <www.naa.org/display/slides/teens.ppt>. In this survey, 1,200 telephone interviews were conducted among teens twelve to seventeen. Four sam-

ples were employed (for each U.S. Census region) in order to ensure appropriate national representation; quotas were set such that the number of interviews conducted in each region matched the national dispersion of the teen population. Each interview lasted an average of twenty minutes.

7. Kaiser Family Foundation, "New Study Finds Kids Spend Equivalent of Full Work Week Using Media" [on-line], November 17, 1999. July 16, 2002. Available from: <http://www.kff.org/content/1999/1535/pressreleasefinal.doc.html>. The study is based on a nationally representative sample of 3,155 children ages two to eighteen, including more than 2,000 written questionnaires completed by children eight and older, more than 1,000 in-home interviews with parents of two to seven-year-olds, and more than 600 week-long media-use diaries maintained by parents (for two to seven-year-olds) or kids (for eight to eighteen-year-olds). The surveys and diaries were completed between November 10, 1998, and April 20, 1999. The study was designed by Kaiser Family Foundation staff in consultation with Stanford University Professor Donald F. Roberts, Jr. and Harris Interactive, Inc. (formerly Louis Harris & Associates).

8. U.S. Department of Education, "A Nation Still at Risk" [on-line], 1999. July 16, 2002. Available from: <http://www.publishers.org/abouta/camp/literacyfacts.htm>.

9. National Institute for Literacy, "Literacy Facts" [on-line], 2001. July 16, 2002. Available from: <http://www.getcaughtreading.org/newsroom/capital_hill/literacy_facts.html>.

10. Cited in Jim Vaccaro, "The Journey to Literacy" [on-line], June 12, 2000. *The Book & the Computer*, Berkeley, California. July 16, 2002. Available from: <http://publishing.about.com/gi/dynamic/offsite.htm?site=http%3A%2F%2Fwww.honco.net%2F100day%2F02%2F2000-0612-vaccaro.html>.

11. Cited in Vaccaro, available from: <http://publishing.about.com/gi/dynamic/offsite.htm?site=http%3A%2F%2Fwww.honco.net%2F100day%2F02%2F2000-0612-vaccaro.html>.

12. Tom Engelhardt, "Reading May Be Harmful to Your Kids," *Harper's Magazine*, June 1991, 57-8.

13. Zipes, *Sticks and Stones*, 8-9.

14. Michael Moorcock, *Wizardry and Wild Romance* (London: Victor Gollancz, 1987), 149.

15. David Denby, "Buried Alive: Our Children and the Avalanche of Crud," *The New Yorker*, July 15, 1996, 48.

16. Denby, 51.

17. Denby, 52. He wrote: "What's lost is the old dream that parents and teachers will nurture the organic development of the child's own interests, the child's own nature. That dream is largely dead. In this country, people possessed solely by the desire to sell have become far more powerful than parents tortuously working out the contradictions of authority, freedom, education, and soul-making."

18. Janet Maslin, "At Last, the Wizard Gets Back to School," *New York Times*, July 10, 2000, B1.

19. Zipes, *Sticks and Stones*, 172.

20. Anthony Holden. Quoted in Sarah Lyall, "Wizard Vs. Dragon: A Close Contest, but the Fire-Breather Wins" [on-line], January 29, 2000. *New York Times*. July 16, 2002. Available from: <http://www.nytimes.com>.

21. Roger Sutton. Quoted in Elizabeth Mehren, "Wild About Harry" [on-line], July 28, 2000. *Los Angeles Times.* July 16, 2002. Available from: <http://www.latimes.com>.

22. Harold Bloom, "Can 35 Million Book Buyers Be Wrong? Yes," *Wall Street Journal*, July 11, 2000.

23. Harold Bloom. Quoted in Jamie Allen, "Harry and Hype" [on-line], July 13, 2000. CNN. Available from: <http://www.cnn.com/2000/books/news/07/13/ potter.hype/>.

24. A *London Review of Books* article, for example, referred to stupid "born-again" Christians (Wendy Doniger, "Spot the Source: Harry Potter Explained," *London Review of Books*; reprinted in *The Guardian*, February 10, 2000, available on-line at <http://www.guardian.co.uk>). A *Jewish World Review* article titled "Casual Censors and Deadly Know-Nothings" called Rowling's critics "barbarians" whose attacks amounted to "ignorance parading as piety" (Suzanne Fields, "Casual Censors and Deadly Know-Nothings" [on-line], December 7, 1999. *Jewish World Review.* July 16, 2002. Available from: <http://www.jewishworldreview.com/cols/fields120799.asp>). Also see Chapter 9, endnote 74.

25. Zipes, *Sticks and Stones*, 173

26. Higgins, 2.

27. This biography of Stine is found on the official Harper Collins publisher's site for children, available from: <http://www.harperchildrens.com/features/nightmare/ bio.htm>.

28. Diana West, "The Horror of R.L. Stine," *American Educator*, fall 1995, 39.

29. Quoted in West, 40.

30. Quoted in West, 40.

31. Review posted by "Sara" at amazon.com.

32. Interview with R.L. Stine by Devon W. and Vicky S., June 2001. Available from: <http://www.teenink.com/Past/2001/June/Interviews/RLStine.html>.

33. R.L. Stine, *Headless Halloween* (Goosebumps Series 2000, #10). Excerpt available from: <http://scholastic.com/goosebumps/books/index.htm>.

34. Michael O'Brien, *A Landscape With Dragons* (San Francisco: Ignatius Press, 1998), 67.

35. Randi Dickson, "Horror: To Gratify, Not Edify," *Language Arts*, 76, no. 2 (November 1998), 120.

36. Associated Press, " 'Goosebumps,' 'Huck Finn,' on List of Banned Books" [on-line], September 26, 1997. *Shawnee News-Star.* July 16, 2002. Available from: <http://www.news-star.com/stories/092697/lfe_bannedbooks.html>.

37. MacNeil/Lehrer Productions, "Pulp Friction" news segment [on-line], February 13, 1997. July 16, 2002. Available from: <http://www.pbs.org/ newshour/bb/education/february97/goose_2-13.html>.

38. See Georgette Brown, "Good vs. Evil—But Which Is Which?," *Sun Herald*, February 28, 1997. In this article, Brown refers to another story ("Ill Literacy Should Cause Goosebumps") in which the father of an eight-year-old expressed his belief that Goosebumps was "no big deal" because at least his son was reading. The *Sun Herald* is a Mississippi Gulf Coast newspaper.

39. R.L. Stine, Interview with Stine, available from: <http://www.cognivision.com/ timecapsule61/timecapsule61/team_10_literature.htm>.

40. Timothy Harper, "Why Kids Love "Goosebumps": An Interview with Fright-Meister R.L. Stine" [on-line], n.d. Familyeducation.com. July 16, 2002. Available from: <http://www.familyeducation.com/article/0,1120,1-313,00.html>.

41. MacNeil/Lehrer, available from: <http://www.pbs.org/newshour/bb/education/february97/goose_2-13.html>.

42. Cheryl Tiu, Tiffany Limsico and Catherine Young, "GenXers' Favorite Reads Growing Up" [on-line], August 28, 2001. *Philippine Daily Inquirer*. July 16, 2002. Available from: <http://www.inq7.net/lif/2001/aug/29/lif_4-1.htm>.

43. West, 41.

44. Steve Russo, "Real Answers with Steve Russo" [on-line], n.d. August 1, 2002. Available from: <http://www.24sevenvideos.com/gb.html>.

45. Marshall, 243.

46. Nicholas Tucker, "Books That Frighten," in Virginia Haviland, ed., *Children and Literature* (New York: Lothrop, Lee & Shepard Co., 1973), 106.

47. J.K. Rowling, *Harry Potter and the Goblet of Fire* (New York: Scholastic, 2001), 642-3: cf. J.K. Rowling, *Harry Potter and the Prisoner of Azkaban* (New York: Scholastic, 1999): "Standing in the doorway, illuminated by the shivering flames in Lupin's hand, was a cloaked figure that towered to the ceiling. Its face was completely hidden beneath its hood. Harry's eyes darted downward, and what he saw made his stomach contract. There was a hand protruding from the cloak and it was glistening, grayish, slimy-looking, and scabbed, like something dead that had decayed in water" (p. 83).

48. Tucker, 108.

49. O'Brien, *A Landscape With Dragons*, 67.

50. Jan Mark, "Another World?: A Sampling of Remarks on Science Fiction and Fantasy—The Story of Golem," in Barbara Harrison and Gregory Maguire, *Innocence & Experience: Essays & Conversations on Children's Literature* (New York: Lothrop, Lee & Shepard Books, 1987), 184.

51. Lillian Smith, *The Unreluctant Years* (Chicago: American Library Association, 1953; 1991 edition), 4.

52. "The Fantasy Myth" [on-line], n.d. *Home School Helper*. July 16, 2002. Available from: <http://www.bjup.com/resources/articles/hsh/0403b.html>.

53. Smith, 6.

54. Joan Aiken, "Between Family and Fantasy: An Author's Perspective on Children's Books," in Virginia Haviland, ed., *The Openhearted Audience: Ten Authors Talk about Writing for Children* (Washington: Library of Congress, 1980), 63.

55. Aiken, 63.

56. Mary Sheehan Warren, "Food for the Soul: Truth, Goodness, and Beauty in Children's Literature" [on-line], n.d. July 16, 2002. Available from: <http://www.catholic.net/rcc/Periodicals/Faith/11-12-98/Childrens.html>.

57. Warren, available from: <http://www.catholic.net/rcc/Periodicals/Faith/11-12-98/Childrens.html>.

CHAPTER FOUR: MIDDLE-EARTH'S MAKER

1. George R.R. Martin, "Introduction," in Karen Haber, ed., *Meditations on Middle-earth* (New York: St. Martin's Press, 2001), 3.

2. Poul Anderson, "Awakening the Elves," in Haber, 21.

3. Deborah Webster Rogers and Ivor A. Rogers, *J.R.R. Tolkien* (Boston: G.K. Hall & Co., 1980), 17.
4. Michael Coren, *J.R.R. Tolkien: The Man Who Created The Lord of the Rings* (Toronto: Stoddart, 2001), 8.
5. Mabel Tolkien. Quoted in Humphrey Carpenter, *Tolkien: The Authorized Biography* (New York: Ballantine Books, 1978; 1985 printing), 10.
6. Carpenter, 10.
7. Carpenter, 15.
8. Michael White, *The Life and Work of J.R.R. Tolkien* (Indianapolis: Alpha, 2002), 14.
9. Joseph Pearce, *Tolkien: Man and Myth* (San Francisco: Ignatius Press, 1998), 14.
10. J.R.R. Tolkien, letter to Sam Gamgee, March 18, 1956, in Humphrey Carpenter, ed., *The Letters of J.R.R. Tolkien* (Boston: Houghton Mifflin, 1981), 244-5.
11. White, 16.
12. J.R.R. Tolkien. Quoted in Carpenter, *The Letters*, 24.
13. J.R.R. Tolkien, letter to W.H. Auden, June 7, 1955, in Robert H. Boyer and Kenneth J. Zahorski, eds., *Fantasists on Fantasy: A Collection of Critical Reflections by Eighteen Masters of the Art* (New York: Avon Books, 1984), 90-1.
14. White, 34.
15. Carpenter, *Authorized Biography*, 44.
16. Coren, 24.
17. J.R.R. Tolkien. Quoted in Carpenter, *Authorized Biography*, 67.
18. Cited in Coren, 31.
19. White, 68.
20. White, 68.
21. G.B.S., letter to J.R.R. Tolkien, July 15, 1916. Quoted in Carpenter, *Authorized Biography*, 95.
22. White, 70.
23. Carpenter, *Authorized Biography*, 110.
24. J.R.R. Tolkien. Quoted in Carpenter, *Authorized Biography*, 94.
25. J.R.R. Tolkien, *The Fellowship of the Ring* (New York: Ballantine Books, 1973; paperback edition), 11.
26. White, 94.
27. White, 97.
28. J.R.R. Tolkien, *The Fellowship*, 236.
29. Wayne G. Hammond and Christina Scull, *J.R.R. Tolkien: Artist & Illustrator* (New York: Houghton Mifflin Co., 1995), 55.
30. Boyer and Zahorski, 76.
31. Coren, 56.
32. C.S. Lewis, diary entry of May 11, 1926, *The Lewis Papers*, Wade Collection, Wheaton College (Wheaton, IL). Quoted in White, 127.
33. Humphrey Carpenter, *The Inklings* (Allen & Unwin, Ltd., 1978; 1979 edition), 52.
34. In his childhood diary, ten-year-old Lewis wrote: "In this abominable place of Romish hypocrites and English liars, the people cross themselves, bow to the Lord's Table (which they have the vanity to call an altar), and pray to the Virgin" (Quoted in Carpenter, *The Inklings*, 50).
35. Coren, 59.

36. A large plaque currently hangs on the wall of The Bird and Baby that reads: "C.S. Lewis, his brother W.H.L., J.R.R. Tolkien, Charles Williams and other friends met every Tuesday morning between the years 1939-1962 in the back room of this their favorite pub. These men, popularly known as the 'Inklings,' met here to drink beer and to discuss, among other things, the books they were writing."
37. Warnie Lewis. Quoted in Coren, 62.
38. White, 133.
39. Tolkien, letter to W.H. Auden, in Boyer and Zahorski, 92.
40. Carpenter, *Authorized Biography*, 193.
41. J.R.R. Tolkien, *The Hobbit* (New York: Ballantine Books, 1965; 1982 revised edition), 2.
42. Tolkien, *The Hobbit*, 18.
43. Tolkien, *The Hobbit*, 302.
44. C.S. Lewis, *Of This and Other Worlds* (London; Geoffrey Bless, 1967), 111.
45. Rayner Unwin. Quoted in Carpenter, *Authorized Biography*, 202-3.
46. Stanley Unwin. Quoted in Carpenter, *Authorized Biography*, 207.
47. Tolkien, letter to W.H. Auden, in Boyer and Zahorski, 93.

CHAPTER FIVE: THE LORE OF THE RINGS

1. Howard Spring, *Country Life*, August 26, 1954. Quoted in Joseph Pearce, 129.
2. Carpenter, *Authorized Biography*, 219.
3. Carpenter, *Authorized Biography*, 219-20.
4. J.R.R. Tolkien, letter to Christopher Tolkien, March 30, 1944, reprinted in Carpenter, *The Letters*, 68.
5. Carpenter, *Authorized Biography*, 222.
6. Rogers and Rogers, 24.
7. C.S. Lewis. Quoted in Carpenter, *Authorized Biography*, 230-1.
8. J.R.R. Tolkien, letter to Stanley Unwin, July 31, 1947, reprinted in Carpenter, *The Letters*, 122.
9. C.S. Lewis, *Time & Tide*, August 14, 1954.
10. Tolkien, *The Fellowship*, 85.
11. Tolkien, *The Fellowship*, 85.
12. *Time*, July 15, 1966. Reprinted in Melissa August, Harriet Barovick, Victoria Rainert, Sora Song, Deirdre Vandyk, "Notebook: 35 Years Ago Today" [on-line], January 14, 2002. July 16, 2002. Available from: <http://www.time.com/time/magazine/notebook/0,9485,1101020114,00.html>.
13. Tom Shippey, *J.R.R. Tolkien: Author of the Century* (New York: Harper Collins, 2000), xx.
14. Pearce, 3.
15. Jeffrey Richards, *Daily Telegram*, February 1, 1997. Quoted in Pearce, 9.
16. Coren, 2.
17. Pearce, 3.
18. Mark Gauvreau Judge, "The Trouble with Harry" [on-line], July 12-18, 2000. *Baltimore City Paper*. July 16, 2002. Available from: <http://www.citypaper.com/2000-07-12/feature2.html>.
19. Gene Hargrove, "An Essay," *Mythlore*, no. 47 (1986). Hargrove explains: "[T]he Maiar who became the wizards of Middle-earth—and who had the same nature as the Valar—were converted to living beings temporarily by the special consent of

Iluvatar: 'For with the consent of Eru they . . . [were] clad in the bodies of Men, real and not feigned, but subject to the fears and pains and weariness of earth, able to hunger and thirst and be slain.' " This article is available from: <http://www.jrrtolkien.org.uk/gene_hargrove_essay.htm>.

20. J.R.R. Tolkien, unsent draft of letter to Robert Murray, November 4, 1954, reprinted in Carpenter, *The Letters*, 202.

21. Richard L. Purtill, *J.R.R. Tolkien: Myth, Morality, and Religion* (San Francisco: Harper & Row, 1984), 110-1.

22. J.R.R. Tolkien, note on letter to Milton Waldman, c. 1951, reprinted in Carpenter, *The Letters*, 159.

23. J.R.R. Tolkien, letter to Naomi Mitchison, April 25, 1954, reprinted in Carpenter, *The Letters*, 180.

24. Tolkien, letter to Murray, in Carpenter, *The Letters*, 207.

25. Tolkien, letter to Murray, in Carpenter, *The Letters*, 207.

26. Tolkien, letter to Murray, in Carpenter, *The Letters*, 205.

27. J.R.R. Tolkien, letter to Michael Straight, c. Jan./Feb. 1956, reprinted in Carpenter, *The Letters*, 235.

28. J.R.R. Tolkien, letter to A.E. Couchman, April 27, 1966, reprinted in Carpenter, *The Letters*, 368.

29. Tolkien, letter to Murray, in Carpenter, *The Letters*, 205.

30. Tolkien, *The Fellowship*, 76, 81.

31. Glover, Willis B. "The Christian Character of Tolkien's Invented World," *Criticism* no. 13 (winter 1971): 39-53. Quoted in Dan Graves, "Christian Elements and Symbols in Tolkien's 'The Lord of the Rings' " [on-line], n.d. August 1, 2002. Christian History Institute. Available from: <http://www.gospelcom.net/chi/BRICABRF/tolkien.shtml# anchor2370461>.

32. This is verified in a variety of places. See, for example, FAQs about Tolkien, available from: <http://tolkien.slimy.com/>.

33. Tolkien, letter to Murray, in Carpenter, *The Letters*, 205.

34. J.R.R. Tolkien, letter to Naomi Mitchison, September 25, 1954, reprinted in Carpenter, *The Letters*, 197-8.

35. J.R.R. Tolkien, unsent draft of letter to Peter Hastings, September 1954, reprinted in Carpenter, *The Letters*, 193-4.

36. Shippey, 238-9, 242.

37. White, 214.

38. White, 214; cf. J.R.R. Tolkien, letter to Robert Murray, December 2, 1953, reprinted in Carpenter, *The Letters*, 172.

39. White, 214.

40. Mark Eddy Smith, *Tolkien's Ordinary Virtues: Exploring the Spiritual Themes of* The Lord of the Rings (Downers Grove: InterVarsity Press, 2002).

41. Kurt Bruner and Jim Ware, *Finding God in* The Lord of the Rings (Wheaton, IL: Tyndale House, 2001), xiv.

42. White, 216.

43. John Tolkien, in *A Film Portrait of J.R.R. Tolkien* (Visual Corporation, ltd., 1992), a video production.

44. J.R.R. Tolkien, letter to Camilla Unwin, May 20, 1969, reprinted in Carpenter, *The Letters*, 400.

45. Tolkien, letter to Murray, December 2, 1953, in Carpenter, *The Letters*, 172.

46. J.R.R. Tolkien, letter to W.H. Auden, May 12, 1965, in Carpenter, *The Letters*, 355.
47. Tolkien, *Tree and Leaf*, 50.
48. Tolkien, *Tree and Leaf*, 40-1.
49. J.R.R. Tolkien, letter to Waldman, in Carpenter, *The Letters*, 147.
50. Reconstructed in Carpenter, *Authorized Biography*, 151.
51. C.S. Lewis. Quoted in Smith, 13.
52. Manlove, 163.
53. Tolkien, *Tree and Leaf*, 62-3.
54. J.R.R. Tolkien, "On Fairie Stories," in *The Monsters & the Critics and Other Essays*, 156.
55. J.R.R. Tolkien, letter to Christopher Tolkien, November 7-8, 1944, reprinted in Carpenter, *The Letters*, 100.
56. J.R.R. Tolkien, letter to Christopher Tolkien, in Carpenter, *The Letters*, 101.
57. Tolkien, *The Fellowship*, 321.
58. Colin Gunton, *Kings Theological Review*, 12, no. 1 (1989): 8. Cited in Pearce, 117.
59. Tolkien, *The Fellowship*, 320-1.
60. John Emerich Edward Dalberg Acton, letter to Bishop Mandell Creighton, 3 April 1887, see *Life and Letters of Mandell Creighton* (1904), vol. 1 , ch. 13.
61. Graves, available from: <http://www.gospelcom.net/chi/BRICABRF/tolkien.shtml#anchor2370461>.
62. Paul H. Kocher, *Master of Middle Earth* (Boston: Houghton Mifflin, 1972), 76.
63. Kocher, 79.
64. J.R.R. Tolkien, letter to Waldman, in Carpenter, *The Letters*, 146.
65. Purtill, 110
66. J.R.R. Tolkien, letter to Hastings, in Carpenter, *The Letters*, 192.
67. J.R.R. Tolkien, letter to Mitchison, September 25, 1954, in Carpenter, *The Letters*, 200. cf., Tolkien, letter to Hastings, in Carpenter, *The Letters*, which reads : "[Elves] have certain freedoms and powers we should like to have, and the beauty and peril and sorrow of the possession of these things is exhibited in them," 189.
68. Purtill, 104.
69. Tolkien, *The Fellowship*, 427.
70. J.R.R. Tolkien, letter to Waldman, in Carpenter, *The Letters*, 146.
71. Tolkien, "On Faerie Stories," in Christopher Tolkien, 142.
72. Tolkien, *The Hobbit*, 11. The other kind of magic that exists in Middle-earth is magic within various objects (e.g., weapons, rings, helmets, mirrors, etc.). These objects receive special qualities through science or technology. They are created in accordance with the laws of nature as found in Middle-earth.
73. Tolkien, letter to Mitchison, in Carpenter, *The Letters*, 200.
74. J.R.R. Tolkien, *The Return of the King* (New York: Ballantine Books, 1965; 1983 edition), 299.
75. Tolkien, *The Return*, 341.
76. Tolkien, *The Fellowship*, 317.
77. Patrick Grant, "Tolkien: Archetype and Word," *Cross Currents* (winter 1973): 365-80. Available from: <http://www.crosscurrents.org/tolkien.htm>.
78. Joseph Pearce, in "J.R.R. Tolkien's Take on the Truth," interview with Pearce by Zenit, available from: <http://www.leaderu.com/humanities/zenit-tolkien.html>.
79. An excellent series of related articles is available from: <http://www.leaderu.com/focus/tolkien.html>.

CHAPTER SIX: TWENTY-FIRST-CENTURY MAGICK

1. This statement was pulled from an advertisement for the lecture "True Magical Practices and Harry Potter," August 4, 2000. It was delivered at The Gnostic Society Center in Hollywood, California. The entire lecture is available from: <http://www.gnosis.org/gnostsoc.htm>.

2. Early indicators of the America's turn toward religiosity appeared as early as 1987 in a *Better Homes and Gardens* survey of 80,000 readers. Sixty-two percent of those polled said that in recent years they had "begun or intensified personal spiritual study and activities." The informal study also found that fifty percent of the respondents thought spirituality was gaining influence on American family life. Other findings were equally significant: 96% believed in God (although interpretations of "God" varied); 89% looked forward to an "eternal life"; 81% felt they would be reunited with loved ones after death (Kate Greer, "Are American Families Finding New Strength In Spirituality?," *Better Homes and Gardens*, January 1988, 16-9.

3. Martin Marty. Quoted in Timothy Jones, "Great Awakenings," *Christianity Today*, November 8, 1993, 24.

4. Barbara Kantrowitz, "In Search of the Sacred," *Newsweek*, November 28, 1994, 55; Bob McCullough, "The New Spin Is Spirituality," *Publishers Weekly*, May 16, 1994; Eugene Taylor, "Desperately Seeking Spirituality" *Psychology Today*, November/December 1994, 57.

5. Kantrowitz, 54.

6. Cecile S. Holmes (Religious News Service), "Seeking Spirituality, Americans Are Picking and Choosing Their Religion," *Salt Lake Tribune*, February 12, 2000, citing George Gallup, Jr. and D. Michael Lindsay, *Surveying the Religious Landscape: Trends in U.S. Beliefs* (Harrisburg, PA: Morehouse Publishing, 2000), available from: <http://www.sltrib.com> (archives).

7. Holmes, available from: <http://www.sltrib.com> (archives).

8. Robert Marquand, "Religious Reading Digs Deeper" [on-line], August 27, 1997. *Christian Science Monitor*. July 16, 2002. Available from: <http://www.csmonitor.com/durable/1997/08/27/feat/feat.1.html>.

9. Claire Moore, "Reading Religion: Rising Religious Books Sales Reflect Americans' Spiritual Search" [on-line], September 24, 2000. ABCnews.com. July 16, 2002. Available from: <http://www.abcnews.go.com/sections/us/DailyNews/religiousbooks000917.html>.

10. Terry Mattingly, "Buying St. Nostradamus" [on-line], n.d. July 16, 2003. Available from: <http://tmatt.gospelcom.net/column/2001/10/10/>.

11. Data obtained by the Gallup Organization, for instance, shows that belief in biblical authority has "fallen to an all-time low," with 2001 statistics showing that only twenty-seven percent of the those polled believe the Bible contains "the actual Word of God in all instances." In 1963, the figure was sixty-five percent (see Mattingly, available from: <http://tmatt.gospelcom.net/column/2001/10/10/>). In 2001, more than 29.4 million Americans said they had no religion—more than double the number in 1990—according to the American Religious Identification Survey 2001 (ARIS). People with no religion now account for 14% of the nation, up from 8% when The Graduate Center of the City University of New York, authors of the ARIS, conducted its first survey of religion in 1990 (Cathy Lynn Grossman, "Charting the Unchurched In America" [on-line], March 7, 2002. *USA Today*. July

16, 2002. Available from: <http://www.usatoday.com/life/2002/2002-03-07-no-religion.htm>).

12. Mattingly, available from: <http://tmatt.gospelcom.net/column/2001/10/10/>.

13. "Belief in the Beyond," *USA Today*, April 20, 1997. Quoted in Matt Nesbit, "New Poll Points to Increase in Paranormal Belief" [on-line], 1998 *Skeptical Inquirer*, 22, no. 5. July 16, 2002. Available from: <http://www.csicop.org/articles/poll/>. This survey is subject to a margin of error of plus or minus 3-5%.

14. Mircea Eliade, *Occultism, Witchcraft and Cultural Fashions* (Chicago: University Press, 1976), 1.

15. Official Web site of Covenant of the Goddess, "CoG: Commonly Asked Questions" [on-line], n.d. July 16, 2002. Available from: <http://www.cog.org/wicca/faq.html#MANY>. Well-known Wiccan high priestess, Phyllis Curott, author of *The Book of Shadows: A Modern Woman's Journey into the Wisdom of Witchcraft and the Magic of the Goddess*, claims there are between 3 and 5 million persons adhering to "witchcraft and Goddess spirituality" (see "Blair Witch Offends Witches: A Practicing Witch on the Summer's Hottest Flick" [on-line], August 18, 1999 ABCnews.com. July 16, 2002. Available from: <http://abcnews.go.com/sections/us/DailyNews/chat_curott990818.html>).

16. Catherine Edwards, "Wicca Casts Spell on Teen-Age Girls" [on-line], October 25, 1999. *Insight* (Washington, D.C.), 15, no. 39. July 16, 2002. Available from: a number of sites including: <http://home-4.tiscali.nl/~t968103/silver_circle/scn_8.htm>; <http://www.angelfire.com/wi2/andromedawicca/news2.html>; <http://www.angelfire.com/ca6/armorofgod/spells.html>.

17. Leslie A. Shepard, ed., *Encyclopedia of Occultism & Parapsychology* (Detroit: Gale Research, 1991), 2:1207.

18. Julien Tondriau, *The Occult: Secrets of the Hidden World* (New York: Pyramid Communications, 1972), 5.

19. In an attempt to better understand the highly complex and multi-faceted world of the occult, sociologists have divided occultists into three separate categories:
   • Minimal Observers, who express only a passing interest in strange occurrences such as flying saucers, land and sea monsters and parapsychological phenomena. Their activities are characterized by an absence of mysticism, supernaturalism and anti-scientific thought.
   • Moderate Participants, who seek to understand mysterious causal relationships between events—i.e., they express an interest, for example, in numerology, sun-sign astrology and palmistry.
   • Entrenched Believers, who are concerned with complex occult belief systems: e.g., witchcraft, Satanism, ritual magic and other mystical traditions. They often question or contradict scientific validation of an event or relationship, and thus may see themselves as competitors to science.

20. Recently such origins have been challenged by religion scholars; see Charlotte Allen, "The Scholars and the Goddess" [on-line], January 2001. *The Atlantic Monthly*. 287, no. 1; 18. July 16, 2002. Available from: <http://www.theatlantic.com/issues/2001/01/allen.htm>; cf. "Hollywood Spirituality," *E! Entertainment Television*, July 25, 1999.

21. From "Book of Deities," available from: <http://www.spiritonline.com/gods/>. August 1, 2002.

22. The Pagan Federation On-line, "Traditions of the Pagan Religion" [on-line], n.d. July 16, 2002. Available from: <http://www.paganfed.demon.co.uk/info-trad.htm>.

23. Susan Harwood Kaczmarczik, Br'an Arthur Davis-Howe, T.O. Radzykewycz, Ailsa N.T. Murphy, Cecilia Henningsson, "Alt.Pagan Frequently Asked Questions" [on-line], January 25, 1993. July 16, 2002. Available from: <http://www.faqs.org/faqs/paganism-faq/>.

24. According to influential witch Margot Adler, the word "wicca" is the original Anglo-Saxon spelling for the modern English word "witch" (*Drawing Down the Moon: Witches, Druids, Goddess-Worshippers and Other Pagans in America Today* [Boston: Beacon Press, 1979], 11).

25. Craig Hawkins, *Witchcraft: Exploring the World of Wicca* (Grand Rapids: Baker Books, 1996), 21. Hawkins writes:

> Witchcraft . . . [is] an antidogmatic, antiauthoritarian, diverse, decentralized, eclectic, experience-based, nature-oriented religious movement whose followers are polytheists and/or pantheists and/or panentheists, and in some sense believe in or experience and/or invoke and/or worship the Mother Goddess and generally her consort the Horned God as well. . . . Witches: Individuals who practice or concur with the views or experiences of witchcraft. Most view divinity as immanent in nature, seeing all life as sacred, thus, denying any sacred/secular distinction. They are nature-oriented and also see no ultimate distinction between matter and spirit—the material and the spiritual. They may believe in or invoke a pantheon of gods and goddesses, but they primarily experience, and/or invoke, and/or worship the Mother or Triple Goddess and her male consort, the Horned God. Witches generally practice multiple forms of divination, participate in trance and other altered states of consciousness, and perform magical spells and incantations. Most observe seasonal holidays and festivals (e.g., the summer and winter solstices). Most believe in some form of reincarnation.

26. Directly quoted from Hawkins, 32.

27. Ronald Hutton, *The Pagan Religions of the Ancient British Isles* (Oxford: Blackwell, 1991), 335.

28. Edwards, available from: <http://home-4.tiscali.nl/~t968103/silver_circle/scn_8.htm>; <http://www.angelfire.com/wi2/andromedawicca/news2.html>; and <http://www.angelfire.com/ca6/armorofgod/spells.html>.

29. Helen Berger, *A Community of Witches* (Columbia, SC: University of South Carolina Press, 1999), 92.

30. Starhawk, *The Spiral Dance* (San Francisco: Harper San Francisco, 1979; 1989 edition), 76.

31. Edwards, available from: <http://home-4.tiscali.nl/~t968103/silver_circle/scn_8.htm>; <http://www.angelfire.com/wi2/andromedawicca/news2.html>; and <http://www.angelfire.com/ca6/armorofgod/spells.html>.

32. Edwards, available from: <http://home-4.tiscali.nl/~t968103/silver_circle/scn_8.htm>; <http://www.angelfire.com/wi2/andromedawicca/news2.html>; and <http://www.angelfire.com/ca6/armorofgod/spells.html>.

33. Susan Greenwood, *Magic, Witchcraft, and the Otherworld* (Oxford: Berg, 2000), 182, 203-4.

34. It is important to remember that witchcraft and neopaganism are not synonymous with Satanism, which is an altogether different form of occultism.

35. Pauline Bartel, *Spellcasters* (Dallas: Taylor Trade Publications, 2000), 154; cf. Hawkins, 28.

36. Hawkins, 52-3.

37. Shepard, 2:1569. Scott Cunningham in his book *Wicca: A Guide for the Solitary Practitioner* advises: "If you can't find a ritual to your liking or that fits your needs, create one" (p. 174-5).

38. Shepard, 2:1569.

39. Leo Martello, *Witchcraft: The Old Religion* (Secaucus, NJ: Citadel Press, 1973), 12.

40. Scott Cunningham, *The Truth about Witchcraft Today* (St. Paul: Llewellyn Publications, 1988), 23.

41. Cunningham, *The Truth about Witchcraft Today*, 3.

42. Aleister Crowley, *Magick in Theory and Practice* (New York: Dover Publications, 1976 edition), 12.

43. Allen, 18.

44. Jo Pearson. Quoted in "Bewitching the Academy," *Fortean Times* (#157), May 2002, 25.

45. Catherine Edwards, "Wicca Infiltrates the Churches" [on-line], November 12, 1999. *Insight* (Washington, D.C.), 15, no. 45. July 16, 2002. Available from: <http://www.confessingumc.org/wicca_story2.html>; <http://www.ucmpage.org/articles/wicca_story2.html>.

46. Those doubting of this assertion by Barnes and Noble marketing executives need only go the Internet's barnesandnoble.com or amazon.com retail sites and enter the word "divination," "occult" or "witch" into its search engine. Within seconds the request will pull up thousands of titles.

47. Edwards, "Wicca Casts," available from: <http://home-4.tiscali.nl/~t968103/silver_circle/scn_8.htm>; <http://www.angelfire.com/wi2/andromedawicca/news2.html>; and <http://www.angelfire.com/ca6/armorofgod/spells.html>.

48. B.A. Robinson, "Teenagers and Wicca" [on-line], n.d. July 16, 2002. Available from: <http://www.religioustolerance.org/wic_teen.htm>.

49. Karen MacPherson, "Book Trend Casts Spell over Young Readers" [on-line], n.d. *Pittsburgh Post-Gazette*. July 31, 2001. Available from: <http://www.post-gazette.com/ae/20010731witchbooks0731p3.asp> and <http://www.cincypost.com/2001/aug/14/witch081401.html>.

50. MacPherson, available from: <http://www.post-gazette.com/ae/20010731witchbooks0731p3.asp> and <http://www.cincypost.com/2001/aug/14/witch081401.html>.

51. MacPherson, available from: <http://www.post-gazette.com/ae/20010731witchbooks0731p3.asp> and <http://www.cincypost.com/2001/aug/14/witch081401.html>.

52. Only eleven volumes had been released as of April 2002. The remaining books were slated to be released by January 2003.

53. Cate Tiernan, *Book of Shadows* (New York: Puffin Press, 2001), 82, 130, 141.

54. Tiernan, 182-3.

55. Tiernan, 24, 27-30, 61, 94, 152-3.

56. Tiernan, 107.

57. Tiernan, 40-3, 96-8, 119.

58. Tiernan, 50, 52.

59. Tiernan, 47, 147, 187.

60. "What Is Sweep" [on-line], n.d. July 16, 2002. Available from: <http://www
.catetiernan.homestead.com/catetiernan.html>. Accurate Wiccan beliefs and rituals are sprinkled liberally throughout the text. The book presents more than enough
information for a teenager to start training as a Wiccan (pp. 24, 27-30, 78, 136-7,
182-3).

61. Author Cate Tiernan has consistently maintained that she is not a practicing
Wiccan. Nevertheless, her books demonstrate an in-depth, working knowledge of
the Craft. Moreover, Tiernan makes several statements in *Book of Shadows*, for instance, that seek to not just explain away concerns about Wicca, but present
Wiccan propaganda against Christianity (pp. 49-50, 102-3, 106, 116, 152, 153).
One such instance is where Tiernan has a character claiming that Roman Catholicism actually borrowed the traditions of Christmas and Easter from Wicca. This is
historically absurd and may belie an agenda on Tiernan's part.

62. Allen, available from: <http://www.theatlantic.com/issues/2001/01/allen.htm>.
Allen's article also provides this fascinating information:

> In 1999 Ronald Hutton, a well-known historian of pagan British reli-
> gion who teaches at the University of Bristol, published *The Triumph of
> the Moon*. Hutton had conducted detailed research into the known pagan
> practices of prehistory, had read Gardner's unpublished manuscripts, and
> had interviewed many of Gardner's surviving contemporaries. Hutton,
> like [Philip Davis], could find no conclusive evidence of the coven from
> which Gardner said he had learned the Craft, and argued that the "an-
> cient" religion Gardner claimed to have discovered was a mélange of ma-
> terial from relatively modern sources. Gardner seems to have drawn on
> the work of two people: Charles Godfrey Leland, a nineteenth-century
> amateur American folklorist who professed to have found a surviving cult
> of the goddess Diana in Tuscany, and Margaret Alice Murray, a British
> Egyptologist who herself drew on Leland's ideas and, beginning in the
> 1920s, created a detailed framework of ritual and belief. From his own ex-
> perience Gardner included such Masonic staples as blindfolding, initia-
> tion, secrecy, and "degrees" of priesthood. He incorporated various
> Tarot-like paraphernalia, including wands, chalices, and the five-pointed
> star, which, enclosed in a circle, is the Wiccan equivalent of the cross.
>   Gardner also wove in some personal idiosyncrasies. One was a fond-
> ness for linguistic archaisms: "thee," "thy," "'tis," "Ye Bok of ye Art Mag-
> ical." Another was a taste for nudism: Gardner had belonged to a nudist
> colony in the 1930s, and he prescribed that many Wiccan rituals be carried
> out "skyclad." This was a rarity even among occultists: no ancient pagan
> religion is known, or was thought in Gardner's time, to have regularly
> called for its rites to be conducted in the nude. Some Gardnerian innova-
> tions have sexual and even bondage-and-discipline overtones. Ritual sex,
> which Gardner called "The Great Rite," and which was also largely un-
> known in antiquity, was part of the liturgy for Beltane and other feasts
> (although most participants simulated the act with a dagger—another of
> Gardner's penchants—and a chalice). Other rituals called for the binding
> and scourging of initiates and for administering "the fivefold kiss" to the
> feet, knees, "womb" (according to one Wiccan I spoke with, a relatively
> modest spot above the pubic bone), breasts, and lips. . . .

Historians have overturned another basic Wiccan assumption: that the group has a history of persecution exceeding even that of the Jews. The figure Starhawk cited—nine million executed over four centuries—derives from a late-eighteenth-century German historian; it was picked up and disseminated a hundred years later by a British feminist named Matilda Gage and quickly became Wiccan gospel (Gardner himself coined the phrase "the Burning Times"). Most scholars today believe that the actual number of executions is in the neighborhood of 40,000. The most thorough recent study of historical witchcraft is *Witches and Neighbors* (1996), by Robin Briggs, a historian at Oxford University. Briggs pored over the documents of European witch trials and concluded that most of them took place during a relatively short period, 1550 to 1630, and were largely confined to parts of present-day France, Switzerland, and Germany that were already racked by the religious and political turmoil of the Reformation. The accused witches, far from including a large number of independent-minded women, were mostly poor and unpopular. Their accusers were typically ordinary citizens (often other women), not clerical or secular authorities. In fact, the authorities generally disliked trying witchcraft cases and acquitted more than half of all defendants. Briggs also discovered that none of the accused witches who were found guilty and put to death had been charged specifically with practicing a pagan religion.

63. "Which T*Witch R U?" [on-line], n.d. August 1, 2002. Available from: <http://www.scholastic.com/titles/ twitches/whichtwitch.htm>.

64. "Which T*Witch R U?" Available from: <http://www.scholastic.com/titles/ twitches/magickarchive.htm>.

65. "Karsh's Magick Tips," [on-line], n.d. August 1, 2002. Available from: <http://www.scholastic.com/titles/ twitches/magick.asp>. This Web site is where children can go to enter their own spells. To access the submitted spells, click on "spellbook." It links to <http://www.scholastic.com/titles/twitches/spellbook.htm>.

66. There exists an obvious similarity between these magick spells submitted by children and the Wiccan spells used by adult witches. For example, in *Easy Enchantments: All the Spells You'll Ever Need for Any Occasion*, author Lexa Rosean shares the "Prosperity Water Spell," a modern spell she designed by blending a number of ancient customs. The ingredients are: ten pennies, "preferably ones found facing heads-up on a road or street"; one empty, clear jar; spring water; green food coloring; one green candle; and potting soil. Rosean writes: "Once you have your ten pennies, place them in an empty clear jar. Fill the jar with spring water and three drops of green food coloring. On the next full moon leave the jar (lid off) under the light of the moon. You may place it on a windowsill where the moon is sure to shine, or in a garden or terrace. If you do not have access to any of these places, go outside with the jar and hold it up to the light of the full moon for at least thirteen minutes. The longer the jar is exposed, the more powerful the potion, but thirteen minutes is the minimum amount of time required to empower the water. You must close the lid on the jar and take it inside before sunrise. . . ." Rosean's spell continues in a manner that virtually mirrors the kind of instruction given by the children submitting spells to the T*Witch Web site.

67. Among the most popular works of Wiccan fiction for children/teens are: *Beyond the Burning Time* (Kathryn Lasky), *Enter Three Witches* (Kate Gilmore), *Gallows Hill* (Lois Duncan), *The Other Ones* (Jean Thesman), *The Time of the Witch* (Mary Downing Hahn), *Wise Child* (Monica Furlong) and *Witch Week* (Diana Wynne Jones).

68. Patrick Goodenough, "Paganism Finds Growing Interest Among UK Children" [on-line], August 25, 2000. CNSnews.com. July 16, 2002. Available from: <http://www.cnsnews.com/ForeignBureaus/archive/For20000825b.html>.

69. Advertisement at Silver Ravenwolf's Web site, available from: <http://www.silverravenwolf.com/enchantm.htm>.

70. Advertisement at Silver Ravenwolf's Web site, available from: <http://www.silverravenwolf.com/enchantm.htm>.

71. Edwards, "Wicca Casts," available from: <http://home-4.tiscali.nl/~t968103/silver_circle/scn_8.htm>; <http://www.angelfire.com/wi2/andromedawicca/news2.html>; and <http://www.angelfire.com/ca6/armorofgod/spells.html>.

72. Robinson, available from: <http://www.religioustolerance.org/wic_teen.htm>.

73. *New Worlds of Mind and Spirit* (Llewellyn Publications), September/October, 1996, 6.

74. Phyllis Curott. Quoted in "Blair Witch Offends Witches: A Practicing Witch on the Summer's Hottest Flick" [on-line], August 18, 1999. ABCnews.com. July 16, 2002. Available from: <http://abcnews.go.com/sections/us/DailyNews/chat_curott990818.html>.

75. Edwards, "Wicca Casts," available from: <http://home-4.tiscali.nl/~t968103/silver_circle/scn_8.htm>; <http://www.angelfire.com/wi2/andromedawicca/news2.html>; and <http://www.angelfire.com/ca6/armorofgod/spells.html>.

76. Goodenough, available from: <http://www.cnsnews.com/ForeignBureaus/archive/For20000825b.html>.

77. Philip Davis. Quoted in Edwards, "Wicca Casts," available from: <http://home-4.tiscali.nl/~t968103/silver_circle/scn_8.htm>; <http://www.angelfire.com/wi2/andromedawicca/news2.html>; <http://www.angelfire.com/ca6/armorofgod/spells.html>.

78. Ruth La Feria, *The Daily Journal* (New York Times News Service), February 15, 2000, A9. Quoted in Wittman, available from: <http://www.catholic.net/rcc/Periodicals/Homiletic/2000-10/wittman.html>.

79. Goodenough, available from: <http://www.cnsnews.com/ForeignBureaus/archive/For20000825b.html>.

80. Andy Norfolk. Quoted in Goodenough, available from: <http://www.cnsnews.com/ForeignBureaus/archive/For20000825b.html>.

81. "Never Seen a Ghost? Then TV May Be Your Teacher" [on-line], October 17, 1997. *Purdue News*. July 16, 2002. Available from: <http://www.purdue.edu/UNS/html4ever/971017.Sparks.survey.html>.

82. Glenn Sparks, quoted in "Never Seen a Ghost?" available from: <http://www.purdue.edu/UNS/html4ever/971017. Sparks.survey.html>.

83. "Never Seen a Ghost?" available from: <http://www.purdue.edu/UNS/html4ever/971017.Sparks.survey.html>.

84. Thomas Hargrove and Guido H. Stempel, "Ghosts, Ghouls, and Goblins Haunt Americans' Imaginations" [on-line], October 27, 1999. *San Francisco Examiner*. July 16, 2002. Available from: <http://www.examiner.com>.

85. Steven D. Greydanus, "Harry Potter Vs. Gandalf: An In-Depth Analysis of the Literary Use of Magic in the Works of J.K. Rowling, J.R.R. Tolkien, and C.S. Lewis" [on-line], n.d. DecentFilms.com. July 16, 2002. Available from: <http://decentfilms.com/commentary/magic.html>.

86. Adapted from W. Elwyn Davies, *Principalities and Powers* (Minneapolis: Bethany House, 1976), 303-4; cf. Josh McDowell and Don Stewart, *Handbook of Today's Religions* (San Bernardino, CA: Here's Life Publishers, 1983; 1992 edition), 153.

87. Phyllis Curott. Quoted in Edwards, "Wicca Casts," available from: <http://home-4.tiscali.nl/~t968103/silver_circle/scn_8.htm>; <http://www.angelfire.com/wi2/andromedawicca/news2.html>; <http://www.angelfire.com/ca6/armorofgod/spells.html>.

88. Michael O'Brien, "Interview in Catholic World Report (special Tolkien issue)" [on-line], December 2001. Studiobrien.com. July 16, 2002. Available from: <http://studiobrien.com/cfiles/talks/006.html>.

89. Higgins, *Beyond Words*, 22-3.

90. Higgins, *Beyond Words*, 22-3.

CHAPTER SEVEN: HARRY POTTER: MAGICK AND MORALITY

1. "Harry Potter and the Goblet of Fire," news article by The Children of Artemis (a neopagan/Wiccan group), available from: <http://www.witchcraft.org/pastnews.html>.

2. Yolen, 95.

3. J.K. Rowling. Quoted in Chuck Colson, "Witches and Wizards: The Harry Potter Phenomenon" [on-line], November 2, 1999. *Breakpoint Commentary*, #91102. July 16, 2002. Available from: <http://www.gbgm-umc.org/prospect/colson.htm>; cf. Ed Vitagliano, "Absolute Magic?: Witchcraft in Entertainment Challenges Christians to Defend Their Views" [on-line], February 2002. *AFA Journal (American Family Association)*. July 16, 2002. Available from: <http://www.afa.net/journal/february/2002/harrypotter.asp>.

4. J.K. Rowling, *Harry Potter and the Sorcerer's Stone* (New York, NY: Scholastic Press, 1997), 58.

5. Yolen, 26.

6. J.K. Rowling, interview with Barnes and Noble, March 19, 1999, available from: <http://www.burrow-jp.com/library/original/03191999.html>. During an appearance at a New Jersey School, Rowling stated: "Before I even started writing the books I knew quite a lot about folklore and magic" (audio file available from: <http://www.montclairkimberley.org/jkrowling/media/answers/answer4 aud.mov>).

7. Ian Potter and Vikki Potter. Quoted in Danielle Demetriou, "Harry Potter and the Source of Inspiration" [on-line], July 1, 2000. *Electronic Telegraph*. July 16, 2002. Available from: <www.telegraph.co.uk>; cf. "Potter Novelist Reveals Characters' Inspiration Ian 'Harry' Potter Had a Thing about Slugs' " [on-line], July 1, 2000. *National Post*. July 16, 2002. Available from: <http://uk.geocities.com/pottermovie/interviews.htm>. Vikki recalls: "Our favorite thing to dress up as were witches. We used to dress up and play witch all the time. My brother would

dress up as a wizard. Joanne [J.K.] was always reading to us. . . . [W]e would make secret potions for her. She would always send us off to get twigs for the potions."

8. J.K. Rowling, interview, *Nickelodeon Magazine* (c. 2000), available from: <http://expage.com/page/jkinterview> and <http://www.geocities.com/harrys_hideout/cat0007.html>.

9. J.K. Rowling, radio interview, October 12, 1999, *Talk Connection*, WBUR (Boston, MA).

10. Rowling's views on "seven" have been confirmed by several persons, including editor Walton Beacham. In his introduction to Beacham Publications' educational resource book *Exploring Harry Potter*, he remarks: "Ms. Rowling has spoken extensively about her plans for future Potter novels, and stated that the magical number seven will see the conclusion of Harry's education at Hogwarts" (Walton Beacham, in Elizabeth Schafer, *Exploring Harry Potter* [Osprey, FL: Beacham Publishing, 2000], 4, statement available from: <www.beachampublishing.com>. Also, Rowling's ex-husband (Jorge Arantes) revealed her beliefs in London's *Daily Express*, saying that she "had planned the full series of seven books because she believed the number seven has magical associations" (Jorge Arantes. Quoted in Peter Fearon, "A Dark Flashback in 'Potter' Author's Tale" [on-line], July 11, 2000. *New York Post.* July 16, 2002. Available from: <http://wwwnypost.com> and <http://www.foxnews.com>).

11. Rowling's views echo Blavatsky's articles "The Number Seven" [on-line], June 1880 *Theosophist.* July 16, 2002. Available from: <http://theosophy.org/tlodocs/hpb/NumberSeven.htm> and "The Number Seven and Our Society" [on-line], September 1880. *Theosophist.* July 16, 2002. Available from: <http://theosophy.org/tlodocs/hpb/NumberSevenAndOurSociety.htm>. Blavatsky's article titled "The Number Seven" quotes a German journal, *Die Gegenwart*, as follows:

> The number *seven* was considered sacred not only by all the cultured nations of antiquity and the East, but was held in the greatest reverence even by the later nations of the West. The astronomical origin of this number is established beyond any doubt. . . . [and is related to] the planets which the whole antiquity numbered as *seven*. In course of time these [planets] were transformed into *seven* deities. The Egyptians had *seven* original and higher gods; the Phœnicians *seven* kabiris; the Persians, *seven* sacred horses of Mithra; the Parsees, *seven* angels opposed by *seven* demons, and *seven* celestial abodes paralleled by *seven* lower regions. To represent the more clearly this idea in its concrete form, the *seven* gods were often represented as one *seven*-headed deity. The whole heaven was subjected to the *seven* planets; hence, in nearly all the religious systems we find *seven* heavens.

She also pointed out these supposedly magical aspects to the number seven:
- Ancient Egyptians believed in seven states of soul purification.
- Buddhists teach seven stages of progressive development of the disembodied soul.
- In Mithraism, an ancient mystery religion, there were seven gates, seven altars, seven mysteries.

- Priests of many Asian nations were sub-divided into seven degrees; seven steps led to the altars, and in the temples burnt seven candles in seven-branched candlesticks.

- Arabian legends assert that seven angels cool the sun with ice and snow, lest it should burn the earth to cinders; and seven thousand angels set the sun in motion every morning.

- Eastern antiquity valued seven principal rivers (Nile, Tigris, Euphrates, Oxus, Yaksart, Arax and Indus), seven famous treasures, seven cities full of gold, and seven marvels of the world.

12. J.K. Rowling, video interview for Scholastic Press, available from Scholastic at <http://www.scholastic.com>.

13. During this interview the Q & A exchange reads: "Does everyone have a little magic in them? Even if they are Muggles? . . . J.K. Rowling: I think we do (outside the books), but within my books—do you really think there's any magic in Uncle Vernon?," available from: <http://www.angelfire.com/mi3/cookarama/aolintfall00.html>.

14. Doreen Valiente, *The Rebirth of Witchcraft* (Custer, WA: Phoenix Publishing, 1989), 92.

15. Valiente, 92.

16. J.K. Rowling. Quoted in Judy O'Malley, *Booklinks* (American Library Association), July 1999. Available from: <http://www.angelfire.com/mi3/cookarama/amlibjul99int.html>.

17. Craig Hawkins, *Witchcraft: Exploring the World of Wicca* (Grand Rapids: Baker, 1996), 74. Examples of published Grimoires include *The Wicca Spellbook* by Gerina Dunwich; *The Witches Workbook* by Ann Grammary; *The Wiccan Guide to Witches Ways* by Claire Lorde and Simon Lorde; and *Witches, Potions and Spells* by Kathryn Paulsen.

18. See Jeff Jenson, "Fire Storm: Interview with J.K. Rowling" [on-line], August 4, 2000. *Entertainment Weekly.* July 16, 2002. Available from: <http://www.ew.com/ew/daily/0,2514,3590,00.html>.

19. It should be noted that despite her interest in occultism, Rowling is a member of the Church of Scotland (see Joanna Carey, *Guardian Unlimited*, February 16, 1999, available from: <http://www.guardian.co.uk/Archive/Article/0,4273,3822242,00.html>). Church membership, of course, does not always reflect one's innermost religious convictions, especially in this modern era when "Christian" witches are prevalent throughout the denominations of Christendom (see Appendix B). Additionally, though, she has recently begun calling herself a Christian who believes "in God, not magic" (J.K. Rowling, quoted in Anne LeVeque, "Harry Potter Author, 'I Believe in God, Not Magic' " [on-line], January 20, 2000. *Catholic News Service.* July 16, 2002. Available from: <http://www.geocities.com/lumen_dei/rowling.html>). As one news article explains: "Rowling told a Canadian reporter that she is a Christian and that this 'seems to offend the religious right far worse than if I said I thought there was no God. Every time I've been asked if I believe in God, I've said, yes, because I do. But no one ever really has gone any more deeply into it than that and, I have to say that does suit me. . . . If I talk too freely about that, I think the intelligent reader—whether 10 or 60—will be able to guess what is coming in the books.' " (Terry Mattingly, "Rowling 'Quote' Came From Onion Web Site," [on-line], November 8, 2001. *Abilene Reporter.* July 16, 2002. Available from:

<http://www.reporternews.com/2001/religion/matt1125.html>). Beyond such innocuous comments, however, Rowling has remained vague about her faith, explaining neither her concept of "God" nor her definition of the term "Christian." And when given opportunities to discuss such topics, she has not done so, choosing instead to make rather flippant comments such as "Well, as it happens, I believe in God, but there's no pleasing some people" (J.K. Rowling, interview, America On-line, May 4, 2000, available from: <http://www.geocities.com/harrypotter518/aolchat.htm> and <http://www.iharrypotter.net/jkrowling/chats/aol.html>. She even side- stepped a question from one fan, who directly asked about John Milton's *Paradise Lost* and its "boring" portrayal of God, as opposed to its interesting portrait of Satan. Rowling made no mention of God, nor did she directly answer the question. She instead declared that Harry was good and was not boring, adding that she was not "bored by *goodness* [emphasis added]" (J.K. Rowling, interview with Evan Solomon, *CBC Newsworld*, July 13, 2000, available from: <http://cbc.ca/programs/ sites/hottype_rowlingcomplete.html>. The relevant portion of this transcript reads: "Solomon: Some people say good characters are boring and evil characters are always the more interesting. There's the famous line about Milton and *Paradise Lost*: God is a bore and the devil is interesting. Rowling: Well, Harry is good. I personally do not find Harry boring at all. He has his faults. Ron and Hermione are very good characters . . . [N]o, I'm not bored by goodness").

20. Okelle, "Harry Potter and the Witch Conspiracy" [on-line], n.d. About.com. July 16, 2002. Available from: <http://paganwiccan.about.com/library/weekly/aa080800a.htm>.

21. In a 2000 article, for instance, Rowling said: "I truly am bemused that anyone who has read the books could think that I am a proponent of the occult. . . . I don't believe in witchcraft, *in the sense* that they're talking about, at all [emphasis added]" (J.K. Rowling. Quoted in Audrey Woods, "Success Stuns Harry Potter Author" [on-line], July 6, 2000. *Associated Press.* July 16, 2002. Available from: <http://www.cesnur.org/recens/potter_030.htm>; cf. Audrey Woods, "J.K. Rowling Basks in Universal Appeal" [on-line], n.d. *Houston Chronicle.* July 16, 2002. Available from: <http://www.chron.com/cs/CDA/story.hts/special/potter/596463>). On another occasion, she explained that when it comes to the magic that appears in her series, she "does not believe in magic *in that way* [emphasis added]" (J.K. Rowling. Quoted in Judy O'Malley, *Booklinks* (American Library Association), July 1999, available from: <http://www.angelfire.com/mi3/cookarama/amlibjul99 int.html>). Elsewhere J.K. has remarked: "I don't believe in magic *in the way I describe it in my books.* I mean, I don't believe in *the wand waving sort of magic* [emphasis added]" (J.K. Rowling, interview, America On-line, May 4, 2000, available from: <http://www.geocities.com/harrypotter518/aolchat.htm>). A similar statement was made in yet another interview: "I don't believe in it [i.e., magic] in the way that I describe in my books" (Tim Bouquet, "J.K. Rowling: The Wizard Behind Harry Potter," [on-line], December 2000. *Reader's Digest*, UK Edition. July 16, 2002. Available from: <http://www.angelfire.com/mi3/cookarama/readigukintdec00 .html>). The public has tended to overlook Rowling's obvious qualifiers. She says she does not believe in witchcraft "in the sense" her critics talk about it, and rejects the "wand waving sort of magic" present in her books. But is there another "sense" in which Rowling does believe in occult powers? Of all the different forms of

magick other than the storybook "wand waving sort of magic," might there be some kind of magick she sees as real?

22. Janet Farrar and Stewart Farrar, *A Witch's Bible Compleat* (New York: Magickal Childe Publishing, 1984), 2:110. This volume reads: "Magic . . . is obeying laws that the observer has not yet understood. A sixteenth-century scientist, for example . . . if he could have seen television might well have branded it as supernatural."

23. Mark McGarrity, "Harry Potter's Creator Meets Her Public" [on-line], October 16, 1999. *The Star-Ledger* (New Jersey). July 16, 2002. Available from: <http://www.montclairkimberley.org/jkrowling/buzz.html> (audio file available of Rowling's Q & A on which the news article is based is available from: <http://www.montclairkimberley.org/jkrowling/media/answers/answer4aud.mov>).

24. During one radio call-in interview, for instance, a self-professed Magus (male witch) hailed Rowling with the Wiccan greeting, "Blessed Be." He then asked her if she was a fellow member of the Craft. When Rowling said no, he seemed shocked and replied, "[Y]ou've done you're homework quite well." This particular caller went on to express his love for the Harry Potter books not only because it contained so much occultism, but also because of its positive portrayal of magick. The series actually had served to make his daughter more comfortable with his own practices as a witch-magickian (see *The Connection*, radio interview with J.K. Rowling, October 12, 1999, a real audio version is available from: <http://archives.theconnection.org/archive/1999/12/1228a.shtml>).

25. J.K. Rowling, interview with Evan Solomon, *CBC Newsworld*, July 13, 2000, available from: <http://cbc.ca/programs/sites/hottype_rowlingcomplete.html> and <http://www.angelfire.com/mi3/cookarama/cbcint2.html>. This interview reads: "[T]he two groups of people who seem to think in Britain that I'm wholeheartedly on their side are people who support the boarding school system and practicing witches—Wiccans!—which are not two groups that one would expect to find allied in any way. And, in fact, they are both wrong. I don't believe in boarding schools.... And I'm neither a practicing witch, nor do I believe in magic."

26. J.K. Rowling. Quoted in Jenson, available from: <http://www.ew.com/ew/daily/0, 2514,3590,00.html> and <http://www.angelfire.com/mi3/cookarama/ewinter .html>. This interview reads: "People who send their children to boarding schools seem to feel that I'm on their side. I'm not. Practicing wiccans think I'm also a witch. I'm not."

27. J.K. Rowling, interview, Vancouver Writers' Festival, October 25, 2000, available from: <http://www.cbc4kids.ca/general/words/harrypottercontest/default.html>. During another interview, Rowling showed equal contempt for those objecting to her books: "[A]re we talking about the religious right again? If so, I'd say "hogwash" was a pretty good description!" (J.K. Rowling, Yahooligans Chat, October 20, 2000, available from: <http://www.angelfire.com/mi3/cookarama/yahoolintoct00pt2.html>).

28. Duke University News Service, "'Harry Potter,' 'Lord of the Rings' Tap into Fairy Tales, Fascination with Medieval History, Say Two Duke Scholars" [on-line], November 27, 2001. July 16, 2002. Available from: <http://www.dukenews.duke.edu/ human/potter.htm>.

29. J.K. Rowling, interview with Barnes and Noble, September 8, 1999, available from: <http://www.geocities.com/aberforths_goat/September_1999_Barnes_Noble.htm>, <http://www.burrow-jp.com/library/original/09081999.html>; <http://www.mugglemagic.net/interview1.htm>.

30. J.K. Rowling, interview, *The Diane Rehm Show* (WAMU), audio file available from: <http://www.wamu.org/dr/shows/drarc_991018.html#wednesday>.

31. Rowling, interview, *The Diane Rehm Show*, available from: <http://www.wamu.org/dr/shows/drarc_991018.html#wednesday>.

32. J.K. Rowling, author appearance at Montclair Kimberley Academy, audio file available from: <http://www.montclairkimberley.org/jkrowling/media/answers/answer4aud.mov>.

33. J.K. Rowling, interview, *Larry King Live*, available from: <http://www.cnn.com/TRANSCRIPTS/0010/20/lkl.00.html>.

34. Rowling, interview, *Larry King Live*, available from: <http://www.cnn.com/TRANSCRIPTS/0010/20/lkl.00.html>.

35. J.K. Rowling, Yahoolagans Chat, available from: <http://www.angelfire.com/mi3/cookarama/yahoolintoct00pt2.html>.

36. Allan Zola Kronzek and Elizabeth Kronzek, *The Sorcerer's Companion* (New York: Broadway Books, 2001), back cover.

37. Deepti Hajela, "Potter Charms Modern-Day Witches" [on-line], May 30, 2000. *Associated Press*. July 16, 2002. Available from: <http://www.cesnur.org/recens/potter_024.htm>.

38. Sarah the Swamp Witch, posted comment available from: <http://www.dutchie.org/Tracy/advice.html>. Another witch explained: "For those who believe that the practice of magic does not involve deity, then witchcraft (with a small 'w') might be the more appropriate term" (Dana, posted comment available from: <http://www.dutchie.org/Tracy/advice.html>). A third witch agreed: "As far as I am concerned, a "witch" (please note small caps) does not have any pre-defined deity(s) they 'must' worship" (Cserrilyn Sadar, posted comment available from: <http://www.dutchie.org/Tracy/advice.html>).

39. Wren Walker. Quoted in David Yonke, "Some Fear Road to Hell Paved with 'Harry Potter' " [on-line], November 24, 2001. *Bradenton Herald*. July 16, 2002. Available from: <http://www.cesnur.org/2001/potter/nov_16.htm>. Reference to the "w" issue also can be found in Isaac Bonewits, *Witchcraft: A Concise History* (PocketPCpress: 1971; 2001 edition), available from: <http://www.neopagan.net/Witchcraft-Classifying.html>. It reads: "witchcraft-with-a-small-w: The beliefs and practices of those modern persons following one or more varieties of Neopagan Witchcraft who refuse to admit it." Some neopagans have confused the Harry Potter issue when it comes to whether or not the series promotes Witchcraft. During interviews with the media, such persons adamantly declare how absurd it is to assert that Rowling's books contain Wiccan beliefs. But what these individuals are saying is in reference to specific Wiccan doctrines, which indeed are not in the books. At the same time, however, they fail to comment on the real forms of occultism in the books (witchcraft) that are practiced by Wiccans. They also do not address the accuracy with which Rowling portrays such practices (e.g., spellcasting). For denials of Wicca in Harry Potter from Wiccans, see Ben Roy, "Wiccans Dispute Potter Claims" [on-line], October 26, 2000. *Citizen On-line* (Newfound Area Bureau), posted at The Witch's League for Public Awareness. July 16, 2002. Available from: <http://www.celticcrow.com/news/potter1026.html>.

40. Colin Covert, "A Genuine Touch of Magic" [on-line], November 16, 2001. *Star Tribune* (Minneapolis-St. Paul). July 16, 2002, 22E. Available from: <http://www.startribune.com> (archives).

41. Covert, "A Genuine Touch of Magic," available from: <http://www.startribune.com> (archives).

42. Moon Pixie, message #1435, November 24, 2001, posted at Pagan Perspectives, available from: <http://www.witchvox.net/perspect/q068_hpm.html?-token.skip=12>.

43. Moon Pixie, available from: <http://www.witchvox.net/perspect/q068_hpm.html?-token.skip=12>.

44. Starling, message #1420, November 22, 2001, posted at Pagan Perspectives, available from: <http://www.witchvox.net/perspect/q068_hpm.html?-token.skip=24>.

45. See the Wicce Women Web site at <http://wiccewoman.homestead.com/BooksMain.html>. The many neopagans and Wiccans listed with Rowling include: Margot Adler (*Drawing Down the Moon*), Vivianne Crowley (*Principles of Wicca*), Scott Cunningham (*Living Wicca*), Phyllis Curott (*Book of Shadows*), Gerald Gardner (*Witchcraft Today*), Silver Ravenwolf (*Teen Witch*), Starhawk (*The Spiral Dance*) and Doreen Valiente (*An ABC of Witchcraft*).

46. See "The Inner Sanctum of Wicca and Witchcraft" Web site at <http://www.witchway.net/witchcraft/list.html>. The "Harry Potter Books" category appears in this site's "Witch's Wares, Occult Store" amid numerous occult categories: e.g., "Wiccan/Witchcraft Books;" "Astrological Books;" "Tarot and Rune Books;" and "Tarot Card Sets."

47. IO, *The Harry Potter Witchcraft Spellbook*, available from: <http://www6.aeonflux.net/~io/index.html>.

48. IO, available from: <http://www6.aeonflux.net/~io/index.html>.

49. Phyllis Curott. Quoted in Buck Wolf, "Witches Bless Harry Potter" [on-line], n.d. ABCnews.com. July 16, 2002. Available from: <http://abcnews.go.com/sections/us/WolfFiles/wolffiles122.html>.

50. Kronzek and Kronzek, 32-4, 149-53.

51. Kronzek and Kronzek, 28-31.

52. See the "Myth Buster" Web site regarding Wicca, available from: <http://www.darkforce.com/wicca/myths.htm>.

53. Rowling, *Sorcerer's Stone*, 291. Anton LaVey labeled as nonsense any differentiations between white (good) and black magick (evil), saying: "White magic is supposedly utilized only for good or unselfish purposes, and black magic, we are told, is used only for selfish or 'evil' reasons. Satanism draws no such dividing line. Magic is magic, be it used to help or hinder" (Anton LaVey, *The Satanic Bible* [New York: Avon Books, 1969], 51).

54. Rosemary Ellen Guiley, *The Encyclopedia of Witches & Witchcraft* (New York: Checkmark Books, 1999), 5-6.

55. Rowling, *Sorcerer's Stone*, 66.

56. See list of initiation degrees at Ordo Anno Mundi Web site at <http://www.angelfire.com/realm/oam/init.htm>

57. The vast array of occult practices, phenomena, lore, objects and personalities are far too numerous to list. A few notable instances, however, are necessary to document: divination (e.g., astrology—Book I, 254, 257), clairvoyance (Book IV, 17, 576-7), magick (throughout Books I-IV), herbology (Book I, 133), potions (Book I, 136-7), spirit channeling (Book III, 324), necromancy (Rowling's characters are constantly communicating with the spirit realm via ghosts, magical creatures, and enchanted objects (books, mirrors, etc.). They regularly commune with ghosts including Professor Binns (one of Hogwarts' teachers), Peeves (a malevo-

lent spirit), Moaning Myrtle (a murdered Hogwarts student), and Nearly Headless Nick (Gryffindor's resident apparition).

58. Raven Grimassi, *Encyclopedia of Wicca & Witchcraft* (St. Paul: Llewellyn Publications, 2000), 405.

59. Dawn Marie Nikithser, message #1375, November 19, 2001, posted at Pagan Perspectives, available from: <http://www.witchvox.net/perspect/q068_ hpm.html?-
token.skip=66>.

60. Kronzec and Kronzec, xiii.

61. Kronzec and Kronzec, 1, 4, 10, 36, 41, 56, 120, 159, 182, 191, 221, 249.

62. Shepard, 2:1282.

63. Kurt Seligmann, *Magic, Supernaturalism, and Religion* (New York: Pantheon
Books, 1948; 1971 edition), 96.

64. Rowling, *Sorcerer's Stone*, 220.

65. Helene Vachet, "Harry Potter and the Perennial Quest" [on-line], November-
December 2001. *Quest Magazine*. July 16, 2002. Available from: <http://www
.theosophical.org/theosophy/questmagazine/novdec2001/vachet/>. Helene Vachet recently retired from the Los Angeles School District as an assistant principal
and a teacher of "Myths and Magic." She is a third-generation theosophist and past
president of Besant Lodge in Hollywood. She is particularly interested in mythology, fantasy literature and Jungian psychology. The Theosophical Society is made
up of nondogmatic persons who tend to adopt only those ideas that satisfy their
own sense of what is real and important. Theosophy is a way of looking at life
rather than a creed. Modern Theosophy, however, generally presents the following ideas:

   • reincarnation,
   • karma (or moral justice),
   • the existence of worlds of experience beyond the physical,
   • the presence of life and consciousness in all matter,
   • the evolution of spirit and intelligence as well as of physical matter,
   • the possibility of our conscious participation in evolution,
   • the power of thought to affect one's self and surroundings,
   • the reality of free will and self-responsibility,
   • the duty of altruism, a concern for the welfare of others and
   • the ultimate perfection of human nature, society and life.

66. Rowling, *Sorcerer's Stone*, 219.

67. Maurice Magre, *Magicians, Seers, and Mystics* (Kila, MT: Kessinger Publishing, 1997;
transl. Reginald Merton), available from: <http://www.alchemylab.com/
flamel.htm>. Rowling also mentions Flamel's wife, Perenelle. Again, this is not fictitious. Nicholas' wife, in agreement with the J.K.'s "fantasy" novel, was named
Perenelle (also spelled Petronelle). Rowling even correctly identifies the approxi-
mate era of their lives. Book I takes place in late 1991-1992 (a school year cycle), a
date easily discerned by calculating subtle time markers in Book II (*Harry Potter
and the Chamber of Secrets*). In *Sorcerer's Stone*, Flamel is 665 years old. This number
subtracted from 1991/92 comes to the year 1326/27 for Flamel's birth (as recorded
by Rowling). In the real world, Flamel was born in 1330, give or take a few years (see
Shepard, 1:594).

68. Children are not simply reading such religion-related comments and giving them
no thought. In a letter to www.yabooks.com, a fifteen-year-old wrote the follow-

ing observation in reference to Rowling's books: "They deal with death, but in a positive way—in the first book, Dumbledore tells Harry, Ron, and Hermione that death is just like a rest after a very long day" ("Young Adult 'Save Harry Potter' Comments: Page 1," available from: <http://www.yabooks.com>).

69. Magre, available from: <http://www.alchemylab.com/flamel.htm>.
70. Starhawk, *The Spiral Dance* (San Francisco, CA: Harper San Francisco, 1979; 1989 edition), 124.
71. Rowling, interview with Barnes and Noble, September 8, 1999, available from: <http://www.geocities.com/aberforths_goat/September_1999_Barnes_Noble.htm>, <http://www.burrow-jp.com/library/original/09081999.html>; and <http://www.mugglemagic.net/interview1.htm>; cf. "Some of the magic in the books is based on what people used to believe really worked, but most of it is my invention" (J.K. Rowling, interview with Barnes and Noble, March 19, 1999, available from: <http://www.burrow-jp.com/library/original/03191999.html>).
72. Francis Bridger, "What's So Wrong about Harry" [on-line], November 16, 2001. *Church of England Newspaper*. July 16, 2002. Available from: <http://www.youth.co.za/theedge/reviews/reviewsPC06.asp>.
73. Shepard, 2:1569.
74. Shepard, 2:1569.
75. Kronzcc and Kronzec, 154.
76. "What's in a Name," Booklist, available from: <http://www.theninemuses.net/hp/a.html>; cf. Encyclopedia Potterica, "Name and Word Origins," available from: <http://www.harrypotterfans.net/potterica/origins.html> and "Harry Potter Derivatives," available on-line at <http://www.sugarquill.net/archivehp/ccgp/derivatives.html>. One interview exchange regarding Avada Kedavra reads as follows: "Tanya asks: Where do you come up with the words that you use, the names of the classes and spells and games, etc. For example, the Patronus Expectumous, was it? Jkrowling_bn: . . . Mostly I invent spells, but some of them have particular meanings, like 'Avada Kedavra.' I bet someone out there knows what that means" (J.K. Rowling, Yahoolagans Chat, October 20, 2000, available from: <http://www.angelfire.com/mi3/cookarama/ yahoolintoct00pt2.html>).
77. Rowling, *Sorcerer's Stone*, 217.
78. Shepard, 2:1569.
79. Shepard, 2:1569.
80. Rowling, *Sorcerer's Stone*, 171.
81. "[P]eople in the portraits along the corridors whispered and pointed as they passed" (*Sorcerer's Stone*, p. 128); "They walked past muttering portraits and creaking suits of armor" (*Chamber of Secrets*, p. 83); "[T]hey reached the passage where the secret entrance to Gryffindor Tower was hidden, behind an oil painting of a very fat woman in a pink silk dress. 'Password?' she said as they approached" (*Chamber of Secrets*, p. 83-4).
82. The Chemical Wedding of Christian Rosenkreutz (1616), available from: <http://www.sacred-texts.com/eso/chemical/chemical.htm>. It reads: "[T]here were up and down the room wonderful images, which moved themselves, as if they had been alive. . . . There began such a marvellous kind of vocal music, that I could not tell for sure whether it was performed by the virgins who still stayed behind, or by the images themselves."

83. This information is available on-line at the official A.M.O.R.C. Rosicrucianism Web site, "Our Traditional and Chronological History," <http://www.rosicrucian.org/rosicruc/mastery/6-history.html>.

84. See <http://www.amazon.com/exec/obidos/ASIN/0933999356/qid=10208712 45/sr=8-1/ref=sr_8_7_1/002-5233221-0591239>. For information on Rosicrucianism, see the A.M.O.R.C. welcome page at <http://rosicrucian.org/rosicruc/mastery/1-welcome.html#challenges>.

85. J.K. Rowling. Quoted in Kathleen Koch, "Success of Harry Potter Bowls Author Over" [on-line], October 21, 1999. CNN. July 16, 2002. Available from: <http://www.cnn.com/books/news/9910/21/rowling.intvu/>.

86. "Potter Prompts Course in Witchcraft" [on-line], February 18, 2002. *BBC News.* July 16, 2002. Available from: <http://news.bbc.co.uk/hi/english/education/newsid_1827000/1827166.stm>.

87. "Ultra Sound: Social History of the Mosh Pit," *MTV*, aired May 4, 2002.

88. "MTV Defends Itself after Youth Burned in 'Copycat' Incident" [on-line], January 29, 2001. CNN.com. July 16, 2002. Available from: <http://www.cnn.com/2001/SHOWBIZ/TV/01/29/mtv.fire.02/index.html>. MTV disavowed all responsibility for the incident, saying: "It is made extremely clear throughout the show, through the use of written and verbal warnings, that none of the stunts featured should be tried at home. The show airs with a TV-MA rating and warnings throughout that specifically state, 'The following show features stunts performed by professionals and/or total idiots under very strict control and supervision. MTV and the producers insist that neither you or anyone else attempt to recreate or perform anything you have seen on this show.' " This MTV program has featured young men being pushed down a flight of stairs in a laundry basket; being hurled from a shopping cart into bushes; getting zapped by an electronic dog collar; leaping into a plastic pool full of elephant dung; complaining to a waitress after slipping dog poop onto their restaurant plate. The program also has shown a kid running into an intersection and knocking a skateboarder off his wheels, onto his butt, in the middle of the street and a man riding a child's plastic big wheel bike into the street in front of a car (see John Kiesewetter, "Real Jackasses Are MTV Programmers" [on-line], n.d. *The Cincinnati Enquirer.* July 16, 2002. Available from: <http://enquirer.com/editions/2001/02/18/tem_kiesewetter_real.html>).

89. Dean Schabner, "The Makings of a Jackass Kid" [on-line], n.d. ABCnews.com. July 16, 2002. Available from: <http://abcnews.go.com/sections/us/DailyNews/jackass010508.html>. In another incident, "a teenager tried to reproduce a prank that showed a regular cast member lunging a fast-food drive-thru window and stealing someone's order before it makes it to the customer. In the non-broadcast amateur version of this stunt, the wanna-be Jackass snapped the hourly-wage employee's wrist clean back and broke [it]" (Viki Reed, "MTV and the Mutilation Done" [on-line], March 4, 2001. *Disinformation.* July 16, 2002. Available from: <http://www.disinfo.com/pages/article/id924/pg2/>).

90. Dan Weiss, "Wrestling with Perversity: America's Love Affair with the WWF" [on-line], winter 2000. *Doublethink.* July 16, 2002. Available from: <http://www.americasfuture.org/doublethink/winter2000/d/winter2000.pdf>.

91. "Harry Potter Makes Boarding Fashionable" [on-line], December 13, 1999. *BBC News.* July 16, 2002. Available from: <http://news.bbc.co.uk/hi/english/education/newsid_563000/563232.stm>.

92. "Harry Potter Makes Boarding Fashionable." August 2, 2002. Available from: <http://news.bbc.co.uk/hi/english/education/newsid_563000/ 563232.stm>.
93. "Harry Potter Makes Boarding Fashionable." August 2, 2002. Available from: <http://news.bbc.co.uk/hi/english/education/newsid_563000/563232.stm>.
94. "Siberian Potter Fans Drink Poisonous Potion" [on-line], April 20, 2002. *BBC News*. July 16, 2002. Available from: <http://news.bbc.co.uk/hi/english/world/monitoring/media_reports/newsid_1941000/1941152.stm>.
95. "Siberian Potter Fans Drink Poisonous Potion," available from: <http://news.bbc.co.uk/hi/english/world/monitoring/media_reports/newsid_1941000/1941152.stm>.
96. "Like Mike—Don't Try This at Home," [on-line], June 28, 2002. Reuters. August 1, 2002. Available from: <http://www.reuters.com/news_article.jhtml?type+search&StoryID=114 2357>.
97. Schabner, available from: <http://abcnews.go.com/sections/us/DailyNews/jackass010508.html>.
98. Schabner, available from: <http://abcnews.go.com/sections/us/DailyNews/jackass010508.html>.
99. Peter Smith. Quoted in "Harry Potter 'Occult' Warning" [on-line], November 5, 2001. *BBC News*. July 16, 2002. Available from: <http://news.bbc.co.uk/hi/english/education/newsid_1638000/1638887.stm>.
100. Smith. Quoted in "Harry Potter 'Occult' Warning." Available from: <http://news.bbc.co.uk/hi/english/education/newsid 1638000/1638887.stm>; cf. Tracy McVeigh, "Teachers Warn of Occult Dangers in Potter Movie Magic" [on-line], November 4, 2001. *The Observer* (England). July 16, 2002. Available from: <http://www.observer.co.uk/uk_news/story/0,6903,587261,00.html>.
101. John Andrew Murray, "Harry Dilemma" [on-line], n.d. *Teachers In Focus*. July 16, 2002. Available from: <http://www.ers-neunkirchen.de/potter/dilemma.htm>.
102. Elizabeth A. Wittman, "Occult Trends in Children's Literature" [on-line], n.d. *Homiletic & Pastoral Review*. July 16, 2002. Available from: <http://www.catholic.net/rcc/Periodicals/Homiletic/2000-10/wittman.html>.
103. Greydanus, available from: <http://decentfilms.com/commentary/magic.html>.
104. Michael O'Brien, "Why Harry Potter Goes Awry" [on-line], December 6, 2001. Zenit News Agency. July 16, 2002. Available from: <http://www.youth.co.za/theedge/reviews/reviewsPC07.asp> and <http://www.catholiceducation.org/articles/arts/al0120.html>.
105. Heather, Message #1432, November 24, 2001, available from: <http://www.witchvox.net/perspect/q068_hpm.html?-token.skip=12>.
106. Lori, Message #1398, November 20, 2001, available from: <http://www.witchvox.net/perspect/q068_hpm.html?-token.skip=48>.
107. Jason, Message #1372, November 19, 2001, available from: <http://www.witchvox.net/perspect/q068_hpm.html?-token.skip=72>.
108. DaraLuz, Message #1367, November 19, 2001, available from: <http://www.witchvox.net/perspect/q068_hpm.html?-token.skip=78>.
109. Linda, Message #1390, November 20, 2001, available from: <http://www.witchvox.net/perspect/q068_hpm.html?-token.skip=54>.
110. Riannon Silvermoon, Message #1378, November 19, 2001, available from: <http://www.witchvox.net/perspect/q068_hpm.html?-token.skip=66>.

111. St. Parker, "Magick or Madness" [on-line], n.d. *Journal of Eclectic Magick*. July 16, 2002. Available from: <http://eclecticmagick.com/potter.php>. A 2001 Reuters news article included similar comments from Wiccan Ruth Shelton. This story noted: "Meanwhile real life witches have praised the Harry Potter stories as painting their practices in a good light and raising their oft-maligned profile. Ruth Shelton, 43, of New York, has been a practicing witch for 27 years. . . . [S]he balks when asked if Harry Potter's world of Hogwarts bears any similarities to her own. '[Witches] don't have quite the same array of fantasy characters or live in a world completely apart from the mundane world,' she said. But are they realistic? 'She [i.e., Rowling] has treated all of the fantasy realm and the magic she works with the utmost respect,' Shelton said. Shelton is also curious about Rowling's own practice and says that members of her coven think that the books 'can open people up to alternative practices, that have rich lore, history and morality' " (Sarah Tippitt, "Harry Potter Film: Invitation to Join Occult?" [on-line], November 17, 2001. *Reuters*. July 16, 2002. Available from: <http://in.news.yahoo.com/ 011117/ 14/18ycr.html>).

112. James Woudhuysen, "The Magic of Mobile" [on-line], May 9, 2001. *Spiked*. July 16, 2002. Available from: <http://www.spiked-on-line.com/Articles/00000002 D0A7.htm>.

113. Andy Norfolk. Quoted in "Potter Fans Turning to Witchcraft" [on-line], August 4, 2000. Available from: <http://www.thisislondon.co.uk/dy-namic/news/story.html?in_review_id=306029&in_review_text_id= 250010>; cf. Robert Mendick, "Witches Take Pagan Message to Youth" [on-line], April 2, 2000. *The Independent* (England). July 16, 2002. Available from: <http://www.independent.co.uk/story.jsp?story=7241>.

114. Kronzek and Kronzek, xiv.

115. Sirona Knight has written more than a dozen books on witchcraft and neopaganism. She has also been contributing editor for *Magical Blend* magazine for the past three years and a featured writer for *New Age Retailer* and *Aquarius* magazines.

116. Sirona's Books, advertisement available from: <http://www.dcsi.net/~bluesky/ bs3.htm>.

117. Sirona Knight, *The Witch and Wizard Training Guide* (Secaucus, NJ: Citadel Press, 2001), back cover. See <www.amazon.com/exec/obidos/tg/stores/detail/ -/books/0806522135/reader/ 7/002-0260620-8900824#reader-link>.

118. Knight, 2-3.

119. Reviewer: A reader from Vermilion, OH, USA, "A Great Introduction into the Magical World" [on-line], January 22, 2002. July 16, 2002. Available from: <http://www.amazon.com/exec/obidos/tg/stores/detail/-/books/0806522135/ glance/102-2981260-4553757>.

120. Available from: <http://www.amazon.com/exec/obidos/tg/stores/detail/-/books/ 0806522135/glance/102-2981260-4553757>.

121. Available from: <http://www.amazon.com/exec/obidos/tg/stores/detail/-/ books/0806522135/glance/102-2981260-4553757>.

122. "The Real Witches' Handbook," advertisement available from: <http:// witchcraft.org/books/KateWest.htm>.

123. Rowling has stated on many occasions that she has never heard of any child ex-pressing a desire to be a witch/wizard or get involved with occultism:

- "I have yet to meet a single child who's told me that they want to be a Satanist, or are particularly interested in the occult because of the book" (J.K. Rowling, Quoted Nicole Martin, "Children Are Safe with Harry Potter, Author Tells Critics" [on-line], October 18, 1999. *Electronic Telegraph*. July 16, 2002. Available from: <http://www.northernlight.com>).
- "I've never met a single child who asked me about the occult" (J.K. Rowling. Quoted in Linton Weeks, "Charmed I'm Sure" [on-line], October 20, 1999 *The Washington Post*. July 16, 2002. Available from: <http://www.washingtonpost.com/wp-srv/style/books/features/rowling1020.htm>); and
- "[N]ot even one time has a child come up to me and said, 'Ms. Rowling, I'm so glad I've read these books because now I want to be a witch'" (J.K. Rowling. Quoted in Koch, see endnote #86, available from: <http://www.cnn.com/books/news/9910/21/rowling.intvu/>).

124. Rachel G. Quoted in "What Are You Reading" [on-line], n.d. July 16, 2002. Available from: <http://apps.scholastic.com/tabadvisors/reading.asp>.
125. Quoted in Bill Adler, comp., *Kid's Letters to Harry Potter from around the World* (New York: Carroll & Graf Publishers, Inc., 2001), 32.
126. Quoted in Bill Adler, 95
127. Quoted in Bill Adler, 55.
128. Quoted in Bill Adler, 51.
129. Letters to the Editor, "What Readers Think about 'Goblet'" [on-line], July 26, 2000. *San Francisco Chronicle*. August 1, 2002. Available from: <http://www.sfgate.com>.
130. Lily, "Rave Reviews," as of January 2001 this post was available from: <http://hosted.ukoln.ac.uk/stories/gallery/reviews/rowling/rowling-stone.htm>.
131. Robert Knight, "A Few Thoughts about Harry" [on-line], November 21, 2001 *Culture and Family*. July 16, 2002. Available from: <http://cultureandfamily.org/report/2001-11-21/o_knight.shtml>.
132. <http://www.the-leaky-cauldron.org/2002_03_31_archive.html> is only one of many Web sites that provide a link to Harry's horoscope. Another fan Web site would be <http://harrypotter.searchbeat.com/>.
133. Schermer makes available Harry's horoscope chart at <http://www.astrologyalive.com/HPChart.html>.
134. Schermer makes available her interpretation of Harry's horoscope at <http://www.astrologyalive.com/HPChart.html#Interpretation>. Her recommendations of occult books through a Harry Potter Web page can be accessed by going to <http://www.astrologyalive.com/HPBooks.html> and clicking on the "For Astrology Books" link.
135. "Real Magick: The Science of Wizardry," advertised by Discovery Channel at <http://dsc.discovery.com/convergence/realmagick/realmagick.html>.
136. The document "Exclusive Download: Harry Potter" that is posted at this Internet resource Web site includes the following exercises (available from: <http://www.beachampublishing.com>):
    - "Look up the names mentioned on the wizard cards [in *Sorcerer's Stone*] . . . and list whether they are real or fictional. If they are historical figures, write a paragraph about each magician, witch, or wizard."

- "Learn about the role of witchcraft [i.e., real witchcraft] in different cultures. Either make a costume for yourself . . . or use construction paper to design the attire of witches in a specific geographic location."
- "[W]rite a poem, short play, literary non-fiction, or other form of expression about magic or witchcraft."

137. "Exclusive Download: Harry Potter," available from: <http://www.beachampublishing.com>.
138. "Exclusive Download: Harry Potter," available from: <http://www.beachampublishing.com>.
139. "Exclusive Download: Harry Potter," available from: <http://www.beachampublishing.com>.
140. Rowling has explained this during several interviews. For example, she has stated: "The magical world of Hogwarts is like the real world only distorted. We're not going off to a different planet. It's a fantastic world which has to exist shoulder to shoulder with the real world" ("J.K. Rowling: Harry Potter and Me Special" [on-line], n.d. July 16, 2002. Available from: <http://www.mugglenet.com/jkrshow.shtml>).
141. J.K. Rowling. Quoted in Malcolm Jones, "The Return of Harry Potter!" [on-line], July 1, 2000. *Newsweek*. July 16, 2002. Available from: <http://www.angelfire.com/mi3/cookarama/newswkint00.html>; and <http://tww.darkmark.com/interview11.shtml>.
142. See Bill Adler, 32, 51, 55, 95.
143. J.K. Rowling, interview with Scholastic Books, Chat #2, October 16, 2000, available from: <http://www.scholastic.com/harrypotter/author/transcript2.htm> and <http://www.angelfire.com/mi3/cookarama/scholintoct00.html>.
144. Rowling, interview with Scholastic, available from: <http://www.scholastic.com/harrypotter/author/transcript2.htm> and <http://www.angelfire.com/mi3/cookarama/scholintoct00.html>.
145. Daniel McGrory, "Children Seduced by Forces of Satanism on the Internet" [on-line], August 28, 2001. *The Times* (London). July 16, 2002. Available from: <http://www.abanes.com/SatanismTimes.html>.
146. McGrory, available from: <http://www.abanes.com/SatanismTimes.html>.
147. McGrory, available from: <http://www.abanes.com/SatanismTimes.html>.
148. Celia Rees, *Witch Child* (Cambridge, MA: Candlewick Press, 2001); cf. "Witch Reports On Occult Power" [on-line], October 28, 2000. *The Independent*. Available from: <http://www.independent.co.uk/story.jsp?story=46495>.
149. "Witch Reports On Occult Power," available from: <http://www.independent.co.uk/story.jsp?story=46495>.
150. J.K. Rowling, "Elizabeth Hurley Talks about Playing the Devil in 'Bedazzled'; J.K. Rowling Discusses the Surprising Success of 'Harry Potter' " [on-line], October 20, 2000. *Larry King Live*. July 16, 2002. Available from: <http://www.cnn.com/TRANSCRIPTS/0010/20/lkl.00.html>.
151. A 1999 Knight-Ridder news article, for instance, reported that Harry Potter is the perfect role model to teach children lessons of endurance, kindness, wisdom and love (see Richard Scheinin, "Christians of All Stripes in Harry Potter's Corner" [on-line], November 27, 1999. *Abilene Reporter*. July 16, 2002. Available from: <http://www.reporternews.com/1999/religion/harry1127.html>).

152. Alan Jacobs, "Harry Potter's Magic" [on-line], January 2000. *First Things*, 35-8. July 16, 2002. Available from: <http://www.firstthings.com/ftissues/ ft0001/reviews/jacobs.html>.

153. Nicholas Bury. Quoted in "Harry Potter Goes to Church" [on-line], August 8, 2000. BBC News Service. July 16, 2002. Available from: <http://news.bbc.co.uk/ hi/english/entertainment/newsid_871000/871240.stm> (and numerous other Web sites). An open letter to the public written by Bury is available from: <http://gloucestercathedral.uk.com/sub_pages/harry%20potter/ harry%20Potter%20the%20dean_writes.htm>.

154. Quoted in Robert Knight, *The Age of Consent* (Dallas: Spence Publishing, 1998),10.

155. Robert Knight, *The Age of Consent*, 11.

156. William Watkins, *The New Absolutes* (Minneapolis: Bethany House, 1996), 28.

157. J.K. Rowling. Q & A Session, Vancouver Writer's Festival, October 25, 2000.

158. Charles Taylor, "The Plot Deepens" [on-line], July 10, 2000. *Salon.com*. July 16, 2002. Available from: <http://www.salon.com/books/review/2000/07/10/potter/ index.html>.

159. Between pages 140 and 225 of *Harry Potter and the Sorcerer's Stone*, Harry breaks Hogwarts school rules eight times: 1) rides a broom against a teacher's directive (pp. 147-9); 2) agrees to a wizard's duel using magic (p. 153); 3) sneaks out at night (p. 173); 4) sneaks out again at night (p. 205); 5) peruses books in the Dark Arts section of the library (pp. 205-6); 6) sneaks out for a third time at night (p. 210); 7) sneaks out for a fourth time at night (p. 212); 8) goes into the Forbidden Forest (p. 225).

160. Rowling, *Goblet of Fire*, 722.

161. Rowling, *Prisoner of Azkaban*, 355-6.

162. Rowling, *Prisoner of Azkaban*, 284.

163. Rowling, *Prisoner of Azkaban*, 204.

164. Rowling, *Prisoner of Azkaban*, 351-2.

165. Rowling, *Prisoner of Azkaban*, 192.

166. Rowling, *Prisoner of Azkaban*, 193.

167. Rowling, *Goblet of Fire*, 55, 88, 367.

168. Rowling, *Goblet of Fire*, 88-9, 117.

169. Rowling, *Goblet of Fire*, 117.

170. Rowling, *Chamber of Secrets*, 31.

171. Rowling, *Chamber of Secrets*, 39, 66.

172. Rowling, *Goblet of Fire*, 45.

173. Rowling, *Goblet of Fire*, 61.

174. Rowling, *Sorcerer's Stone*, 80.

175. Rowling, *Sorcerer's Stone*, 80.

176. Several examples of Hagrid's excessive drinking are as follows: "Harry watched Hagrid getting redder and redder in the face as he called for more wine, finally kissing Professor McGonagall on the cheek" (*Sorcerer's Stone*, pp. 203-4). "'Hagrid told that stranger how to get past Fluffy . . . it must've been easy, once he'd got Hagrid drunk' " (*Sorcerer's Stone*, p. 266). "Dumbledore led them in a few of his favorite [Christmas] carols, Hagrid booming more and more loudly with every goblet of eggnog he consumed" (*Chamber of Secrets*, p. 212). "It was Hagrid, making his way up to the castle, singing at the top of his voice, and weaving

slightly as he walked. A large bottle was swinging from his hands. . . . They watched Hagrid meander tipsily up to the castle" (*Prisoner of Azkaban*, p. 405).

177. " 'I think you've had enough to drink, Hagrid,' said Hermione firmly. She took the tankard from the table and went outside to empty it" (*Prisoner of Azkaban*, 121).

178. Rowling, *Sorcerer's Stone*, 59, 64.

179. Rowling, *Sorcerer's Stone*, 230-3.

180. On page 64 of *Sorcerer's Stone*, for example, Hagrid makes the following request: " 'If I was ter—er—speed things up a bit, would yeh mind not mentionin' it at Hogwarts?' " Harry replies, "Of course not" because he is "eager to see more magic." Later in the book, Hagrid actually allows Harry, Ron and Hermione to smuggle his illegal dragon out of Hogwarts, with the help of Ron's brother (a Hogwart's graduate) and some of Ron's older post-graduate friends (*Sorcerer's Stone*, p. 237).

181. Dumbledore breaks Hogwarts rules in *Sorcerer's Stone* by allowing Harry to play Quidditch and also by allowing him to have his own broomstick. These are seemingly minor infractions, to be sure, but they belie two of the overriding themes of Harry Potter: 1) rules are made to be broken, especially by those who have either enough power or cunning; and 2) the ends justifies the means.

182. Rowling, *Chamber of Secrets*, 125.

183. This insightful observation was first raised by Michael O'Brien in his important work, *A Landscape With Dragons*, 68.

184. J.K. Rowling. Quoted in Deirdre Donahue, "Harry Potter's Appeal: Proof Positive," *USA Today*, December 2, 1999. Available from: <www.usatoday.com>.

185. Rowling, *Goblet of Fire*, 645.

186. Jennifer G., "Harry Potter: Magical or Harmful?: The Beloved Wizard—Revisited!" [on-line], n.d. July 16, 2002. Available from: <http://www.momson-line.com>.

187. Novelist Michael O'Brien concisely notes the problem with Rowling's moral landscape: "Lip service is paid to a code of ethics—never really spelled out—but in fact the undermining of those ethics is reinforced at every turn. Harry's faults are rarely punished, and usually by the negative authority figures in the tale. The positive authority figures actually reward Harry for his disobedience when it brings about some perceived good. His lies, his acts of vengeance, and his misuse of his powers are frequently ignored. The message of 'the end justifies the means' is dominant throughout" (Michael O'Brien, "Author Michael D. O'Brien Critiques a Literary Phenomenon" [on-line], n.d. July 16, 2002. Available from: <http://www.warmbooks.com/html/miscellaneous/ZENIT-NEWS-POTTER.htm#obrien>).

188. Michael Pearce, "J.R.R. Tolkien's Take on the Truth," available from: <http://www.leaderu.com/humanities/zenit-tolkien.html>.

189. Dr. Curt Brannan, "What about Harry Potter" [on-line], n.d. July 16, 2002. Available from: <http://www.tbcs.org/papers/article04.htm>. Brannan is associated with The Bear Creek School, a Christian Liberal Arts educational institution.

190. Greydanus, available from: <http://decentfilms.com/commentary/magic.html>. Greydanus lists what he calls the "Seven Hedges" of protection present in The Lord of the Rings. According to Greydanus, these "hedges" prove that parents can be consistent in their thinking by accepting Tolkien, while at the same time rejecting Harry Potter. Greydanus writes: "At the very least, then, these seven 'hedges' disprove the claim of some Harry Potter fans that parents cannot consistently disap-

prove of the magic in Harry Potter while approving of Tolkien and Lewis. There is no slippery slope here, but a substantial differentiation. One may still choose to accept Harry Potter as well as Tolkien and Lewis—or one may choose to reject them all—but at any rate there's no arguing that acceptance of Tolkien and Lewis is inconsistent with rejection of Harry Potter. Here are the seven hedges in Tolkien and Lewis:

- Tolkien and Lewis confine the pursuit of magic as a safe and lawful occupation to *wholly imaginary realms*, with place-names like Middle-earth and Narnia—worlds that cannot be located either in time or in space with reference to our own world, and which stand outside Judeo-Christian salvation history and divine revelation. By contrast, Harry Potter lives in *a fictionalized version of our own world* that is recognizable in time and space, in a country called England (which is at least nominally a Christian nation), in a timeframe of our own era.

- Reinforcing the above point, in Tolkien's and Lewis's fictional worlds where magic is practiced, the existence of magic is an *openly known reality* of which the inhabitants of those worlds are as aware as we are of rocket science—even if most of them might have as little chance of actually encountering magic as most of us would of riding in the space shuttle. By contrast, Harry Potter lives in a world in which magic is a *secret, hidden reality* acknowledged openly only among a magical elite, a world in which (as in our world) most people apparently believe there is no such thing as magic.

- Tolkien and Lewis confine the pursuit of magic as a safe and lawful occupation to characters who are numbered among the *supporting cast*, not the protagonists with whom the reader is primarily to identify. By contrast, Harry Potter, a student of wizardry, is the title *character and hero* of his novels.

- Reinforcing the above point, Tolkien and Lewis include cautionary threads in which exposure to magical forces proves to be a *corrupting influence* on their protagonists: Frodo is almost consumed by the great Ring; Lucy and Digory succumb to temptation and use magic in ways they shouldn't. By contrast, the practice of magic is Harry Potter's *salvation* from his horrible relatives and from virtually every adversity he must overcome.

- Tolkien and Lewis confine the pursuit of magic as a safe and lawful occupation to characters who are *not in fact human beings* (for although Gandalf and Coriakin are human in appearance, we are in fact told that they are, respectively, a semi-incarnate angelic being and an earthbound star.) In Harry Potter's world, by contrast, while some human beings (called "Muggles") lack the capacity for magic, others (including Harry's true parents and of course Harry himself) do not.

- Reinforcing the above point, Tolkien and Lewis emphasize the pursuit of magic as the safe and lawful occupation of characters who, in appearance, stature, behavior and role, embody a certain *wizard archetype*—white-haired old men with beards and robes and staffs, mysterious, remote, unapproachable, who serve to guide and mentor the heroes. Harry Potter, by contrast, is a wizard-in-training who is in many crucial respects the *peer* of many of his avid young readers, a boy with the same problems and interests that they have.

- Finally, Tolkien and Lewis devote no narrative space to the process by which their magical specialists *acquire* their magical prowess. Although study may be assumed as part of the back story, the wizard appears as a finished product with powers in place, and the reader is not in the least encouraged to think about or dwell on the process of acquiring prowess in magic. In the *Harry Potter* books, by contrast, Harry's *acquisition of mastery over magical forces* at the Hogwarts School of Wizardry and Witchcraft is a central organizing principle in the story-arc of the series as a whole."

191. Brian M. Carney, "The Battle of the Books—No Contest. Tolkien Runs Rings Around Potter" [on-line], November 30, 2001. *Wall Street Journal.* July 16, 2002. Available from: <http://www.cesnur.org/tolkien/010.htm>. Carney also provides a pointed comparison between Tolkien's use of a magical Ring in his story as opposed to Rowling's use of the Philosopher's Stone: "Contrast Tolkien's careful use of the ring with Ms. Rowling's rather flippant use of another great artifact of legend, the philosopher's stone. Alchemists believed the stone would turn lead into gold. As a bonus, it was also thought to confer eternal life. The conceit of 'Harry Potter' is that such a stone has been made and the bad guy wants it. This is a setup worthy of Tolkien; indeed, it mimics his tale in vital respects. But Ms. Rowling's story manages to bring to light none of the moral dilemmas—of mortality, wealth, power—that the existence of the stone naturally suggests. The reader simply accepts as given that both sides want it, no particular importance is assigned to its powers and Harry never shows any interest in using it. He merely wants to keep it away from the bad guy. Once that's accomplished, the stone drops out of the story, like a token at the end of some video game."

192. Marcia Montenegro. Quote in Martha Kleder, "Harry Potter: Seduction of the Occult" [on-line], November/December 2001. *Family Voice.* July 16, 2002. Available from: <http://www.cwfa.org/library/_familyvoice/2001-11/06-12.shtml>.

193. O'Brien, *A Landscape with Dragons*, 110.

194. Greydanus, available from: <http://decentfilms.com/commentary/magic.html>.

CHAPTER EIGHT: RALLYING BEHIND ROWLING

1. James Morone, "What the Muggles Don't Get: Why Harry Potter Succeeds While the Morality Police Fail" [on-line], July/August 2001. *Brown Alumni Magazine.* July 16, 2002. Available from: <http://www.brownalumnimagazine.com/storydetail.cfm?ID=210>.

2. Chris Mooney, "Muddled Muggles: Conservatives Missing the Magic in Harry Potter" [on-line], July 11, 2000. *The American Prospect.* August 1, 2002. Available from: <http://www.prospect.org/webfeatures/2000/07/mooney-c-07-11.html>.

3. Ina Hughes, "Bible Thumpers in a Dither over Harry Potter" [on-line], December 8, 2001. *Knoxville News-Sentinel.* July 16, 2002. Available from: <http://www.knoxnews.com/kns/news_columnists/article/0,1406,KNS_359_901524,00.html>.

4. One particularly outrageous set of rumors about Rowling and her books was circulated in 2000-2001 via the Internet's e-mail system. Countless conservative Christians spread false information relating to numerous anti-Christian (and terribly offensive) comments allegedly made by Rowling to a British newspaper. Moreover, the false information included horrendous statements from children supposedly turning to Satanism due to the Harry Potter books. As it turned out, the bogus information originated from a satirical article posted at The Onion, an Internet site of parody that lampoons social and cultural controversies.

5. Bob Hostetler, "Wild About Harry?" [on-line], November 2, 2001. *Hamilton [Ohio] Journal-News*. July 16, 2002. Available from: <http://www.bobhostetler.com/writing/article023.html>.

6. " 'Harry Potter' Rich With Christian Allusions, Says BU Prof" [on-line], October 25, 2001. *Baylor University Tip Sheets*. July 16, 2002. Available from: <http://pr.baylor.edu/tipsheet/>.

7. Mike Hertenstein, "Harry Potter Vs. the Muggles: Myth, Magic & Joy" [on-line], n.d. *Cornerstone*, 30, issue 121. July 16, 2002. Available from: <http://www.cornerstonemag.com/imaginarium/features/muggle.html>.

8. Chuck Colson, "Witches and Wizards: The Harry Potter Phenomenon" [on-line], November 2, 1999. *Breakpoint Commentary*, #91102. July 16, 2002. Available from: <http://www.gbgm-umc.org/prospect/colson.htm>.

9. Alan Jacobs, "Harry Potter's Magic" [on-line], January 2000. *First Things*, 35-8. July 16, 2002. Available from: <http://www.firstthings.com/ftissues/ft0001/reviews/jacobs.html>.

10. Chris Gregory, "Hands Off Harry Potter!" [on-line], n.d. *Salon.com*. July 16, 2002. Available from: <http://www.salon.com/books/feature/2000/03/03/harry_potter/>.

11. Michael Miller, "Burning Books, Ideas Is the Real Sorcery" [on-line], April 20, 2001. *South Florida Business Journal*. July 16, 2002. Available from: <http://southflorida.bizjournals.com/southflorida/stories/2001/04/23/ editorial2.html>.

12. Michael G. Maudlin, "Virtue on a Broomstick" [on-line], September 4, 2000. *Christianity Today*. July 16, 2002. Available from: <http://www.christianitytoday.com ct/2000/010/37.117.html>.

13. Michael G. Maudlin, "Saint Frodo and the Potter Demon" [on-line], February 18, 2002. *Christianity Today*. July 16, 2002. Available from: <http://www.christianitytoday.com/ct/2002/106/13.0.html>.

14. Ted Olsen, "Positive About Potter" [on-line], December 13, 1999. *Christianity Today*. July 16, 2002. Available from: <http://christianitytoday.aol.com/ct/1999/150/12.0.html>.

CHAPTER NINE: JUST THE FACTS: BYPASSING THE PROPAGANDA

1. Edmund Kern, "Harry Potter, Stoic Boy Wonder" [on-line], November 16, 2001. *The Chronicle Review*. July 16, 2002. Available from: <http://chronicle.com/free/v48/i12/12b01801.htm>.

2. Winston Churchill, Speech before the House of Commons. Quote by The Churchill Society (London), available from: <http://www.churchill-society-london.org.uk/wscminor.html>.

3. Alan Jacobs, "Harry Potter's Magic" [on-line], January 2000. *First Things*, 35-38. July 16, 2002. Available from: <http://www.firstthings.com/ftissues/ft0001/reviews/jacobs.html>.

4. J.K. Rowling. Quoted in "J.K. Rowling: Harry Potter and Me Special" [on-line], n.d. July 16, 2002. Available from: <http://www.mugglenet.com/jkrshow.shtml>.

5. J.K. Rowling, interview with South West News Service, available from: <http://www.swns.com/vaults/rowling.htm>.

6. Rowling, *Chamber of Secrets*, 130-1. Another example of cruelty displayed by "good" characters can be found in passages where Moaning Myrtle—the ghost of a girl murdered many years earlier at Hogwarts—is ridiculed and mocked. She suffered emotionally when at Hogwarts and haunts a school lavatory. Students continue to make fun of her for being a fat, pimple-faced girl, who must endure an afterlife marked by depression and rage. Hermione jokes: "[I]t's awful trying to have a pee with her wailing at you" (*Chamber of Secrets*, p. 133).

7. One seven-year-old wrote to a newspaper in Britain, "I like Harry Potter because he is rather cheeky—he isn't always good" (Jasmine Wark, letter to the editor, *London Times*, June 29, 2000, available on-line at <http://www.timesonline.co.uk>). Another nine-year-old said: "I think all the characters are very well described, especially Harry and his friends Ron and Hermione. Together they are very mischievous" (Anastasia Wark, letter to the editor, *London Times*, June 29, 2000, available from: <http://timesonline.co.uk>). Eleven-year-old Megan Campanelle told the *New York Times* she likes reading the Potter series because it's "like we're reading about ourselves. . . . They like to do stuff like we like to do. They like to get in trouble" (Megan Campanelle. Quoted in Jodi Wilgoren, "Don't Give Us Wizards" [on-line], November 1, 1999. *New York Times*. July 16, 2002. Available from: <http://www.nytimes.com).

8. Dawn Marie Nikithser, message #1375, November 19, 2001, posted at Pagan Perspectives, available from: <http://www.witchvox.net/perspect/q068_hpm.html?-token.skip=66>.

9. Merlyn, "Magick: High and Low" [on-line], n.d. August 1, 2002. Available from: <http://www.connectionsjournal.com/files/archives/rootsreligion/magickhilo.html>.

10. Steven D. Greydanus, in "Harry Potter vs. Gandalf," makes an excellent case for why it is logically consistent to reject Rowling, while at the same time accepting Lewis and Tolkien, available from: <http://decentfilms.com/commentary/magic.html>. Regarding Hertenstein's argument, consider how closely it mirrors Rowling's own words: "If we are going to object to depicting magic in books, then we are going to have to reject C.S. Lewis. We're going to have to get rid of the 'Wizard of Oz.' There are going to be a lot of . . . classic children's literature [which] is not going to be allowed to survive that" (J.K. Rowling, "Elizabeth Hurley Talks About Playing the Devil in 'Bedazzled'; J.K. Rowling Discusses the Surprising Success of 'Harry Potter' " [on-line], October 20, 2000. *Larry King Live*. July 16, 2002. Available from: <http://www.cnn.com/TRANSCRIPTS/0010/20/lkl.00.html>).

11. *The Steinerbooks Dictionary of the Psychic, Mystic, Occult*, 62.

12. Alan Cochrum, "Harry Potter and the Magic Brew-Haha" [on-line], December 18, 1999. *Fort-Worth Star Telegram*. July 16, 2002. Available from: <http://www.dfw.com/mld/dfw/> (archives).

13. Harold Bloom, "Can 35 Million Book Buyers Be Wrong? Yes," *Wall Street Journal*, July 11, 2000. Also see chapter 3, endnotes #20-#23.

14. Hertenstein, available from: <http://www.cornerstonemag.com/imaginarium/features/muggle.html>.

15. Hertenstein, available from: <http://www.cornerstonemag.com/imaginarium/features/muggle.html>.

16. Gillian Tindall, *A Handbook on Witches* (New York: Castle Books, 1945; 1965 edition), 111-2.

17. Rowling, *Chamber of Secrets*, 234.

18. Rowling, *Chamber of Secrets*, 92-4, 234.

[She] grasped one of the tufty plants firmly, and pulled hard. . . . Instead of roots, a small, muddy, and extremely ugly baby popped out of the earth. The leaves were growing right out of his head. He had pale green, mottled skin, and was clearly bawling at the top of his lungs. Professor Sprout took a large plant pot from under the table and plunged the Mandrake into it, burying him in dark, damp, compost. . . .

The Mandrakes didn't like coming out of the earth, but they didn't seem to want to go back into it either. They squirmed, kicked, flailed their sharp little fists, and gnashed their teeth; Harry spent ten whole minutes trying to squash a particularly fat one into a pot. . . .

[Eventually] the Mandrakes were becoming moody and secretive, meaning they were fast leaving childhood.

"The moment their acne clears up, they'll be ready for repotting again. . . . And after that. it won't be long until we're cutting them up and stewing them."

19. Rowling, *Prisoner of Azkaban*,121. This scene wherein Hagrid is drunk is only one of many such episodes throughout the series.

20. Rowling, *Goblet of Fire*, 111.

21. Rowling, *Chamber of Secrets*, 116, 118.

22. Rowling, *Chamber of Secrets*, 136-7.

23. Rowling, *Prisoner of Azkaban*, 50.

24. Rowling, *Goblet of Fire*, 195. Rowling brings up "bubotuber pus" again on page 541.

25. Rowling, *Goblet of Fire*, 201.

26. Rowling, *Goblet of Fire*, 84.

27. Rowling, *Sorcerer's Stone*, 260.

28. Rowling, *Prisoner of Azkaban*, 162.

29. Shepard, 1:662.

30. Shepard, 1:664.

31. Rowling, *Prisoner of Azkaban*, 324.

32. Rowling, *Prisoner of Azkaban*, 324.

33. Rowling, *Prisoner of Azkaban*, 324.

34. Shepard, 2:1066.

35. Shepard, 2:1066.

36. Rowling, *Goblet of Fire*, 655, 687.

37. Rowling, *Goblet of Fire*, 15.

38. Rowling, *Goblet of Fire*, 119-20.

39. Rowling, *Goblet of Fire*, 465.

40. Rowling, *Goblet of Fire*, 143, 531, 589, 595, 603, 638, 611, 642, 656, 690

41. J. K. Rowling, Stories from the Web interview, <http://www.storiesfromtheweb.org/stories/rowling/interview.htm>; cf. Emily Farache, "Darker and Scarier Harry Potter Going Hollywood?" [on-line], September 25, 1999. July 16, 2002. Available from: <http://www.eonline.com>.

42. Steve Bonta, "Harry Potter's Hocus Pocus" [on-line], August 28, 2000. *The New American*. July 16, 2002. Available from: <http://www.thenewamerican.com.

43. J.K. Rowling. Quoted in Bonta, available from: <http://www.thenewamerican.com>.

44. Mary Ann Grossman, "Newest Harry Potter Adventure a Bit Thick with Wizard History" [on-line], July 9, 2000. *St. Paul (Minnesota) Pioneer Press*, 1A. July 16,

2002. Available from: <http://www.pioneerplanet.com>; cf. Connie Fletcher, "Longer and Darker, But More Riveting" [on-line], July 26, 2000. MSNBC. July 16, 2002. Available from: <http://www.msnbc.com>.

45. Lee Siegel, "Fear of Not Flying" [on-line], November 4, 1999. *The New Republic.* July 16, 2002. Available from: <http://www.tnr.com/current/siegel112299.html>.

46. Pam Ciepichal, "Goblet of Fire Delivers Twists, Turns" [on-line], n.d. *Pencil News (MSNBC).* July 16, 2002. Available from: <http://www.msnbc.com.

47. Deepti Hajela, "Potter in Fine Form" [on-line], July 8, 2000. ABCnews.com. July 16, 2002. Available from: <http://www.abcnews.com>.

48. Mark Lawson, "Hype at Its Hottest, But Rowling May Survive It" [on-line], July 10, 2000. *The Guardian.* July 16, 2002. Available from: <http://www.guardian unlimited.co.uk>.

49. J.K. Rowling. Quoted in David Kirkpatrick, "Harry Potter and the Quest for the Unfinished Volume" [on-line], May 5, 2002. *New York Times.* July 16, 2002. Available from: <http://www.nytimes.com/2002/05/05/business/05HARR.html> (must be a registered user).

50. See Internet articles produced by the A.M.O.R.C. on-line at <http://home.pi.net/ ~amorc.nl/enontsta.html> and <http://www.rosicrucian.org/rosicruc/mastery/ 6-history.html>.

51. Magre, available from: <http://www.alchemylab.com/flamel .htm>.

52. "Meet J.K. Rowling" [on-line], October 16, 2000 interview with Scholastic. July 16, 2002. Available from: <http://www.scholastic.com/harrypotter/author/ transcript2.htm>.

53. Grimassi, 3. This source reads: "ALCHEMY is an occult science of transformation and transmutation. As such it reflects the esoteric nature of Wicca/Witchcraft. In medieval times alchemical practices outwardly focused largely on the transmutation of base metals into gold. To occultists this process symbolized the spiritual process by which one could gain enlightenment—the refinement of the spirit."

54. An article in *An International Journal for the Philosophy of Chemistry*, 4, no. 1 (1998): 63-80, reads: "[I]t was advantageous to accentuate alchemy as donum dei [gift of God] in order to not attract the unwanted attention of the church. It was a kind of mimicry, and as will be shown later, this attitude persisted for an unexpectedly long time."

55. Rosemary Ellen Guiley, *The Encyclopedia of Witches and Witchcraft* (New York: Checkmark Books, 1999), 214.

56. Richard Cavendish, ed., *Man, Myth and Magic* (New York: Marshall Cavendish, 1970; 1995 edition), 1682-3.

57. Aleister Crowley, *Moonchild* (1917), 150. Available from: <http://www.hermetic.com/crowley/moonchild/mc11.html>.

58. "What Is Wicca," available from: <http://www.geocities.com/RainForest/2111/ whatiswicca.html>.

59. Branwen, "A Traditional Witch: Guidelines for a Magickal Life," [on-line], n.d. August 1, 2002. Available from: <http://www.branwenscauldron.com/witch_ethics.html>.

60. Guiley, 213.

61. Doreen Valiente, *An ABC of Witchcraft* (New York: St. Martin's Press, 1973), 271.

62. Guiley, 213; Valiente, 271.

63. Grimassi, 232.

64. Guiley, 213: "High magic, which calls upon the aid of beneficent spirits, is akin to religion"; cf. Grimassi, 232.

65. "Types of Magick," available from: <http://www.freethinkers.freeserve.co.uk/ Pagan/magicktypes.html>.

66. Grimassi, 232; cf. "Arcana Mundi" (Baltimore & London: Johns Hopkins University Press, 1985).

67. Muse, "Magic: The Highs and Lows," available from: <http://www.sophiaswisdom .com/para_magic.html>.

68. Muse, "Magic: The Highs and Lows," available from: <http://www.sophiaswisdom .com/para_magic.html>. This Sophia Net article explains: "Low magic is the magic that deals with acquiring things in the material world. Low magic is also referred to as practical magic. Most of the magic used today fits into this classification. Witchcraft, astrology, planetary magic, ceremonial magic, invocations and conjurations, necromancy, satanism, demonology, spell casting, the making of charms and talismans, curses, use of incense, candles and all forms of divination are examples of low magic/practical magic. Low magic can be what's called creative or white magic or it can be destructive and in that case is referred to as black magic. Rather then saying that black magic is evil, it might be more appropriate to say that black magic usually deals in excesses. Excessive pride, excessive lust, pride and hatred are the fuel that fires black magic. High Magic deals with the realm of spirit. High magic is otherwise known as transcendental magic. Kabbalah, Yoga, transcendental meditation and Taoism all fall into the category of high magic. High magic uses the doctrine of mind over matter. Those that practice high magic do so without thought of personal glory, being more concerned with the unifying of spirit and matter. High magic is neither white nor black, but transcends both. It is the middle path of mind and body. A true mage practicing high magic is neither good nor bad but has stuck a balance that rings through time and space to the here and now."

69. All kinds of sinners came to Jesus and believed he was the Messiah. But just because prostitutes, astrologers, tax collectors and adulterers came to Him, that does not mean that their sinful actions were acceptable. The Bible in both the Old Testament and the New Testament repeatedly condemns astrology, divination and magick. When it comes to the Wise Men (Greek text, magi), we know nothing about them, except that after they saw Him they left the area. That's it. The Bible does not say that after they visited Him they continued practicing the astrology and divination associated with their priestly caste. Obviously, just because they were astrologers did not mean they could not, or should not, have visited Christ. In other words, the Magi were watching their stars and saw something very curious—i.e., the star of Bethlehem—and wanted to see what it was because of things they had heard about a Jewish Messiah. It would be as if a police man guarding a stretch of highway saw smoke rising in the distance and drove in that direction to see what was going on. They found Jesus and accepted Him as their true Messiah as well. What makes them admirable is that they visited and accepted Jesus, the Messiah of a religion that condemned their profession as astrologers. Would they actually continue being astrologers after their conversion? Why would they do such a thing when Judaism so blatantly condemned astrology? To continue as astrologers would make no sense. Interestingly, two other individuals referred to in the original Bible texts as being astrologers or "magi" are Simon (Acts 8:9-11) and Bar-Jesus (Acts 13:6). Both are presented as evil charlatans. The difference between them and the wise men who came to Christ, was that Simon and Bar-Jesus

rejected the Christian message of Jesus, whereas the wise men were open to Jesus being the Messiah and apparently accepted Him as such, then most likely left their profession as astrologers (this is assumed because both the Old and New Testaments, as well as the Jews, were so clearly against astrology).

70. Harry Potter contains many examples of magic being used by good characters for bad purposes, yet these instances are rarely mentioned by Potter fans. Consider the following partial list:

- In Book I (pp. 59, 90) Hagrid performs an illegal spell against Harry's cousin, Dudley. (He gives Dudley an extremely painful pig's tail that has to be surgically removed.) This is not even done because Dudley acts improperly toward Hagrid. It is done to punish Mr. Dursley for insulting Dumbledore. Rather than attacking Mr. Dursley, Hagrid takes revenge on Dudley as a way of more gravely hurting the boy's father.

- Also in *Sorcerer's Stone*, when a timid boy named Neville tries to prevent Ron and Harry from sneaking out of the dorm, Hermione (now as much a rule-breaker as her friends), puts a full "Body-Bind" spell on him: "Neville's arms snapped to his sides. His legs sprang together. His whole body rigid, he swayed where he stood, and then fell flat on his face, stiff as a board" (p. 273).

- In Book III, Harry uses the magic of his invisibility cloak to exact a little revenge on his nemesis, Draco Malfoy. "The opportunity was too perfect to miss," Rowling tells us on page 280. "Harry crept silently around behind Malfoy, Crabbe, and Goyle, bent down, and scooped a large handful of mud out of the path. . . . Malfoy's head jerked forward as the mud hit him; his silver-blond hair was suddenly dripping in muck." Harry continued enjoying himself by sneaking "along the path, where a particularly sloppy puddle yielded some foul-smelling, green sludge. SPLATTER. Crabbe and Goyle got some this time."

- In Book IV, Fred and George Weasley use magic (an Engorgement Charm) to create "Ton-Tongue Toffee," which when eaten, causes some rather horrific results. They give the toffee to Dudley: "A horrible gagging sound erupted and Aunt Petunia started screaming. . . . Dudley was no longer standing behind his parents. He was kneeling beside the coffee table, and he was gagging and sputtering on a foot-long, purple, slimy thing that was protruding from his mouth. . . . Harry realized that the foot-long thing was Dudley's tongue. . . . [George later asked his father] "How big did his tongue get?" . . . "It was four feet long before his parents would let me shrink it!" Harry and the Weasleys roared with laughter again (pp. 48-9, 53).

71. Julia Keller, "Should Harry Potter Be Expelled from the Classroom?" [on-line], November 28, 1999. *The Holland [West Michigan] Sentinel*. July 16, 2002. Available from: <http://www.hollandsentinel.com/stories/112899/fea_potter.html>.

72. Elizabeth Schafer, "The Bad Boy Censors Want to Kick Out of School: Harry Potter's Enemies" [on-line], November 18, 1999. *TomPaine.commonsense*. July 16, 2002. Available from: <http://www.tompaine.com/feature.cfm/ID/2564>.

73. Wendy Doniger, "Spot the Source: Harry Potter Explained," *London Review of Books*, February 10, 2000; reprinted in *The Guardian*, February 10, 2000, available from: <http://books.guardian.co.uk/lrb/articles/0,6109,135352,00.html>.

74. Suzanne Fields, "Casual Censors and Deadly Know-Nothings" [on-line], December 7, 1999. *Jewish World Review*. July 16, 2002. Available from: <http://www

.jewishworldreview.com/cols/fields120799.asp>. Equally caustic was a story from Scripps Howard News Service (David Waters, "Not Every Christian Horrified by Harry Potter" [on-line], July 5, 2000. July 16, 2002. Available from: <http://www.cesnur.org/recens/potter_039.htm>), which dubbed the conservative Family Friendly Libraries a "House of Slytherin" organization and called Lindy Beam of Focus on the Family a "squib" (i.e., in the Harry Potter series, a non-magical person resulting from a genetic abnormality and who, as a result if their non-magicalness, tends to be resentful, bitter and bad-tempered). There also was a scathingly sarcastic commentary posted to the Internet's CBS-News Channel 2000.com Web site (Betsy Gerboth, "Feeling Demonic? It's Harry Potter's Fault" [on-line], n.d. July 16, 2002. Available from: <http://www.thebakersfieldchannel.com/culture shocked/136476/detail.html>), which misrepresented an evangelical critique of Rowling. The author of this CBS opinion piece, Betsy Gerboth, lambasted the evangelical analysis, alleging that it not only condemned childrens' imagination, but put forth the idea that "[c]hildren who are unhappy should just put up or shut up." After implying that concerned parents are illiterate, Gerboth added some patently anti-Christian comments:

> Have you ever noticed that the longer you let these people spout their sanctimony, the less they make sense? . . . I'm sure a lot of you are even now leaping head-first into your e-mail programs to tell me that . . . I am not only an idiot, but also condemned for all eternity to burn in the fiery pit of hell. Or something like that. . . . The books are fantasies. Don't understand the word? Look it up. Perhaps what the anti-Harry factions are most frightened of is that their children will read books like Rowling's, develop their own imaginations—and learn to make up their own minds—and reject the fanatical teachings of those who would like to decide what every child should and shouldn't read, based on their own narrow beliefs.

75. Judy Blume, "Is Harry Potter Evil?" [on-line], October 22, 1999. *New York Times.* July 16, 2002. Available from: <http://www.judyblume.com/articles/harry_potter_oped.html>.

76. Gene Edward Veith, "Censoring 'Kum Ba Ya' " [on-line], September 2, 2000. *World Magazine.* July 16, 2002. Available from: <http://www.worldmag.com/world/home.asp>.

77. Charges of sexism and the propagation of unflattering female stereotypes have come from various sectors of society. Consider the following two reviews from non-religions, secular writers:
   • Once I opened "The Sorcerer's Stone," I was hooked. . . . Believe me, I tried as hard as I could to ignore the sexism. I really wanted to love Harry Potter. But how could I? Harry's fictional realm of magic and wizardry perfectly mirrors the conventional assumption that men do and should run the world. From the beginning of the first Potter book, it is boys and men, wizards and sorcerers, who catch our attention by dominating the scenes and determining the action. . . . Harry is supported by the dignified wizard Dumbledore and a colorful cast of male characters. Girls, when they are not downright silly or unlikable, are helpers, enablers and instruments. No girl is brilliantly heroic the way Harry is, no woman is experienced and wise like Professor Dumbledore. In fact, the range of female personalities is so limited that neither women nor girls play on

the side of evil. But, you interject, what about Harry's good friend Hermione?
. . . Hermione is a smart goody-goody who annoys the boys by constantly re-
minding them of school rules. Early on, she is described as "a bossy
know-it-all," hissing at the boys "like an angry goose." Halfway through the
first book, when Harry rescues her with Ron's assistance, the hierarchy of
power is established. We learn that Hermione's bookish knowledge only goes
so far. At the sight of a horrible troll, she "sinks to the floor in fright . . . her
mouth open with terror." Like every Hollywood damsel in distress, Hermione
depends on the resourcefulness of boys and repays them with her complicity.
By lying to cover up for them, she earns the boys' reluctant appreciation. . . .
Ron's younger sister Ginny, another girl student at Hogwart's, can't help
blushing and stammering around Harry, and she fares even worse than
Hermione. "Stupid little Ginny" unwittingly becomes the tool of evil when
she takes to writing in a magical diary. . . . Again and again, we see girls so
caught up in their emotions that they lose sight of the bigger picture. We watch
them "shriek," "scream," "gasp" and "giggle" in situations where boys retain
their composure. Again and again, girls stay at the sidelines of adventure while
the boys jump in. . . . The only female authority figure is beady-eyed,
thin-lipped Minerva McGonagall, professor of transfiguration and deputy
headmistress of Hogwart's. . . . Although she makes a great effort to keep her
feelings under control, in a situation of crisis she loses herself in emotions because she lacks Dumbledore's vision of the bigger picture. When Harry returns from the chamber of secrets, she clutches her chest, gasps and speaks
weakly while the all-knowing Dumbledore beams. Sybill Trelawney is the
other female professor we encounter. She teaches divination, a subject that includes tea-leaf reading, palmistry, crystal gazing—all the intuitive arts commonly associated with female practitioners. Trelawney is a misty, dreamy,
dewy charlatan, whose "clairvoyant vibrations" are the subject of constant
scorn and ridicule. The only time she makes an accurate prediction, she doesn't
even know it because she goes into a stupor [a channeling trance]. . . . There are
"funny little witches," "venerable looking wizards" who argue philosophy,
"wild looking warlocks," "raucous dwarfs" and a "hag" ordering a plate of raw
liver. Which would you prefer to be? I rest my case. (Christine Schoefer,
"Harry Potter's Girl Trouble" [on-line], n.d. *Salon.com*. July 16, 2002. Available from: <http://www.salon.com/books/feature/2000/01/13/potter/>);

- "Could it be that the Harry Potter books, written by a woman for her daughter, fit into that chauvinist world of male literature where women are either absent, weak, silly, evil or vaporized by car bombs? . . . Let's take a closer look at
the females in Harry Potter. . . . The women and girls in The Sorcerer's Stone
are weak, whining, b****es. The boys Harry and his friend Ron are the central
characters. The girl is the annoying Hermione, a prissy know-it-all who already read the entire year's schoolwork before school starts and knows all the
answers in class. When the boys want to go exploring in the school at night,
she warns them, but often ends up tagging along. . . . After she answers classroom questions, Ron complains to Harry "It's no wonder no one can stand
her. She's a nightmare, honestly." She overhears this and ends up crying alone
in the bathroom and the boys "quickly put Hermione out of their minds."
While she is weeping alone in the girls' bathroom, a dangerous troll enters. . . .

Hearing her "high petrified scream," the boys come to rescue her. . . . All of the central characters, both good and evil, are men. They make decisions and drive the story. Hermione solves the logical riddle at the end, but she knows that it doesn't really count for much. Harry's boyish daring and bravery are more important. "Hermione's lip trembled and she suddenly dashed at Harry and threw her arms around him. 'Harry—you're a great wizard, you know.' " Bashful Harry replies that he isn't as good as her. She replies 'Me! Books! And Cleverness! There are more important things—friendship and bravery and—oh Harry—be careful!'" Hermione herself belittles her knack at learning and logical skills (Andreas Ramos, "The Trouble with Harry—Teaching Our Children Sexism" [on-line], n.d. *Advancing Women*. July 16, 2002. Available from: <http://www.advancingwomen.com/womsoc/review_potter.html>).

78. Lisa Jackson, "The Return of Harry Potter" [on-line], September/October 2000. *Christian Parenting Today*. July 16, 2002. Available from: <http://www.christianitytoday.com/cpt/2000/005/4.44.html>.

79. Dierdre Donahue, "'Goblet of Fire' Burns Out" [on-line], July 26, 2000. *USA Today*. July 16, 2002. Available from: <http://www.usatoday.com/life/enter/books/potter/hp04.htm>.

80. Stephen King, "Wild About Harry" [on-line], July 23, 2000. *New York Times*. July 16, 2002. Available from: <http://partners.nytimes.com/books/00/07/23/reviews/000723.23kinglt.html>.

81. Kristin Lemmerman, "Gladly drinking from Rowling's 'Goblet of Fire' " [on-line], n.d. CNN.com. July 16, 2002. Available from: <http://www.cnn.com/2000/books/reviews/07/14/review.potter.goblet/>.

82. Jennifer Lee Carrell, "Harry Dares to Grow Up" [on-line], December 3, 2001. *Arizona Daily Star*. July 16, 2002. Available from: <http://www.azstarnet.com/harrypotter/0711potter.html>.

83. Jennifer Currie, "'Goblet of Fire' Not As Good As the Last Harry Potter" [on-line], n.d. *Schoolsnet*. July 16, 2002. Available from: <http://www.schoolsnet.com/cgi-bin/inetcgi/schoolsnet/library/bookArticle.jsp?OID=403944&cat=Books>.

84. John Ezard, "Harry Potter Put to Flight by Darker Forces" [on-line], November 15, 2000. *The Guardian*. July 16, 2002. Available from: <http://books.guardian.co.uk/whitbread2000/story/0,6194,397635,00.html>.

85. Julie Rigby, "Harry Potter and the Goblet of Fire" [on-line], July 2000. July 16, 2002. Available from: <http://www.arcfan.demon.co.uk/sf/books/2000jul.htm>.

86. Yvonne Zipp, "Harry Potter and the Goblet of Fire" [on-line], July 13, 2000 *The Christian Science Monitor*. July 16, 2002. Available from: <http://www.csmonitor.com/durable/2000/07/13/p21s2.htm>.

87. Paul Gray, "Harry's Magic Is Back Again" [on-line], July 24, 2000. *Time*. July 16, 2002. Available from: <http://www.time.com/time/pacific/magazine/20000724/potter.html>.

88. Kimberly Pauley, "Harry Potter and the Goblet of Fire" [on-line], n.d. *Young Adult Books Central*. July 16, 2002. Available from: <http://www.yabookscentral.com/cfusion/index.cfm?fuseAction=books.review&review_id=114>

89. J.R.R. Tolkien, letter to Hastings, in Carpenter, *The Letters*, 193-4.

CHAPTER TEN: QUESTIONS MOST FREQUENTLY
ASKED

1. Jonathan Zimmerman, "Harry Potter and His Censors" [on-line], August 2, 2000. *Education Weekly*. July 16, 2002. Available from: <http://www.edweek.org/ew/ewstory.cfm?slug=43zimmer.h19>.

2. Josh London, "Harry Potter Is Great" [on-line], December 7, 2001. *Spintech*. July 16, 2002. Available from: <http://www.spintechmag.com/2001/jl120701.htm>.

3. James Morone, "What the Muggles Don't Get: Why Harry Potter Succeeds While the Morality Police Fail" [on-line], July/August 2001. *Brown Alumni Magazine*. July 16, 2002. Available from: <http://www.brownalumnimagazine.com/storydetail.cfm?ID=210>.

4. Mem Fox, *Reading Magic: Why Reading Aloud to Our Children Will Change Their Lives Forever* (New York: Harcourt Inc., 2001), 139.

5. ABC and NBC references cited in John Ankerberg, "Questions about Harry Potter" [on-line], n.d. July 16, 2002. Available from: <http://www.johnankerberg.org/hp-articles/hp-questions.htm>.

6. Michael O'Brien, interview with Zenit News Agency, "Why Harry Potter Goes Awry" [on-line], December 6, 2001. July 16, 2002. Available from: <http://www.youth.co.za/theedge/reviews/reviewsPC07.asp>.

7. From conversations with author: Marcia Montenegro, Steve Russo, Dr. Ron Rhodes, Dr. Douglas Groothuis.

8. Rowling, *Goblet of Fire*. Mr. Weasley, "Damn" (Book IV, p. 43), Bill Weasley, "damn" (Book IV, p. 62), Ludo Bagman, "Damn them" (Book IV, p. 127), Snape, "I don't give a damn" (Book IV, p. 470), Cedric, "What the hell" (Book IV, p. 626).

9. Rowling, *Goblet of Fire*, 103.

10. "ABC's of Religion in the Curriculum" [on-line], n.d. *Anti-Defamation League*. July 16, 2002. Available from: <http://www.adl.org/issue_religious_freedom/ABC_Poster.html>.

11. This document is titled "Exclusive Download: Harry Potter," available from: <http://www.beachampublishing.com>.

12. Joseph Campbell. Quoted in Pamela Johnson, "Dark Side of the Force" [on-line], May 3/10, 1997. *World Magazine*. July 16, 2002. Available from: <http://www.worldmag.com/world/issue/05-03-97/>. An excellent critique of Campbell's work is "Myth and the Power of Joseph Campbell," by Doug Groothius in *Christianity that Counts* (Grand Rapids: Baker Books, 1995), 150-62.

13. Elizabeth D. Schafer, *Beacham's Sourcebooks for Teaching Young Adult Fiction: Exploring Harry Potter* (Osprey, FL: Beacham Publishing, 2000), 156-7.

14. Schafer, 128.

15. Schafer, 164.

16. "Exclusive Download: Harry Potter," available from: <http://www.beachampublishing.com>.

17. "Exclusive Download: Harry Potter," available from: <http://www.beachampublishing.com>.

18. J.K. Rowling. Quoted in Malcolm Jones, "The Return of Harry Potter!" [on-line], July 1, 2000. *Newsweek*, 4. July 16, 2002. Available from: <http://www.angelfire.com/mi3/cookarama/newswkint00.html>;

<http://www.geocities.com/aberforths_goat/July_2000_Malcolm_Jones_ Newsweek.htm>; and <http://tww.darkmark.com/interview11.shtml>.

19. Bernice E. Cullinan, *Literature and the Child* (New York: Harcourt Brace Jovaovich, 1989), 280.

20. O'Brien, available from: <http://www.youth.co.za/theedge/reviews/reviews PC07.asp>.

21. Valiente, *An ABC of Witchcraft*, 60.

22. J.D. Douglas and Merril C. Tenney, eds., *The New International Dictionary of the Bible* (Grand Rapids: Zondervan, 1987 edition), 1067.

23. Francis Brown et al., eds. *The New Brown-Driver-Briggs-Gesenius Hebrew and English Lexicon* (Peabody, MA: Hendrickson, 1979), s.v. 3784 and Geoffrey W. Bromiley, *The International Standard Bible Encyclopedia* (Grand Rapids: Eerdmans, 1979; revised edition), vol. 2, s.v. "magic, magician," 213-19.

24. "Never Seen a Ghost?," available from: <http://www.purdue.edu/UNS/html 4ever/971017.Sparks.survey.html>.

25. Cited in Ankerberg, available from: <http://www.johnankerberg.org/hp-articles/ hp-questions.htm>.

26. Cited in Ankerberg, available from: <http://www.johnankerberg.org/hp-articles/ hp-questions.htm>.

27. O'Brien, available from: <http://www.youth.co.za/theedge/reviews/reviews PC07.asp>.

APPENDIX A: WHAT'S SO BAD ABOUT OCCULTISM?

1. Gordon Michael Scallion, interview with Art Bell, *Coast to Coast*, December 8, 1995, Internet transcript available from: <http://www.nhne.com/interviews/ intbellinterview.html>.

2. For an in-depth explanation of all of Scallion's predictions, see Richard Abanes, *End-Time Visions: The Road to Armageddon?* (New York: Four Walls, Eight Windows, 1998), 53-5.

3. Abanes, 56-8.

4. Roland Seidel, "Astrology Overview" [on-line], n.d. *The Skeptic*. July 16, 2002. Available from: <http://www.skeptics.com.au/journal/astrol.htm>.

5. Elliot Miller, *A Crash Course on the New Age Movement* (Grand Rapids: Baker Books, 1989), 36.

6. Jason Barker, "Youth and the Occult" [on-line], 1998. *The Watchman Expositor*, 15, no. 6. July 16, 2002. Available from: <http://www.watchman.org/occult/ teenwitch.htm>.

7. Randall Tedford, "An Answer to the Call: Something Has to Be Done" [on-line], May 14, 1999. July 16, 2002. Available from: <http://www.oakridger.com/stories/ 051499/opE_0515990010.html>.

8. Lori Gray, "Preventing Violence," *Education Report*, January 6, 1998; cf. Reid Kimbrough and John Evans, *Pathological Maturity* (Cincinnati: Custom Publishing, 1999).

9. For more information on this important work, see the reading material available from: <http://www.amazon.com>, <http://www.barnesandnoble.com> and <http://vig .prenhall.com/catalog/academic/product/1,4096,0130847844,00.html# toc>.

10. Norvin Richards. Quoted in "Satanic Crimes on the Rise in Alabama" [on-line], n.d. *Associated Press*. July 16, 2002. Available from the Alabama Center for Justice: <http://www.alabamacenterforjustice.com/devilwor.htm>.

APPENDIX B: TODAY'S "CHRISTIAN" WITCHES

1. Mitch Pacwa, *Catholics and the New Age* (Ann Arbor: Servant Publications, 1992), 11. Quoted in Elizabeth A. Wittman, "Occult Trends in Children's Literature" [on-line], n.d. *Homiletic & Pastoral Review.* July 16, 2002. Available from: <http://www.catholic.net/rcc/Periodicals/Homiletic/2000-10/wittman.html>.

2. Mitch Pacwa. Quoted in Edwards, "Wicca Infiltrates" [on-line], n.d. August 2, 2002. Available from: <http://home-4.tiscali.nl/~t968103/silver_circle/scn_8.htm>; <http://www.angelfire.com/wi2/andromedawicca/news2.html>; <http://www.angelfire.com/ca6/armorofgod/spells.html>.

3. Catechism of the Catholic Church, #2115-2117, available from: <http://www.catholicdoors.com/catechis/cat2052.htm#2115>.

> All forms of *divination* are to be rejected: recourse to Satan or demons, conjuring up the dead or other practices falsely supposed to "unveil" the future. Consulting horoscopes, astrology, palm reading, interpretation of omens and lots, the phenomena of clairvoyance, and recourse to mediums all conceal a desire for power over time, history, and, in the last analysis, other human beings, as well as a wish to conciliate hidden powers. They contradict the honor, respect, and loving fear that we owe to God alone.
>
> All practices of *magic or sorcery*, by which one attempts to tame occult powers, so as to place them at one's service and have a supernatural power over others—even if this were for the sake of restoring their health—are gravely contrary to the virtue of religion. These practices are even more to be condemned when accompanied by the intention of harming someone, or when they have recourse to the intervention of demons. Wearing charms is also reprehensible. *Spiritism* often implies divination or magical practices; the Church for her part warns the faithful against it.

4. Pearson, "Bewitching the Academy," *Fortean Times*, 25.

5. Waterwheel, quoted in Edwards, "Wicca Infiltrates," available from: <http://www.confessingumc.org/wicca_story2.html>; <http://www.ucmpage.org/articles/wicca_story2.html>.

6. Mary Hunt. Quoted in Edwards, "Wicca Infiltrates," available from: <http://www.confessingumc.org/wicca_story2.html>; <http://www.ucmpage.org/articles/wicca_story2.html>.

7. For example, at a 1998 "Feminist Retreat" sponsored by the Dakota Conference of the United Methodist Church (UMC), the guest speaker was Judith Duerk—a favorite lecturer at neopagan and gatherings. Duerk's book, *Circle of Stones*, is often listed among standard works on Wicca/paganism and feminist spirituality. One review of it states: "In *Circle of Stones*, women will find a guide for attending to the Goddess within" (Meris Morrison, "Woman's Journey to Herself," available from: <http://www.state.vt.us/libraries/b733/BrooksLibrary/reviews2.htm#womans>). Participants at the UMC retreat also were given drums to facilitate meditative states wherein they contemplated the powers of their femininity (see Tom Graffagnino, "UMC Sponsored Women's Event Returns to Wiccan/Witchcraft Spirituality—Bishops Informed," available on-line at <http://www.ucmpage.org/news/neopaumc1.html>).

8. Russ Wise, "The Goddess and the Church," Probe Ministries Leadership U, request from <http://www.leaderu.com/orgs/probe/docs/godd-chu.html>.
9. James Walker, "Can a Christian Church Be a Cult," *The Watchman Expositor*. 11, no. 5 (1994): 3.
10. Quoted in Edwards, "Wicca Infiltrates," available from: <http://www.confessingumc .org/wicca_story2.html>; <http://www.ucmpage.org/ articles/wicca_story2.html>.
11. Quoted in Edwards, "Wicca Infiltrates," available from: <http://www.confessingumc .org/wicca_story2.html>; <http://www.ucmpage.org/ articles/wicca_story2.html>.
12. Quoted in Edwards, "Wicca Infiltrates," available from: <http://www.confessingumc .org/wicca_story2.html>; <http://www.ucmpage.org/ articles/wicca_story2.html>.
13. See the main page of Foundry United Methodist Church at <http://www .foundryumc.org/leadership.html> and Dumbarton United Methodist Church at <http://www.gbgm-umc.org/DumbartonDC/>.
14. Russ Wise and Tal Brooke, "Goddess Worship" [on-line], winter 1998/99. *SCP Journal*, 23:2. July 16, 2002. Available from: <http://worthynews.com/goddess.htm>.
15. Wise and Brooke, available from: <http://worthynews.com/goddess.htm>.
16. Edwards, "Wicca Infiltrates," available from: <http://www.confessingumc.org/ wicca_story2.html>; <http://www.ucmpage.org/ articles/wicca_story2.html>.
17. Stephen Hand, "The Witch of Boston College," in Conflict of Faith, (St. Paul, MN: Remnant Press, 1999), excerpt available from: <http://www.geocities.com/ Athens/Thaca/3251/genwomen.html>.

[Daly] is a self-admitted butch-Lesbian who so looks the part that one would think her pictures were designed to be a caricature. . . . [S]he regularly "conjures" the presence of many deceased womyn [*sic*] at the beginning of her lectures. . . . [Her] philosophic motto is "to sin is to be." She refuses to bend the knee to the "patriarchal" Father, God, insisting that worship is "not kneeling in front of so-and-so but swirling in energy." . . . She calls this "Energy"—the "mother-triple-goddess"—by many names: Isis, Hera-Demeter-Kore, Thetis-Amphitrite-Kore and others. Daly is often photographed holding a battle-ax, which she calls the symbol of lesbianism. . . . [S]he will not allow male students to speak in her class room under the pretext that Patriarchy has done too much talking already. When some dare to raise their hands she either ignores or openly rebukes them. So much for feminist "diversity" Mary Daly's hatred of men has gone to such execrable extremes as to allow her, in perfect seriousness, to see in the Infancy Narratives and the Incarnation the "rape" of Mary—and, symbolically, the "rape of all matter"—by the Patriarchal deity. . . . She generally distrusts men who want to take up women's causes and prefers that "womyn" [*sic*] take up the battle ax's [*sic*] themselves.

18. Mary Daly. Quoted in Wise and Brooke, available from: <http://worthynews.com/ goddess.htm>.
19. Quoted in Edwards, "Wicca Infiltrates," available from: <http://www.confessingumc .org/wicca_story2.html>; <http://www.ucmpage.org/ articles/wicca_story2.html>.
20. Walker, 5.
21. Statements made by various other key figures at the conference were highly revealing:

- Francis Wood (National Council of Churches) and Elizabeth Bettenhausen (Evangelical Lutheran Church in America) both promoted abortion rights and homosexuality.
- Virginia Mollenkott (National Council of Churches) claimed that woman are equal with Jesus, and that his death was not a blessing, but was "the ultimate in child abuse."
- Aruna Gnanadson (World Council of Churches) and Dolores Williams (professor at Union Theological Seminary in New York) both painted the idea of Christ's atonement as an abusive patriarchal system with the comment, "I don't think we need folks hanging on crosses dripping blood and weird stuff."
- Chinese feminist Kwok Pui-Lan (World Council of Churches) explained that the Chinese reject the sinfulness of humans and dismiss Christ in favor of Confucius, who emphasized "the genuine possibility for human beings to achieve moral perfection and sainthood." She also rejected the doctrine of the Trinity.

22. Walker, 6.
23. Walker, 6.
24. "1998 Re-Imagining Revival," *The Watchman Expositor*. 15, no. 4 (1998): 3.

OTHER BOOKS
BY RICHARD ABANES

Cults, New Religious Movements, and Your Family
Defending the Faith: A Beginner's Guide to Cults
Journey into the Light: Exploring Near Death Experiences
End-Time Visions: The Doomsday Obsession
Embraced by the Light and the Bible
Harry Potter and the Bible

Richard Abanes can be contacted on the web at:
www.abanes.com